C0-APP-575

Introduction to
Home Economics

EILEEN ELLIOTT QUIGLEY
Dean and Professor Emeritus
School of Home Economics, Southern Illinois University

Introduction to

Home Economics

SECOND EDITION

Macmillan Publishing Co., Inc.
New York

Collier Macmillan Publishers
London

Copyright © 1974, Eileen Elliott Quigley
Printed in the United States of America

All rights reserved. No part of this book may be reproduced
or transmitted in any form or by any means, electronic or
mechanical, including photocopying, recording, or any information storage and retrieval system, without permission in
writing from the Publisher.

Earlier edition copyright © 1969
by Eileen Elliott Quigley

Macmillan Publishing Co., Inc.
866 Third Avenue, New York, New York 10022

Collier-Macmillan Canada, Ltd.

Library of Congress Cataloging in Publication Data

Quigley, Eileen Elliott
   Introduction to home economics.
   Bibliography: p. 355.
   1. Home economics. I. Title.
TX167.Q5 1974   640   73–1043
ISBN 0–02–397200–9

Printing: 1 2 3 4 5 6 7 8   Year: 4 5 6 7 8 9 80

Preface

Having taught and studied home economics college freshmen for a number of years, I have become aware of many of the reasons why some succeed and others fail. No textbook has aimed directly at these reasons for success and failure, although many college instructors in home economics do discuss and have the students study materials relating to these factors. The specific purposes of this book are to aid the student in (1) achieving an understanding of and appreciation for home economics as a profession through study of its objectives and history, the organizations within it, and the services it renders; (2) clarifying his major objectives through an understanding of the many professional opportunities, their advantages and disadvantages, and the personal and professional qualifications required; and (3) realizing the importance of certain attitudes, skills, and habits necessary to the achievement of both short- and long-range goals and providing the basic information necessary for these in the areas of studying, taking notes, writing term papers, and taking examinations, as well as in the areas of basic health, personality development, acceptable social usage, and critical thought about the bases for his modus operandi.

Throughout the revision the main stress has been on updating; this shows in every chapter, although some sections have required more changes than others. Most of the illustrations have been changed, as needed, to show various activities of the professional and to illustrate professional involvement with specific groups within our culture. The chapter on the history of home economics was not only updated but changed to include some indications for the future and to challenge the student to think of the various and great potentials in this ongoing profession. The title and content of Chapter 3 were changed (1) to indicate that more men are entering the home economics profession and should be encouraged to do so; (2) to point out the new major areas that need professionally trained men and women; and (3) to show, in many careers, the changing emphasis in the types of activities in which the profession might engage.

Some changes reflect the additional needs and interests of students. Some examples of these are to be found, though not exclusively, in

Chapter 5, "Developing Good Health Practices," especially in the section on "Medication and Drugs: Their Use and Misuse." Chapter 7, "The Ethical Dimension of a Career," reflects the students' interests in this subject and points up where and how it is applicable to their own situations.

This book does not aim at answering all the questions on any subject. It is directed toward an introduction to the field of home economics, some *basic review*, and orientation to college. If this book provides some bases for critical thinking and a challenge for continued study, it will have served its purpose.

My appreciation is expressed to many friends in the business and education worlds for their contributions to the text and review of parts of the manuscript. Appreciation must also be expressed to the many home economics students of Southern Illinois University who have made my teaching and this book seem worthwhile.

Pompano Beach, Florida   E. E. Q.

Contents

Tables and Charts

Illustrations

Part I

Understanding Your
Objectives, Career
Possibilities, and
Requirements

Introduction

What is home economics? What are its objectives and origins? Who had the organizational ability and dedication to begin a whole new profession? What is the status of the profession today? What career opportunities are open to a home economist? What are the requirements for entering a home economics profession?

These are some of the questions that motivated the writing of this section. Chapter 1, "Understanding Your Objectives and Those of the Profession," suggests your need for objectives as a student of home economics, as a professional home economist, and as a member of the American Home Economics Association. The goals of the profession in regard to improvement of the lives of individuals and families has received primary emphasis.

"The History of Home Economics, with Some Indications for the Future" begins with an example of the instructions of the Greek husband Ischomachus to his wife pertaining to her role and responsibilities in the home. The chapter shows the awakening of the need for science in the home and briefly describes the Lake Placid Conferences and some of the accomplishments of the profession since the conferences.

In Chapter 3, "Careers for Men and Women in Home Economics," many of the career opportunities are considered. Any home economics career combines well with homemaking. Without doubt, home economics is the "career with a double future."

Preparation for a Career in Home Economics

1

Understanding Your Objectives and Those of the Profession

Objectives are a form of direction, clarified in one's mind so that, knowing what one wants to accomplish, he may choose his approach and activities accordingly. You set objectives when you choose to enter a university and decide upon a major area and a profession. There are many more objectives to be formed, such as when you register for a class: what do you want to achieve from that class? These are some of the objectives you have as a student; you will also want to choose objectives as a future home economist and as a member of a professional association.

An interesting question regarding *college goals* was posited in an informal, limited survey at the Southern Illinois University, Carbondale Campus, when 118 students were interviewed by members of the Student Advisory Council to the Dean of the School of Home Economics. The results, which follow, may help other students formulate individualized long-term goals. Of the 118 students, 41 were home economics majors. The goals are listed in descending order in relation to the number of times they were mentioned—for all majors, including home economics students, and specifically for home economics students.

The purpose in choosing and recording goals is to have a basis for decisions in college or life in general. When one does not have this purpose in mind, he is likely to wander somewhat aimlessly. When studying has meaning and purpose, the chances for success are far greater.

After long-term goals are determined, equally important inter-

COLLEGE GOALS OF SOME UNIVERSITY STUDENTS

All Students	Home Economics Majors
Economic security	Preparation for profession
Preparation for profession	Economic security
Broader outlook	Broader outlook
Knowledge in specific area	Knowledge in specific area
Meeting people	Meeting people
Better job opportunity	Better job opportunity
Preparation for learning	Degree
Aesthetic values	Socialization benefit
Socialization benefit	Experience
Degree	Aesthetic values

mediate ones should be set up. Early success in intermediate goals provides a foundation of success upon which to build.[1] Making "good" grades may be one of your intermediate goals or objectives.

Every university has established, stated purposes. Did you study them before selecting your university? The purposes and objectives of universities do vary, and we suggest that you look in your university catalogue for such statements. You may expect your college program to be geared toward these purposes and objectives. One midwestern university catalogue carries this statement of objectives:

SOUTHERN ILLINOIS UNIVERSITY OBJECTIVES

TO EXALT BEAUTY
In God
  in nature
    and in art;
Teaching how to love the best
  but to keep the human touch;

TO ADVANCE LEARNING
In all lines of truth
  wherever they may lead
Showing how to think
  rather than what to think
Assisting the powers
  of the mind
In their self-development;

[1] C. d'A. Gerken, *Study Your Way Through School* (Chicago: Science Research Associates, Inc., 1953), p. 6.

TO FORWARD IDEAS AND IDEALS
In our democracy
Inspiring respect for others
    as for ourselves
Ever promoting freedom
    with responsibility;

TO BECOME A CENTER OF ORDER AND LIGHT
That knowledge may lead
    to understanding
And understanding
    to wisdom.[2]

An eastern university catalogue carries these statements: "The University's basic objective is to produce men and women of intellect and to equip them to use their abilities wisely."[3] A western university catalogue carries these statements: "Education at Brigham Young University is directed toward the development of the whole person, whose life is balanced by many interests and activities, integrated by a knowledge of divine revealed truth, and dedicated to the service of mankind."[4] As the foregoing quotes indicate, a definite variance exists, and your choice of university should include a consideration of these as well as other factors.

Within a university the colleges, schools, divisions, or departments also have stated objectives or purposes, which the home economics student should study to determine the kind of education offered or possible. The illustrations listed as follows are given not as indications of regional objectives but as examples of varying emphases in objectives and hence variance in the kind of education that the student could expect. One set of objectives is better than another only as the stated objectives meet the particular objectives or desires of a specific student.

The general objectives of the school, as established by the Home Economics faculty, are: (1) to prepare men and women as professionals (generalists and specialists) in selected home economics areas of service; (2) to assist home economics majors (and non-majors who elect courses in the school) in their personal development and in their preparation for establish-

[2] *Graduate School Bulletin,* cover page 2. Southern Illinois University Bulletin, Vol. 12, No. 6 (Carbondale, Ill.: Southern Illinois University, 1970).

[3] *Cornell University Announcements,* July 10, 1970, Vol. 62, No. 9 (Ithaca, N.Y.: Cornell University, Sheldon Court), p. 6.

[4] *Catalog of Courses, Brigham Young University Bulletin,* Vol. 67, No. 10 (Provo, Utah: Brigham Young University, 1970–1972), p. 47.

ing homes and families; (3) to provide services at the regional, national, and international levels which promote the aim of home economics. The aim is to strengthen individual and family life through the application of relevant arts and sciences in the interaction of people with their near environment in a setting of continuous social and technological change.[5]

The same eastern university quoted previously has these stated objectives:

The aim of t.. undergraduate program of the New York College of Human Ecology is twofold: to provide, through the facilities of the College and the University, a liberal education in the social and natural sciences, the humanities, and the arts; and to provide specialized instruction, based upon these disciplines, as preparation for professional careers in which the interests and well-being of the individual, the consumer, and the family are paramount.[6]

The western university quoted previously states the objectives of the College of Family Living as these:

The four-year academic program in family living provides a broad liberal education, as well as preparation for a profession. All the colleges of the University contribute to the curriculum, providing background in the arts, humanities, and sciences to be applied and integrated into areas of specialization which may continue through the baccalaureate to an advanced degree. The college contributes to the total University community by offering courses designed to develop insight into and understanding about various aspects of family life.[7]

As to the home economics profession, its members have placed a strong emphasis on objectives for the people of the world. This is true not only now but was also true sixty years ago when at Lake Placid, New York, the founders of the American Home Economics Association pledged support to the "economy of human mind and force," which was believed to be nurtured best in the home. The need for such an objective was apparent in the late nineteenth and early twentieth centuries. Women frequently lacked time and energy for accomplishing their many tasks, as well as the money for purchasing goods, fewer goods were available, and families were often poorly nourished.

[5] *Bulletin,* Southern Illinois University, Vol. 13, No. 5 (Carbondale, Ill.: Southern Illinois University, 1971), p. 5.

[6] *Cornell University Announcements,* New York State College of Human Ecology, 1970–1971, Vol. 62, No. 4 (Ithaca, N.Y.: Cornell University, April 23, 1970), pp. 15–16.

[7] *Catalog of Courses,* Brigham Young University, 1970–1972, op. cit., p. 79.

Today's needs may vary and the further needs of homemakers are becoming apparent. Needs therefore must constantly be studied and objectives redefined. Basically the purpose of home economics in all of its specific phases remains, as stated by the founders of the American Home Economics Association in 1909, ". . . to improve the conditions of living in the home, the institutional household, and the community." Its unique purpose was perhaps best formulated in the definition proposed by the Association of Land-Grant Colleges: "Home economics is that body of subject matter which has to do with the application of the natural and social sciences and arts to the problems of the home and the problems growing out of homes and their interrelationships."[8]

According to a publication prepared by the American Home Economics Association and reiterated at the convention of the association in 1967,

. . . Home economics is the field of knowledge and service primarily concerned with strengthening family life through:
  educating the individual for family living
  improving the services and goods used by families
  conducting research to discover the changing needs of individuals and families and the means of satisfying these needs
  furthering community, national, and world conditions favorable to family living.[9]

Many changes influencing the needs of families have occurred in the twentieth century. One of the major changes is in the role of women, who now receive more education, work outside the home to a greater extent, and take a more active part in the decisions of the family. According to Women's Bureau Bulletin 294, *1969 Handbook on Women Workers:* "Women are marrying young today—half of them marry by age 20.6, and more marry at age 18 than at any other age." A trend toward high mobility has emerged as people move from the country to the city, the city to the suburbs, the South to the North, and the East to the Far West. A change in occupational structure is evident with the rising number of professional people in proportion to unskilled, skilled, and clerical people. Service occupations, too,

[8] Thirty-eighth Annual Convention of the Association of Land-Grant Colleges, *Proceedings,* November 12–14, 1924.

[9] American Home Economics Association, *Home Economics—New Directions, A Statement of Philosophy and Objectives,* prepared by the Committee on Philosophy and Objectives of Home Economics of the American Home Economics Association (Washington: AHEA, June 1959), p. 4.

seem to be increasing as individuals have more money to spend on the tasks that they once did themselves. The number of job opportunities for women is multiplying as employers realize the potential of women in various positions. Scientific work has brought about new discoveries that can aid families, if the discoveries are made relevant and if consumers are helped to analyze the values of these products. As transportation and communication are improved, the world becomes smaller; as nations of people become closer, interracial and international understanding becomes a necessity.

The changes just mentioned, and particularly the changing role of women, indicate that certain role changes have also taken place for men. The day is gone in which homemaking was the responsibility of the wife alone. Men are assuming more responsibility in sharing in homemaking activities, the kind and amount depending on the particular family situation and attitudes. It is clear that women are expecting things other than, but perhaps in addition to, support, protection, and parenthood. Companionship, the sharing of responsibilities, and the understanding of women in general and his wife in particular are assumed by most women to be a part of a man's role today. All the social and economics factors mentioned in the preceding paragraph also impinge upon the role of men, but we find that, for men in particular, tradition, cultural status, and education are strong affective factors in the acceptance or rejection of new or different roles. Today, however, the interacting roles of the woman and the man tend to supplement each other.

Home economists have a responsibility to the individual and to the American family, and increasingly they have an obligation to join home economists of other countries in helping to relieve the problems of the world family. According to the results of a research question studied by Agnes Reasor Olmstead,[10] the seven most frequently accepted responsibilities of the home economist are the family, money management, food, time management, voicing the consumer's needs, the profession, and keeping up to date.

The family is the center of the home economist's world, the object of the profession's goals. It is an institution that has a great effect upon personality and satisfaction. If the home economist can help to strengthen the unity of the home and at the same time increase the appreciation of life, he will have provided a service most

[10] Agnes Reasor Olmstead, "Home Economics' Responsibility to the Family in the Consumer Age," *Journal of Home Economics,* 53 (September 1961), 537–542.

dear to personal life. Within families begin the basic democratic foundations for life. Children and parents, through failures and accomplishments, sickness and health, sadness and happiness, build a life for tomorrow. Home economists set their objectives to help families achieve good physical and mental health; guide and care for children; manage time, energy, and money; set immediate and future goals; adapt new scientific understandings in methods and products; and clothe their families and feed them in an appealing, satisfying way. Health and happiness may be the optimum objectives of the home economist for the family—all families in America and throughout the world.

Home economists strive to contribute to effective living through the following competencies of individuals and families to:[11]

Establish values which give meaning to personal, family, and community living; select goals appropriate to these values.

Create a home and community environment conducive to the healthy growth and development of all members of the family at all stages of the family cycle.

Achieve good interpersonal relationships within the home and within the community.

Nurture the young and foster their physical, mental, and social growth and development.

Make and carry out intelligent decisions regarding the use of personal, family, and community resources.

Establish long-range goals for financial security and work toward their achievement.

Plan consumption of goods and services—including food, clothing, and housing—in ways that will promote values and goals established by the family.

Purchase consumer goods and services appropriate to an overall consumption plan and wise use of economic resources.

Perform the tasks of maintaining a home in such a way that they will contribute effectively to furthering individual and family goals.

Enrich personal and family life through the arts and humanities and through refreshing and creative use of leisure.

Take an intelligent part in legislative and other social action programs which directly affect the welfare of individuals and families.

Develop mutual understanding and appreciation of differing cultures and ways of life, and cooperate with people of other cultures who are striving to raise levels of living.

[11] *Home Economics—New Directions*, op. cit., p. 9.

The first types of goals considered in this chapter were those of a student and those of home economists for the family. The third goal is the objectives of home economists for the profession, that is, to strengthen the profession, thereby increasing its effectiveness with families.

The American Home Economics Association, the voice of the profession, adopted a new statement of objectives of the Association, when the motion was passed by the assembly of delegates to the AHEA convention in June 1966, by stating:

The purpose of the American Home Economics Association shall be to strengthen home economics at all levels and through it the well-being of individuals and families:
Specifically, the Association shall
1. Establish and improve standards of education, research and service for the profession.
2. Represent and speak at the national and international levels for the profession of home economics in the United States.
3. Provide opportunity to members for professional growth.
4. Provide means for exchange of professional knowledge.
5. Alert members to social, economic, and psychological changes having implications for home economics programs.
6. Encourage discussion and debate within the profession on critical issues.
7. Identify trends affecting the profession and provide leadership and means for unified action.
8. Promote cooperative action among its members and with groups having related concerns.
9. Stimulate and encourage research which will provide new knowledge.
10. Encourage and promote legislation designed to aid and promote home economics in its contribution to the well-being of home and family life.

In June 1967, the following statement of purposes of the Association was adopted by the assembly of delegates at the annual convention:

The purposes of the Association shall be to further education and science in home economics. Without in any way limiting the foregoing, but in expansion thereof, the Association shall improve and strengthen education in home economics; establish and improve standards of service and scientific research in the public interest in home economics; sponsor and otherwise support seminars, debates, symposia, conferences, and similar professional discussion in home economics; state and disseminate policy for professional guidance at the national and international levels concerning the public interest in home economics; identify and study social, economic, and psychological changes having implications for home economics programs, and bring these changes to the attention of the home economics profession and the public; encourage and promote a sufficiently full and fair exposition of the pertinent facts involving legislation affecting home economics and the improvement of home and family life as to permit an individual or the public to form an independent opinion or conclusion; and promote liaison and other cooperative professional activity with groups having related concerns in behalf of the public interest in home economics.[12]

The 1971 "Fact Sheet" published by the American Home Economics Association succinctly stated its purpose as being "to improve the quality and standards of individual and family life through education, research, cooperative programs, and public information."

With objectives as a student of home economics, as a professional home economist, and as a member of the American Home Economics Association clearly in mind, one can set out to reach what he desires to accomplish. As Theodore C. Blegen said, ". . . the potential of home economics is as great as your hopes and dreams and will and courage can make it."[13]

[12] "Bylaws of the American Home Economics Association," *Journal of Home Economics,* Vol. 59, No. 7 (September 1967), 585.

[13] Theodore C. Blegen, "Potential of Home Economics in Education and the Community," *Journal of Home Economics,* 47 (September 1955), 482.

2

The History of Home Economics, with Some Indications for the Future

The history of any profession is respected by its members. Its early beginnings, its pioneers and leaders, its important dates and events become its foundation as a constitution or laws are the foundation of an organization or a country. The home economics profession is no exception. You, as a future home economist, will take pride in the profession and in its history. Leaders will judge accomplishments in the light of past progress and potential for the future.

Little was written by the Greeks and Romans on the education of women or the need for training in domestic situations. Zenophon wrote a classic example of a man instructing his wife in the Greek wife's duties and responsibilities. The husband, Ischomachus, set forth these duties:

> The Gods, as it seems to me, have plainly adapted the nature of women for works and duties within doors, and that of man for works and duties without doors . . . and over such as have business to do in the house you must exercise a watchful superintendence. . . . Whatever is brought into the house you must take charge of it; whatever portion of it is required for use, you must give out; and whatever should be laid by, you must take account of it and keep it safe. . . . For the divinity knowing that he had given the woman by nature and laid upon her the office of rearing children has also bestowed upon her a greater portion of love for her newly born offspring than on the man.[1]

[1] Isabel Bevier, *Home Economics in Education* (Philadelphia: J. B. Lippincott Company, 1924), p. 63.

14

Throughout the centuries, the practice of the woman's handling the domestic tasks and the rearing of the children has been generally accepted. There are exceptions. The roles are reversed in an African tribe, where the woman hunts and builds, assuming the responsibilities and the hardships, while the man beautifies himself and cares for the children. Pearl S. Buck speaks of the role of the Chinese woman:

> True, woman's place was in the home, but then the seat of power in Chinese society was the home. Unspoiled and without special privilege, Asian women did the practical work of life. She worked in the fields beside her husband and she stood behind the counter if he kept a shop. Men took it for granted that women worked wherever there was work to be done. Under the Communists, woman is expected to take her full place as a citizen, and now the goal is to release her from the home. It is considered reprehensible that a woman should cook for one family, or devote herself to the children of one family. If she wants to be a housewife she should be cooking and caring for the children of many. Under communism men insist that women take full part in the industrial and cultural life of the nation, and they use ruthless means to accomplish the fact.[2]

Yet the heritage of American women came from the Greeks and the Romans to the Western Europeans to the early colonists of America and to the present citizens of the United States. The immigrants of other than European stock with different social customs for their women did not have a striking effect. Thus, the woman in the United States has had the primary role of caring for the home, being a companion to her husband, guiding the children, and doing the many domestic tasks involved. Secondly, she has come in the twentieth century to be a helper or partner in providing the income for the family. The home and family have been the primary responsibility of American women.

The education of women has evolved slowly throughout history. An awareness of the need for educating women in America paralleled the slow realization in Europe. The progressive steps of schools to which girls were entered were dame schools, reading schools, schools of penmanship, double-headed schools (coeducational schools at which the boys and girls came at different hours), private schools, and then in the eighteenth century—the academies. The motives of the promoters of women's education were not always the same. A French priest, Fénelon (1651–1715), the head of a French school for young women, believed that women were weaker both physically

[2] Beverly Benner Cassara (ed.), *American Women: The Changing Image* (Boston: Beacon Press, 1962), p. 4.

and mentally but that they had the grave responsibility of mothering men; therefore they should be educated in order to strengthen their weak minds for their major duty. Others believed that women were as capable as, if not in some ways more capable than, men. Thus, women's opportunity for knowledge grew slowly in various educational channels and because of varying reasons of administrators.

Science had no less a role in the realization of domestic education than did the role of women or the progressively increasing education of women. Walter Buehr in *Home Sweet Home in the Nineteenth Century* realizes this when he says:

One major factor in our nineteenth-century revolution in domestic life was the chronic labor shortage. Every household was then "a long-term storehouse and a large-scale processing plant" that required constant labor almost around the clock. But domestic help—once plentiful when new immigrants were grateful for live-in jobs—became hard to find when growing mill towns offered young people higher wages and greater social status. And hired help became scarcer yet when the opening of the West offered the common man and woman a chance to work their own land and maybe make their own fortune.[3]

A need for labor-saving devices developed and with the need— inventions to ease work. These greatly affected the home.

Count Rumford was one of the early nineteenth-century scientists. Born as Benjamin Thompson in 1753, the Count experimented in physics and later turned his attention to household problems. He was probably the first to apply science to the problems of the kitchen; it has been said that he was the first to propose a home economics movement. In recognition of his great work, a scientific kitchen, shown at the Massachusetts exhibit at the World's Fair in 1893, was named the Rumford Kitchen.

In 1798, home economics was first introduced in the form of sewing to the first graders of Boston schools. It was not until 1872, though, that it was legalized along with other industrial education under a Massachusetts legislative act. This may have been the first teaching of a domestic course in public schools.

The study of household arts was begun at the Troy Female Seminary by Mrs. Emma Willard in 1821. Catherine E. Beecher entered upon the scene in 1822 when she established a private school for

[3] Walter Buehr, *Home Sweet Home in the Nineteenth Century* (New York: Thomas Y. Crowell Company, 1965), p. v.

girls in Connecticut. During the time of her teaching she realized the need for domestic economy and later wrote two books, which became the basic texts of the awakening field.

In 1835, sewing was extended to the second and third graders of the Boston schools. Again the course was extended in 1854, this time to the fourth grade. This gradual extension typifies the entire movement—slowly at first but with increasing speed.

By 1840, Catherine Beecher was ready to write the outstanding book, *A Treatise on Domestic Economy*. Chapters included:

Peculiar Responsibilities of American Women
Difficulties Peculiar to American Women
Remedies for the Preceding Difficulties
On Domestic Economy as a Branch of Study
On the Care of Health
On Cleanliness
On Early Rising
On Domestic Exercise
On Domestic Manners
On the Preservation of a Good Temper in a Housekeeper
On the Habits of System and Order
On Giving in Charity
On Economy of Time and Expenses
On the Construction of Houses
On Fire and Lights
On Washing
On Starching, Ironing, and Cleansing
On the Care of Parlors
On Sewing, Cutting and Mending
On the Care of Yards and Gardens
On the Propagation of Plants[4]

Interesting ideas set forth by Miss Beecher included her answer to the question, "Why cannot mothers teach their own children domestic economy?", her reasoning for the scientific basis for the study, and her early plan for a home management residence. Her answer to the question, still often asked today, shows unusual insight and clarity of argument:

[4] Catherine E. Beecher, *A Treatise on Domestic Economy* (New York: Harper & Brothers, 1859), pp. 11–23.

In reply to the thousand-times-repeated remark, that girls must be taught their domestic duties by their mothers, at home, it may be inquired, in the first place, What proportion of mothers are qualified to teach a "proper" and "complete" system of Domestic Economy? When this is answered, it may be asked, What proportion of those who are qualified, have that sense of the importance of such instructions, and that energy and perseverance which would enable them actually to teach their daughters, in all the branches of Domestic Economy presented in this work?

It may then be asked, How many mothers "actually do" give their daughters instruction in the various branches of Domestic Economy? . . . a large portion of the most intelligent mothers, and those, too, who most realize the importance of this instruction, actually cannot find the time, and have not the energy, necessary to properly perform the duty?[5]

Miss Beecher proposed in her *Treatise* that domestic economy be made a science, equal to other sciences in women's education. Domestic economy should relieve women of the burden of life, she felt, and need not be taught as a practical course, but systematically, like other sciences. Miss Beecher stressed that it could not be "properly" taught until it became a science, a specific branch of study. She proceeded to state that domestic economy is needed by women everywhere at all times. The placement of it as a science would give it dignity in the minds of the young in the vocation. Thus, in 1840 Catherine Beecher reemphasized Count Rumford's earlier conviction.

Miss Beecher also developed the home management residence plan, which has become a general practice in many colleges and universities in home economics curricula. Her plan was for a practice home where students would live with a domestic economy teacher and learn through experience the application of background principles. Miss Beecher's second book, *Domestic Receipt Book*, which was written in 1842, gave practical procedures for those household problems that she had discussed in the *Treatise*. The two volumes became a format for teaching the course in schools. Benjamin R. Andrews stated assuredly that "Her books were the beginning of domestic education."[6]

In 1857, Edward L. Youmans, a chemist, wrote *Household Science*, in which he presented a scientific study of air, heat, food, and light. His definition of household science was considered by Isabel Bevier as the most clear and comprehensive one formed at the time of the

---

[5] Ibid., p. 65.
[6] Keturah E. Baldwin, *The AHEA Saga* (Washington, D.C.: American Home Economics Association, 1949), p. 3.

publication of her book, *Home Economics in Education.* The statement of meaning, which appeared in the preface of Dr. Youmans' book, read, "Household science has to do with the agents, the materials and the phenomena of the household."[7]

The Federal Land-Grant Act or the Morrill Act (1862) greatly encouraged the development of home economics. It provided for colleges "to teach such branches of learning as are related to agriculture and the mechanic arts."[8] Miss Bevier praised the land-grant colleges:

. . . no agency has been more effective [in contributing to the development of home economics] than the land-grant colleges. No other agency has appreciated the possibilities of the subject so clearly or laid for it such broad and deep foundations. As these colleges were among the first to recognize the need for a scientific basis to education for the home, they have been most insistent that this standard should be maintained, and the home economics departments have realized the necessity of maintaining college ideals in the work if they would have the respect of the college community.[9]

The Massachusetts state legislature in 1870 passed an act in which drawing was made obligatory in the public schools of the state. Industrial training had begun. This first act paved the way for the 1872 Massachusetts act that legalized the teaching of sewing and other industrial education. Sewing had been taught in the Boston schools as early as 1798. Therefore the act only legalized what was already in practice, yet the legality of it in a state act shows further awareness and recognition of the importance of the study.

In 1874, the Free Training School for Women had its beginning in New York with Miss Juliet Corson as Superintendent of the Department. This was to become the New York Cooking School. This school has been said to be "the starting point in the movement for improving cookery in this country."[10] Sewing had been already taught for seventy-six years in the United States. The reason for the slow start for the teaching of cooking was not that it was considered less important than sewing, but equipping food laboratories or kitchens was far more costly. The pioneers of home economics had to wait until the public was more accepting before they could undertake projects

[7] Bevier, op. cit., p. 114.
[8] Baldwin, op. cit., p. 93.
[9] Bevier, op. cit., pp. 131–132.
[10] Ibid., p. 135.

that required more funds. After Miss Corson's first school, many cookery schools opened around 1875.

Soon the industrial concept was accepted. In the East, schools of art and design, industrial classes, and cooking and sewing classes were begun. Housekeeping and laundry were included. In the West, departments of domestic economy were introduced in agricultural colleges. The enlarging "sphere of women's activities and responsibilities" resulted in the departments of household science in the land-grant colleges. The pioneering land-grant colleges adopting household science programs were Iowa, Kansas, Illinois, Oregon, and South Dakota.

Mrs. Mary B. Welsh, in an evaluation of the domestic economy classes at Iowa, which began in 1869 and received department status in 1875, ended on this note:

> . . . It is acknowledged to have met a long-existing want, and to have done real service for the young women of the state. It has not only given them manual skill, but it has also increased their respect for all branches of such labor, and added dignity to that part of their life work hitherto considered as menial drudgery.[11]

Classes in sewing were first held in 1873 at Kansas Agricultural College. In 1875 a course of lectures on the scientific aspects of food and changes in composition during the cooking process were begun. The courses evolved into department status and Mrs. Nellie Kedzie took charge of the department in 1882. Her inspiring work led toward full development of the department.

The Illinois Industrial University, later to become the University of Illinois, announced a School of Domestic Science and Art in the 1871–1872 catalogue with classes to begin the following year. Mrs. Lou Allen Gregory was the head of the department from 1874 to 1880. She wrote concerning this field:

> The school was the outgrowth of a conviction that a rational system for the higher and better education of women must recognize their distinctive duties as women—the mothers, housekeepers, and health keepers of the world—and furnish instruction which shall fit them to meet these duties.
>
> As set forth in the catalogue, it was the aim of the school to give to earnest and capable young women a liberal and practical education, which should fit them for their great duties and trusts, making them the equals of their educated husbands and associates, and enabling them to bring the aids of science and culture to the all-important labors and vocations of womanhood.

[11] Ibid., p. 122.

This school proceeded upon the assumption that the housekeeper needs education as much as the house builder, the nurse as well as the physician, the leaders of society as surely as the leaders of senates, the mother as much as the father, the woman as well as the man. We discarded the old and absurd notion that education is a necessity to men, but only an ornament to woman. If ignorance is a weakness and a disaster in the places of business where the income is won, it is equally so in the places of living where the income is expended. If science can aid agriculture and the mechanic arts to use more successfully nature's forces and to increase the amount and value of their products it can equally aid the housekeeper in the finer and more complicated use of those forces and agencies in the home, where winter is to be changed into genial summer by artificial fires, and darkness into day by costly illumination; where the raw products of the field are to be transformed into sweet and wholesome food by a chemistry finer than that of soils, and the products of a hundred manufactories are to be put to their final uses for the health and happiness of life.[12]

The development of home economics in the East followed a somewhat different pattern largely because of a prejudice against coeducation. Thus, instead of schools of domestic science as in land-grant colleges, specific classes, schools of cooking, and other private schools or classes were begun in various large eastern cities. One of the purposes of such undertakings was to create a demand for similar instruction in public schools. Although in 1876 a Centennial Exposition in Philadelphia gave a strong impetus to the movement for manual training (shop for the boys and domestic science for the girls) in the public schools of the East, most instruction in the household sciences remained in private schools.

The Boston Cooking School was the first incorporated American cooking school. It was started in 1879 by the Woman's Education Association, which had been formed in Boston during 1872. The association had standing committees on industrial, aesthetic, moral, and physical education; the industrial committee developed the interest in a cooking school. The Boston Cooking School was first organized to give instruction in budgetary cooking to people of low incomes. An interest could not be developed in that group of people, so after the first season the classes were opened to all who wished to attend. The school ran under different principals until 1902 as the Boston Cooking School; then it was incorporated into Simmons College. One of the principals, Mrs. Mary J. Lincoln, wrote the first cooking textbook in 1887.

During this period between 1870 and 1900 group action brought significant movement to the developing field. One such group was

[12] Ibid., pp. 126–127.

the Kitchen Garden Association, which taught children household arts through play during the 1870's. In 1880, the association was incorporated in New York and, in 1884, it evolved into the Industrial Education Association. Today's Teachers College of Columbia University developed out of the original Kitchen Garden Association.

The National Household Economic Association, which lasted from 1893 to 1903, was organized to awaken the public to the need for bureaus of information for exchange of ideas between employer and employee, to promote scientific knowledge, and to secure skilled labor—all in relation to the home. The group dissolved, inasmuch as the work was being done well by the General and State Federation of Women's Clubs and the Lake Placid Conference.

Ellen H. Richards, a woman with the conviction that the world maintained unnecessary illness and that man lacked much of the joy of life that was due him, was to become the founder of home economics. At Vassar, Mrs. Richards consistently applied scientific facts and discoveries to the problems of the home. Examples of her applications were her new understandings of why egg whites could be beaten to a foam and how a room could be properly ventilated.

Gradually there evolved an interest in controlling external conditions in order to benefit all persons. By 1879, Mrs. Richards had a strong background of knowledge and was ready to lead others. In March of that year, Maria Mitchell invited her to give an address on "Chemistry in Relation to Household Economy" to a group of three hundred women. This was the first of her innumerable lectures. A major point in the speech was Mrs. Richards' three reasons for the introduction of science into household affairs. These were that

1st. It would benefit health.
2d. It would save labor and the wear of material.
3d. It would show us how to obtain the most for our money of the stable articles of daily consumption.[13]

During the same lecture, Mrs. Richards first suggested a domestic organization.

Perhaps the day will come when an association of housekeepers will be formed in each large town or city, with one of their number as a chemist. Some similar arrangement would be far more effective in checking adulteration than a dozen acts passed by Congress.[14]

[13] Caroline L. Hunt, *The Life of Ellen H. Richards* (Washington: American Home Economics Association, 1958), p. 101.
[14] Ibid., pp. 101–102.

Through Mrs. Richards the New England Kitchen was opened in Boston in 1890. The methods used and the cleanliness of the kitchen were open for demonstration and display to the public. The kitchen did not meet its original objective—helping the poor to have economical and nourishing food—but it was a success in its effect upon concern for cleanliness and the nutritional value of food.

Ellen H. Richards organized the Rumford Kitchen at the Massachusetts State exhibit at the World's Fair in Chicago during 1893. The menu at the kitchen showed the nutrients in the food one received. "The Rumford Kitchen was the first attempt to demonstrate by simple methods to the people in general the meaning of the terms proteids, carbohydrates, calories, and the fact there are scientific principles underlying nutrition."[15]

During the following year, 1894, a plan that grew out of the New England Kitchen materialized—the preparation of lunches for school children. The school lunch program in Boston, begun by Mrs. Ellen H. Richards, was the first of its kind in the United States. There were many odds to overcome—competing with local shops and assuming the job of the janitors who had the responsibility of feeding the children—but the program was a success. Mrs. Richards became an authority on school lunches, giving advice to school superintendents and others interested in education.

By 1887, Mrs. Richards had become involved in nutrition investigations with the U.S. Department of Agriculture. Congress passed the Hatch Act that year, to lend support and encouragement to agricultural research and to establish an experiment station in every state and territory with a special department for its organization in the Department of Agriculture. Professor W. O. Atwater was chosen to be the first director of the central office. Today one hears of outstanding research as results of the Agricultural Experiment Stations.

Wilbur O. Atwater is called the father of American nutrition. He realized nutrition was based in science and had prepared himself with a doctorate in chemistry. From the 1929 publication *Home Economists* comes this remarkable reflection about his career.

In 1873 he was called to Wesleyan University, his alma mater, as Professor of Chemistry, a position he retained throughout his increasingly active and varied career as teacher, organizer of the Office of Experiment Stations in the United States Department of Agriculture, head of the nutrition investigations carried on by various state experiment stations in cooperation with the Department, and conductor in his own laboratory of

[15] Ibid., p. 128.

23

an extraordinary amount of fundamental research on the composition and physiological effects of food materials. . . . The Atwater bomb calorimeter and the experiments on metabolism carried on with it are conspicuous examples of the scope, daring and accuracy of his research. His name is now perhaps most widely known for the bulletin "The Chemical Composition of American Food Materials," a compilation of analyses which since 1899 has been in demand all over the world. . . . [T]he animating force behind all his unresting, wide-reaching activities was the belief that the discovery and application of scientific truth is one of the highest forms of human service.[16]

During 1894, Mrs. Richards and Mr. Edward Atkinson prepared, at the request of Professor Atwater, the pamphlet "Suggestions Regarding the Cooking of Food." This was one of the first of the Department of Agriculture's popular bulletins on nutrition, which have made a valuable contribution to public education.

The organization of the home economics movement "may be considered the crowning labor of Mrs. Richards' life, because it brought together her numberless lines of work and directed them toward a well-defined end—education for right living."[17] The organized home economics movement began during the Lake Placid Conference of Home Economics held in 1899, at the Club of Mr. and Mrs. Melvil Dewey.

On September 19, 1899, somewhat more than a year after Mrs. Richards' first visit to the Club, the first Lake Placid Conference on Home Economics was held in a room over the boathouse, which may be described as a fresh-air library. To call it a "library" conveys the idea that it was full of books and periodicals conveniently arranged for use, which is correct, but it gives no suggestion of the splendour of its outlook over the water to the mountains, or of the bracing quality of its air. It was a fit place for the organization into a working group of those who were seeking to learn from Nature through Science how to live.[18]

Eleven persons met at the Lake Placid Club for one week discussing many phases of domestic economy. This was the first of ten years of conferences. During the first meeting of the conference a name for the field of study was discussed. In order to gain recognition of the economic and ethical aspects of the field, the group agreed on "Home Economics" as the official title to be applied to the entire general subject. Ellen H. Richards explained the meaning in the

---

[16] Lita Bane and Mildred R. Chapin, *Introduction to Home Economics* (Boston: Houghton Mifflin Company, 1945), pp. 165–167.

[17] Hunt, op. cit., p. 135.

[18] Hunt, op. cit., p. 143.

name adopted by the conference in the following manner. *Home* stands for "the place of shelter and nurture for the children and for those personal qualities of self-sacrifice for others for the gaining of strength to meet the world." *Economics* stands for "the management of this home on economic lines as to time and energy as well as to mere money."[19]

Those topics that were originally suggested at the conferences are found in the report of the first Lake Placid Conference.

1. A classification of household economics as a working basis.
2. Additions to the bibliographies already printed, with annotations.
3. Provision for the higher education of some selected young women who shall be fitted by the best training for a higher leadership.
4. A compilation of the results of experience in teaching domestic economy in schools of this kind in this country and in Europe.
5. The preparation of a series of papers or brochures in domestic science, which the government may publish and distribute as it now does the bulletins on food and nutrition thru the department of agriculture.
6. The founding of state schools or chairs of household economics in our state universities.
7. The training of teachers of domestic science.
8. What name best interprets this work?
9. Industrial science as a part of the high school curriculum.
10. Some method of cooperation between experiment stations and schools of domestic science.
11. Domestic science in farmers' institutes.
12. How can domestic science help the woman who does her own work?
13. Simplified methods of housekeeping.
14. The discussion of technical details in the conduct of the home which may lead to some agreement on definite and approved methods.
15. Standards of living as affected by sanitary science.[20]

Caroline Hunt gave her philosophy of home economics in a talk entitled "Revaluations" during the first Lake Placid Conference. An individual's value to the world, said Caroline Hunt, depends upon the greatness of his inner life and his ability to express it. His happiness, too, depends upon this expression. Three traits are essential to full expression of the individual: health, efficiency, and opportunity. The individual can be immediately responsible for only part of the attainment of these responsibilities. Through cooperation with others

---

[19] "Proceedings of the Tenth Annual Conference, July 6–10, 1908," *Lake Placid Conference on Home Economics, Conference Proceedings* (Lake Placid Club, N.Y., 1908), p. 22.

[20] "History and Outline of First Conference," *Lake Placid Conference on Home Economics* (Lake Placid, N.Y., 1901), pp. 3–4.

he can make changes in social conditions that will increase freedoms for many, but individually he can increase his own freedom in health, efficiency, and opportunity. The individual's gaining of these freedoms depends "almost entirely upon his values"—the importance he places upon things which affect his life. The individual needs to learn to place his value upon things in relation to his needs. To do this one requires knowledge, in both science and society. "Teachers in home economics hold in their power, to an almost alarming extent, the control of values," a grave responsibility. "They should keep in mind that the world needs the most complete expression of the life of each individual, the fullest exercise of his peculiar talent or talents." For this he needs health, efficiency, and opportunity. "It should be the highest aim of teachers of home economics to help him to obtain the fullest measure of each." We succeed when we simplify life and free energy for self-expression.[21]

"Mrs. Richards' Creed" is well known for its simplicity and the professional goals set forth. The creed reflecting Mrs. Richards' philosophy was printed on a card in the Mary Lowell Stone exhibit—showing how science can be applied to daily living—which was seen at the St. Louis Exposition in 1904.

HOME ECONOMICS STANDS FOR

The ideal home life for today unhampered by the traditions of the past.
The utilization of all the resources of modern science to improve the home life.
The freedom of the home from the dominance of things and their due subordination to ideals.
The simplicity in material surroundings which will most free the spirit for the more important and permanent interests of the home and of society.[22]

During the seventh conference at Lake Placid a summary of the training of home economics teachers was given. As of 1907, 137 institutions were offering complete courses in home economics and 19 institutions incomplete courses. The progress that had been made in the thirty years since the introduction of such training in the land-grant colleges was undoubtedly due in part to the growing public knowledge resulting from the Lake Placid Conference.

Ellen H. Richards summarized the progress and development of the conference and the movement during a talk at the tenth annual conference, "Ten Years of the Lake Placid Conference on Home

[21] Ibid., pp. 79–89.
[22] Baldwin, op. cit., p. 17.

Economics; Its History and Aims." The home, she said, had not been receiving the benefits of the nineteenth-century advances in technology and science as had industry. Few of the new scientific and modern inventions filtered into the home, and woman was hampered by tradition from leaving the home to gain knowledge. Faith in and the realization of the potential of women as a collective force was lacking. Calling attention to the potential of women was a primary aim of the Lake Placid Conferences. "A name and an organized body of knowledge" were realized as the prerequisite of recognition, thus the official title "Home Economics." The basic goal of the field is the "economy of human mind and force," and it was believed that this could be nurtured best in the home, thus the emphasis of home in the title and the study. This emphasis shall remain as long as the nurture best is fulfilled within the home. The conference was believed a success as indicated by the experiments begun, the introduction of homemaking courses in many schools and universities, and the scientific investigations promoted to relieve problems. The many accomplishments of the conference showed "the beginnings of a fundamental education along progressive lines."[23]

On January 1, 1909, the American Home Economics Association became a realization. The charter membership of the AHEA was seven hundred.

By the time of the second annual meeting of the new organization in December 1909, six state and local home economics organizations had become affiliated. In 1971 the membership was about 47,000; 33,000 of these men and women held bachelor's or advanced degrees in home economics or one of its specializations, and 14,000 were student members enrolled in undergraduate programs in home economics. The AHEA then had affiliated home economics associations in each of the fifty states, the District of Columbia, and Puerto Rico. Early members laid down as the purpose of the association "to improve the conditions of living in the home," the institutions, and the community. Anyone "actively interested in home problems" could be a member. A professional journal was provided for, as well as officers, which included a president, three vice-presidents, a secretary-treasurer, an executive committee, and a council. The first elected officers were Mrs. Ellen H. Richards, president, and Dr. Benjamin R. Andrews, secretary-treasurer. Mrs. Richards held the presidency until 1910 when she insisted that she retire. She was then made honorary president.

[23] *Lake Placid Conference on Home Economics, Conference Proceedings,* "Proceedings of the Tenth Annual Conference, July 6–10, 1908," pp. 19–25.

FIGURE 2-1. *Dr. Doris Hanson (right), Executive Director of the American Home Economics Association. The illustration depicts one facet of her varied activities as she appears on the program at annual meeting. Also shown in the picture are Dr. Naomi Albanese, Association Officer (center), and Miss Mildred Davis, Director of Program and Field Services, headquarters staff. (Courtesy of the American Home Economics Association.)*

Volume 1, Number 1, of the *Journal of Home Economics* appeared in February 1909. At first Dr. Benjamin R. Andrews and Dr. C. F. Langworthy edited the journal. Beginning with the fourth issue Mrs. Mary Hinman Abel became editor; she served until 1915. In 1912, Marguerite Lake became the managing editor; in September 1913, she was succeeded by Keturah E. Baldwin, who served until 1945. Her title changed from managing editor to business editor and then to business manager of the American Home Economics Association.

On March 30, 1911, Mrs. Richards died and the association suffered a great loss. The October issue of the *Journal of Home Economics,* 1911, was devoted to the woman whose belief in the home, science, and euthenics—the term Mrs. Richards coined meaning the science dealing with bettering living conditions in order to secure efficiency for man—made possible the developing of such an organization.

Isabel Bevier divided the period of home economics development after 1912 into three stages: development, the "First World War," and reconstruction. During the development stage the public became oriented to home economics and gradually asked for more courses in other areas of the science—the family, home planning, and so on. The leaders had been greatly interested in these other aspects, but the public and administrators required time for recognition of their importance. During this period home economics was connected to some degree with social work.

The Smith-Lever Act of May 1914 provided funds that brought home economics to rural people through cooperative extension. It was designed specifically for adults not attending college. The act provided for federal and state cooperation with county and local people in diffusing useful and practical information on subjects relating to the home and the encouragement of the application of these. The Smith-Lever Act of 1914 is also noteworthy in that home economics was placed on a par with agriculture for federal and state support and in that this was the first systematic effort of the federal government to provide for adult education.

The following illustrates the growth of home economics extension work and recognizes one of the great leaders in the development. Programs varied and developed differently in various states; not all were fortunate enough to have a leader of Mrs. Burns' caliber.

Mrs. Kathryn Van Aken Burns*

by Jeanette B. Dean

Kathryn Van Aken (Burns) became the third state leader of Home Economics Extension in Illinois in 1923. During her 33 years in this position she contributed a professional attitude and high educational standards to the developing program, and she built a solid organization that provided outstanding leadership to the women of Illinois.

At first the work was largely demonstration of a few techniques, with the trained adviser doing the work and assuming responsibility for subject

---

* Written for this volume. Miss Dean was Home Science Advisor (1969–1971) on a University of Illinois/USAID contract at the Uttar Pradesh Agricultural University in India. She served from 1939 to 1954 as Jackson County Home Advisor; was on assignment in India from 1954 to 1956 at the Allahabad Agricultural Institute; and was an Assistant State Leader, Cooperative Extension Service, University of Illinois, Urbana, from 1956 to 1969.

matter and also for organization of the groups. Gradually the women assumed responsibility for details of organization and became actively interested in subject matter. They were no longer content with techniques, but wanted to know the "why" of things. Interest progressed from the demonstration of a new recipe to the relation of food to health. Mrs. Burns guided the developing program on an intellectual level that has always attracted women with high leadership qualities. An unusual number of them have become national leaders in extension associated groups. At the time of her retirement in 1956, 101 of the state's 102 counties were organized into associations having the single purpose of extension education.

Mrs. Burns' belief that extension work should be sound as to educational method and worthwhile as to content, coupled with the guidance that encouraged people to meet the standard, brought a program of which Illinois residents have been justly proud.

During the First World War the necessities of the situation placed heavy emphasis upon the value of home economics training. Women learned to conserve food and materials. A Food Administration begun by President Hoover organized home economists for action. Throughout the war Mr. Hoover relied strongly upon the leaders in the field, and it is interesting to note that he was an honorary member of AHEA.

The Smith-Hughes Act of 1917 appropriated funds for vocational education in agriculture, home economics, and trades and industries and for teacher training in these fields. This education, too, was to be a cooperative effort of the federal government and the states. The act defined home economics education as "That form of vocational education which has for its controlling purpose the preparation of girls and women for useful employment as house daughters and as homemakers engaged in the occupations and management of the home."[24] The results of the act were of great significance to the profession. It hastened and challenged home economics education; led to discussions that attempted to analyze the vocation and its processes; necessitated distinguishing between general and vocational home economics; and brought the development of unit courses. When the George-Reed supplemental act was passed in 1929, money was specifically designated for education in home economics.

No history of home economics, however sketchy, can be complete unless some mention is made of and credit given to the American Vocational Association. Organized in 1906, the association has consistently promoted and supported federal legislation in the vocational areas. Much of the credit for the growth and progress of home eco-

[24] Bevier, op. cit., p. 177.

FIGURE 2-2. *Lowell A. Burkett, Executive Director of the American Vocational Association, being interviewed on TV at an annual conference in Fresno, California. (Courtesy of the American Vocational Association.)*

nomics is attributable to the financial support and the establishment of standards for the various programs through the federal acts. Another feature that gave impetus to progress in home economics programs was the concomitant cooperative planning of policies and methods of procedures by federal, state, and local personnel. These features were consistent in all the vocational programs of the association. The association includes educators in agricultural, business, distributive, home economics, industrial arts, and trade and industrial education. All areas have profited from cooperative action. Today's home economist and other vocational educators would do well to remember that the concept of homemaking as a vocation was one of the most significant developments brought about and promulgated because of federal legislation. We find this thread running consistently through the history of home economics as stated in different ways by different leaders in different eras: that the purpose is to enhance the quality of family living through the best possible use of human and material resources.

The Office of Home Economics was created in 1915 as a division of the U.S. Department of Agriculture. Dr. Charles Langworthy became chief of this office; he had served as chief of nutrition investigations since 1905. The office included, in addition to the human nutrition investigations, textiles and clothing, and household labor and equipment. In 1923 the Office of Home Economics became the Bureau of Home Economics. Dr. Louise Stanley served as chief until 1943 and under her leadership the Bureau gained an international reputation for its work. In 1924 separate divisions were established to conduct research in foods and nutrition, family economics, textiles and clothing, and housing and household equipment. An information division was established to disseminate the findings of the research. In 1943 the Bureau of Home Economics and the Division of Protein and Nutrition were combined into the Bureau of Human Nutrition and Home Economics. Dr. Henry C. Sherman was named chief of the new bureau. In 1957 the U.S. Department of Agriculture expanded still further its work in home economics by the establishment of the Institute of Home Economics in the Agricultural Research Service of the Department of Agriculture. Through its three divisions—Clothing and Housing, Nutrition, and Household Economics—cooperative and independent research was carried on. In 1961 the name was changed to Nutrition and Consumer Use Research, as more accurately reflecting the nature and scope of the home economics research being done in the Department of Agriculture. In 1963, to strengthen the Department's consumer research effort, the Nutrition and Consumer Use Research and the Utilization Research of the Department was merged and the combined program named Nutrition, Consumer and Industrial Use Research (NCIUR). This merger made possible closer collaboration of the consumer-oriented research in food and human nutrition, clothing, and home furnishings and the utilization research into the development of new foods and food processes and new qualities for cotton and wool fabrics. In 1965 Congress discontinued support of research in housing and household equipment. In 1966 the textiles and clothing laboratory became one unit of the Consumer and Food Economics Research Division.

As a result of the First World War there was a slack in internal progress and research, inasmuch as workers had been called away from schools and laboratories. An immediate result of the war affecting the "reconstruction" period was the "opening of new lines of effort for women."[25] Home economists became needed in hotels as well as hospitals, banks, and businesses. Reconstruction meant research, improved training as preparation for research, and councils for the promotion of research. Reconstruction, according to Isabel Bevier, "is always a difficult and delicate task, difficult because often it means the uprooting of cherished traditions and customs; delicate lest in an attempt to give new form to cherished ideals they be destroyed."[26] Reconstruction was "difficult" and "delicate" but home economics advanced through its wise leadership and dedicated followers.

The Purnell Bill of 1925 provided for a more complete funding for agricultural experiment stations. Although home economics was not specifically mentioned in the bill, the funds did give impetus to the development of home economics research. The Bankhead-Jones Bill of 1935 provided additional funds for research.

Four other pieces of federal legislation, furthering other facets of home economics, were enacted during this era. The George-Reed Act of 1929 provided funds for the expansion of home economics and allowed funds for salaries of state supervisors. The George-Ellzey Act of 1934 provided additional funds for vocational education. This act expired in 1937. The George-Deen Act of 1937 provided funds for teachers of adult classes. This act was amended and superseded by the George-Barden Act of 1946, which provided for further expansion of vocational education and included authorization for the use of funds for teacher training and for research in vocational education and a limited amount of funds for equipment.

During 1926, the American Home Economics Association offered a prize for the best design of a symbol for the association, which would suggest "the application of science to the improvement of the home." Mildred Chamberlain won the award with her design incorporating the Betty lamp. According to Helen Atwater the lamp "suggests simple, American homeliness and combines with its idea of light that of the pleasant ordering of the household."[27] In *Home Sweet Home in the Nineteenth Century*, Mr. Buehr described the Betty lamp.

[25] Ibid., p. 179.
[26] Ibid.
[27] Baldwin, op. cit., p. 108.

In the well-settled areas, most homes could boast a "better lamp" than that [the customary grease lamp] or a "Betty lamp," as it came to be called. Its wrought-iron bowl was shaped roughly like a boat. After the householder filled it with fuel—usually lard or other grease—he covered it with a lid. At one end there was a tube in which he placed the wick. From the other end there rose a crescent-shaped arm which he could fit into links in a chain hanging from the rafter. This made it possible for him to raise or lower the light.[28]

The Betty lamp became the official symbol and seal of the American Home Economics Association when the executive board authorized an adaptation of the round design in 1948.

FIGURE 2-3. *The Betty Lamp, official symbol and seal of the American Home Economics Association. (Courtesy of the AHEA.)*

As early as 1916 and 1922 states were encouraged to promote student clubs. They were provided for in the bylaws of the American Home Economics Association. Student groups in both colleges and high schools were admitted into the American Home Economics Association in 1923 as affiliated groups through state organizations.

The Future Homemakers of America (FHA) developed from the high school groups that had been affiliated with the American Home Economics Association. The Home Economics Education Unit of the U.S. Office of Education sponsors FHA, with AHEA as cosponsor. Students in junior and senior high schools who are taking or have taken a home economics course are eligible to join. Total membership in June 1970, was over 600,000 in 12,000 chapters in the United States, Puerto Rico, the Virgin Islands, and American Schools overseas. The goal is to help individuals improve personal, family, and community living.[29]

[28] Buehr, op. cit., p. 88.
[29] *Biennial Report on Future Homemakers of America*, Office of Education, U.S. Department of Health, Education, and Welfare (Washington, D.C.: U.S. Government Printing Office, 1970).

34

Membership in the American Home Economics Association Constitution has undergone considerable revision. In the beginning the membership requirement was simply an interest in problems of the home. By 1940 a new policy brought a special membership requirement.

A degree from a college or university with a major in home economics; or a degree from a college or university with a major in a related field (as biological science, physical science, social science, psychology, related art) and, in addition, evidence satisfactory to the executive committee that through subsequent training or experience the person has become, in interest and practice, a home economist.[30]

The assembly of delegates at the annual convention of the American Home Economics Association in June 1967, and in June 1970, adopted bylaws that again somewhat changed the membership requirements. Eligible for membership are those who hold a bachelor's degree or an advanced degree in home economics or in a specialized area of home economics from an accredited college in the United States or Canada. Also eligible for membership are those who hold a bachelor's or advanced degree in a related subject-matter area from an accredited college or university in the United States or Canada, who have a minimum of two years' experience in home economics.

The American Home Economics Association includes in its organizational structure subject-matter and professional sections embracing the major areas of study and employment. Currently, the subject-matter sections are the following: art; family economics–home management; family relations and child development; food and nutrition; home economics communications; home economics teacher education; housing, furnishings, and equipment; institution administration; and textiles and clothing. The professional sections are the following: colleges and universities; elementary, secondary, and adult education; extension service; health and welfare; home economists in business; home economists in homemaking; research; and student members.

The primary business offices of the AHEA remained in the Mill's Building in Washington, D.C., for many years. In 1948 the offices were moved to the Victor Building. A red brick and limestone Victorian building at 1600 Twentieth Street in Washington was purchased as headquarters November 9, 1950, was dedicated on May 16, 1952, and was used until 1971. The new national headquarters building

---

[30] Baldwin, op. cit., p. 28.

at 2010 Massachusetts Avenue, N.W., was built specifically to serve this purpose and, as stated in the May 1971, *Journal of Home Economics,* "verifies the fact that a building is primarily space for people with a program."

FIGURE 2-4. *Headquarters building at 2010 Massachusetts Avenue, N.W., Washington, D.C. (Courtesy of the AHEA.)*

In the following years the American Home Economics Association and its members cooperated extensively with other groups. At the Midcentury White House Conference on Children and Youth, held in Washington, D.C., in 1950, many AHEA members participated and a postconference of home economists was held. A Special Project on

Family Life Education was held in 1951–1952 by the Grant Foundation, which worked chiefly to strengthen a family-centered concern with home economics. The "Home Economist in Expanding Programs of International Service" was a conference called by the Association in 1954 to give better preparation to home economists going abroad and to help foreign students studying home economics in the United States.[31]

The American Home Economics Association continues to evidence its basic concern with "the attainment and maintenance of the well-being of individuals, families, and homes, and the preservation of values significant in home life"[32] through workshops, conferences, and publications. Illustrative of these are the "National Workshop on Working with Low Income Families," the international conference held by AHEA on "Family Planning," participation in White House conferences on nutrition and on aging, participation in and publications on Project Head Start, and the theme of the 1972 annual meeting of the Association—"Motivation for Involvement."

A note of historical interest is that in 1915 the American Home Economics Association was "authorized to take out membership in the International Office for the Teaching of Domestic Subjects (International Congress on Home Economics)."[33] It may be challenging to realize that the international "federation was organized in 1908 and in 1911 was responsible for the International Congress on Home Economics."[34]

It is interesting to note some of the concerns of the members of the International Federation as indicated by stresses placed in the last three International Congress meetings held in Helsinki, Finland; in Bristol, England; and in Paris, France. An important stress is the opportunity to become acquainted and exchange ideas with other home economists from over sixty countries, thus emphasizing the need for international cooperation. Another point of emphasis was the study of the place and responsibilities of home economics in preserving the inherent values of family life and serving the wider society.

The home economics profession again was advanced by a legis-

---

[31] Mary Hawkins (ed.), *The American Home Economics Association 1950–1954. A Supplement to the AHEA Saga*, by Keturah E. Baldwin (Washington, D.C.: The Association, 1959), p. 29.

[32] Marilyn J. Horn, "Accreditation Second Progress Report," *Journal of Home Economics*, 56:9 (November 1964), p. 660.

[33] Hazel T. Craig, *The History of Home Economics* (New York: Practical Home Economics, 1945), p. 34.

[34] Ibid., p. 38.

lative act, the Vocational Education Act of 1963, which appropriated funds to be used

for vocational education programs to prepare people for employment in any occupational field not requiring a baccalaureate degree. The program may be conducted in comprehensive or specialized high schools, area vocational schools, junior and community colleges or universities that offer terminal vocational programs. . . .

In addition to preparation for homemaking, home economics funds will be directed toward the homemaking skills that hold employment opportunities. A minimum of ten per cent of the home economics funds, under provisions of the Smith-Hughes and George-Barden Acts, must be used for job-oriented training.[35]

Since homemaking education in the high schools had been defined in the Smith-Hughes Act as that education preparing one to be a housedaughter or housewife, little had been done in the public schools to prepare students in home economics for related occupations, employment in these occupations to begin immediately after high school graduation. Thus, home economics education began seeking the help of the other vocational subjects, such as business and agriculture, in which students were already being trained for wage-earning occupations. Workshops began in colleges and universities throughout the country preparing home economics teachers for this new role.

The Economic Opportunity Act of 1964 made possible the creation of such programs as Project Head Start, the Peace Corps, Upward Bound, Community Action Programs, Migrant Worker Programs, VISTA, the Job Corps Training, and the Grandparents Programs. Because they are directly related to work with children and families these have been briefly discussed in the section of this book relating to careers.

The National Vocational Student Loan Insurance Act of 1965, P. L. 89–287, provided for assistance to students desiring vocational training. It was designed to encourage the establishment of loan insurance for such students in business, trade, technical, and other vocational schools. The terms of these loans to students in vocational schools were similar to the student loan insurance provisions of the Higher Education Act.

The Elementary and Secondary Education Act of 1965 had for its purpose to strengthen and improve educational quality and educational opportunities in the nation's elementary and secondary schools.

[35] M. D. Mobley, "A Review of Federal Vocational-Education Legislation 1862–1963," *Theory into Practice*, III: 5 (Columbus: Ohio State University), 167–170.

The Act's five titles were each directed toward a particular problem area. Title I provided financial assistance to local educational agencies for special educational programs in areas having high concentrations of children of low-income families. Funds could be used to hire additional staff, to buy or rent equipment and other teaching aids, to improve the school plant, and to provide in-service training of teachers, supplemental health and food services, and so on. Title II provided for additional school library resources, textbooks, and other instructional resources. Title III provided financing for supplementary educational centers and services. Among the types of services that were provided and that made the difference between a poor school and a good school were special instructions in science, languages, music, and the arts; counseling and guidance; health and social work; access to museums, art galleries, theaters, and technical institutes; and innovative, exemplary programs that served as stimuli to local planning and operation. Title IV amended the Cooperative Research Act and provided funds for the construction of national and regional research facilities and for the expansion of research and development. Title V provided for strengthening state departments of education. Funds could be used to improve educational planning; identify problems and needs; evaluate programs; publish and distribute curriculum materials; conduct research; improve teacher preparation; and train staff.

The Higher Education Act of 1965 is intended to strengthen the educational resources of our colleges and universities and to provide financial assistance for students in postsecondary and higher education. Title I provides for community services and continuing education programs. It is dedicated to taking advantage of the skills and knowledge of the university to work with the community and to enlarging university extension and continuing education programs and bringing them within the economic and geographical reach of more people.

Title II is concerned with college library assistance and library training and research. It provides grants to colleges and universities for books, periodicals, tapes, phonograph records, and so on; for training libraries; and for research and demonstration projects in library science. Title III is concerned with strengthening developing institutions. It is designed to assist small colleges through federal grants to promote faculty improvement programs, new courses and study materials, exchange of faculty and students with other colleges, joint use of libraries and laboratories, and so on.

Title IV is concerned with student assistance. It provides for educational opportunity grants to help college students with exceptional financial needs; for federally subsidized loans to college students; and for transferring the administration of the work-study program, enacted the previous year as part of the Economic Opportunity Act of the Office of Education, and broadening its provisions. Title V is directed toward improving the quality and increasing the number of teachers. It provides for a National Teacher Corps; for fellowships for graduate study for persons pursuing or intending to pursue a career in elementary or secondary teaching; and for grants to and contracts with institutions of higher education to strengthen their graduate teacher-education programs. Berenice Mallory is Head of the Home Economics Unit, Occupational Section, Division of Vocational and Technical Education.

The 1965 amendments to Title V, Social Security Act, P. L. 89–97, Relating to Maternal and Child Health and Crippled Children's Services, together with the provisions for programs under the Maternal and Child Health and Mental Retardation Planning Amendments of 1963, have given a major new impetus to preventive health services and medical care for mothers and children and to meeting the problems of providing such health services in areas with a growing concentration of low-income families.

In order to extend programs and services, the 1965 amendments increased the authorization for grants to states for maternal and child health and crippled children's services, raising the former ceiling for each program of $50 million by steps to $60 million for the fiscal year ending June 30, 1970.

Significance for home economists: Nutrition services are an integral part of these expanded and improved maternal and child health and crippled children's services. More well-trained nutritionists and dietitians are needed to:

- Extend nutrition consultation to the multidiscipline staff of maternal and child health and crippled children's programs in public health agencies at the federal, state, and local levels.
- Provide nutrition services in the special maternity clinics established for high-risk maternity patients; and in the screening, diagnostic, and treatment centers for children.
- Expand and improve consultation given to hospitals and group-care facilities for mothers and children to improve nutrition and food service standards and practices (e.g., hospitals, day-care centers, residential homes).

• Collect data and research information related to the nutritional status and the dietary practices of high-risk maternity patients, children, and youth and to ways of improving them.

Nutritionists, dietitians, and other home economists are already providing services in clinics for mothers and children, in follow-up services in the home, and in group care facilities, such as residential centers, day-care centers, and sheltered workshops. All of these activities should increase and expand. It should be noted, however, that the tendency, at the time of this writing, is toward revenue sharing whereby such expanding *might* be done through federal, state, county, and local support.

Many new occupations have opened for the professional home economists in all forms of research. The Peace Corps and the War on Poverty have utilized the training of home economists to the advantage of peoples throughout the world. The American Home Economics Association and American home economists have done and are doing their part in contributing to "an environment that supports and contributes to the well-being of people, as individuals and as members of a family and society."[36]

The 1968 amendment, P. L. 90–576, to the Vocational Education Act of 1963 contains a separate section, Part F of Title I, authorizing allotments of funds on a matching basis to states for "Consumer and Homemaking Education."[37]

"Consumer and homemaking education" is defined in the "Regulations for State Plan Program," which states must meet to qualify for funding under the provisions of Part F of the Vocational Education Amendments of 1968, as "education designed to help individuals and families improve home environments and the quality of personal and family life. . . . [It] includes instruction in food and nutrition, child development, clothing, housing, family relations, and management of resources with emphasis on selection, use, and care of goods and services, budgeting, and other consumer responsibilities."

Funds allotted to the states for the purpose of Part F of the Amendments may be used for consumer and homemaking programs and for ancillary services and activities to assure quality in these programs. The following requirements must be met for a program to receive approval:

    (a) The program will encourage greater consideration of the social and cultural conditions and needs, especially in economically depressed areas;

[36] Mary Hawkins (ed.), preface to *The AHEA Saga,* op. cit., p. 29.
[37] Public Law 90–576, October 1968. *Vocational Education Amendments of 1968,* "Title I, Part F," p. 22.

(b) The program will encourage preparation for professional leadership in home economics and consumer education;

(c) The program will be designed for youth and adults who have entered or are preparing to enter the work of the home;

(d) The program will be designed to prepare such youth and adults for the role of homemaker or to contribute to their employability in the dual role of homemaker and wage earner; and

(e) The program will include consumer education as an integral part thereof.[38]

Certainly no history of home economics, however brief or however selective, could or should ignore the "McGrath report," entitled *The Changing Mission of Home Economics*. The report was the result of "a study aimed at defining the future role and scope of home economics among[39] the members of the National Association of State Universities and Land-Grant Colleges. "The dominant object of" the report was "to improve the practice of home economics and to expand its beneficial influence on American society.[40] The study covered a two-year period and used the survey and interview methods.

The report indicated that "This study of the programs of home economics in the land-grant colleges and state universities leads to the firm conclusion that it is wiser social policy to help and to encourage home economics to adapt to new social needs than to abandon or dismember it as a field of study or to shift its services to other elements of the American system of higher education. Hence we advocate improving the practice of home economics and extending its beneficial influence to other phases of American life."[41] The historical focus of home economics upon the family is still appropriate and preferable.[42]

". . . 'Family service' remains the integrative center of home economics. . . ."[43] Although "other professions . . . encompass in their purview one or another kind of service to families, none of them so directly aims to serve the overall well-being and maintenance of the family unit as does home economics."[44] Thus, while indicating that

[38] Mary Lee Hurt and Margaret Alexander, "New Challenges," *Journal of Home Economics*, Vol. LXI, No. 10 (December 1969), p. 772.

[39] Earl J. McGrath and Jack T. Johnson, *The Changing Mission of Home Economics* (New York: Teachers College Press, 1968), page ix.

[40] Ibid., p. x.

[41] Ibid., pp. 83–84.

[42] Ibid., p. 84.

[43] Ibid., p. 85.

[44] Ibid., p. 85.

the mission of home economics has not changed in actuality, many very immediate and continuing changes in methods, clientele, and scope are indicated. These changes must be made because of the ". . . social, economic, and educational developments in American and in international life. . . ."[45] Stressed among these developments were urbanization, the increasing numbers of women who combine homemaking and a career outside the home, the number of occupations now open to women, the changing role of the American home-maker, and the new programs in social welfare.[46] Definite recommendations were made for alternatives and adaptations; the Home Economics Commission Task Force generally supported these recommendations but took exception to some of them (or to some of their implications), particularly (4), (5), and (6), which follow. Among the changes recommended in the McGrath study are (1) "the knowledge encompassed within home economics must be made available in more ways to more people."[47] (2) At the undergraduate level, "some specialized majors must be provided, but the present primary need in undergraduate programs is to assure the quality of the broad major in the field—the major most appropriate for students who seek employment as home economists in business or as school teachers of home economics, or for those who enroll to become more effective community volunteer workers or better homemakers."[48] ". . . Home economics at the undergraduate level can best confirm its heritage and meet present challenges by retaining a strong generalist major, while expanding its interdisciplinary base in order to fully comprehend contemporary social problems and those of family life."[49] (3) "At the master's level, home economics should stress professional specialization. . . ." Most ". . . institutions should expand their urban programs considerably, and some should assume greater international responsibilities by creating master's programs specifically for these purposes."[50] (4) At the doctoral level, "in the years ahead . . . the profession and society as a whole would be better served if the offering of the doctorate in home economics continues to be concentrated in a limited number of universities."[51] (5) As to extension service clientele,

[45] Ibid., p. 83.
[46] Ibid., pp. 81–84.
[47] Ibid., p. 85.
[48] Ibid., p. 87.
[49] Ibid., p. 88.
[50] Ibid., p. 92.
[51] Ibid., p. 93.

it was suggested that cooperative extension agents would render more valuable service to American society, if they were to deal more than they now do with persons in urban areas, with the poor, and with the non-white.

The facts about social conditions in the United States clearly indicate that such a shift in the orientation of extension work is patently essential. In a nation in which nearly 70 per cent of the population resides in urban areas, urban dwellers constitute only about one-half of the persons reached by home economics extension projects. While there is no doubt that middle-class families can benefit from increased knowledge of home economics, instruction of this kind is nothing less than essential to the improvement of the living conditions of those persons who are in the lowest economic strata. Moreover, since non-whites constitute a much larger proportion of those in the lowest financial strata than they do of the total population, they should therefore receive increased attention by those designing extension service programs.[52]

(6) As to extension service administration, (a) "the activities of cooperative extension and general extension should ultimately be combined into one structure, with home economics extension becoming an area of continuing education along with the many other subject-matter fields now being made accessible to an ever-growing number of our citizens;"[53] (b) "in each state the extension programs of all the public colleges and universities, and where possible the privately supported institutions as well, should be coordinated by means of a state master plan;"[54] (c) "the administrators of home economics programs must be granted a more decisive voice in budget preparation and hence in the allocation of funds."[55]

(7) As to research, (a) "To assure that the investigations undertaken possess both substance and broad significance . . . it is essential that working relationships be established with productive scholars in other disciplines;"[56] (b) " 'it is recommended that applied research programs in home economics should be dispersed over a wider number of institutions. . . .' "[57] (8) As to organization, (a) "The programs of home economics now under the jurisdiction of schools of agriculture should be freed from this control;"[58] (b) "Since local needs, objectives, and traditions vary widely, no single realignment will automatically produce the most effective structure for every institution.

[52] Ibid., pp. 93–94.
[53] Ibid., p. 94.
[54] Ibid., p. 95.
[55] Ibid., p. 95.
[56] Ibid., p. 96.
[57] Ibid., p. 97.
[58] Ibid., p. 99.

... Perceptive and imaginative advocates of change ... must take the initiative in experimenting with new informal and formal programs and alliances."[59]

The Home Economics Commission Task Force mentioned on page 42 was authorized at the meeting of the National Association of State Universities and Land-Grant Colleges in November 1967. The task force was to be selected and was directed to study, analyze, and implement the findings of the McGrath Report.

THE NASULGC HOME ECONOMICS TASK FORCE[*]

by Flossie M. Byrd

The NASULGC Home Economics Commission Task Force met in Chicago, May 2–4, 1968, "to study, analyze and implement the findings of the McGrath Report." With regard to the concentration of doctoral programs in a limited number of institutions, it was suggested that this would create hardships for many capable persons interested in further study but unable to relocate for this purpose. The development of interinstitutional doctoral programs within the several regions was recommended as a solution to the personnel problem. It was indicated that cooperative extension agents had been and were actively engaged in the development of innovative approaches to the problems of the urban as well as rural low-income families and that these programs were multiethnic in orientation. Further, it was recommended that the focus of cooperative extension should include the identification of new funds for program expansion, the enrichment of training programs through studies dealing with pertinent contemporary issues affecting families, and the inclusion of college and extension home economics personnel on cooperative extension policy-making bodies.

The full text of recommendations of the Task Force was extensive in scope. Member institutions of the NASULGC undertook in-depth study of the areas of concern. Subsequent activity has included the publication of college and university enrollment data with definitive analyses, articles dealing with cooperative extension and community action programs, and a definition of home economics for the 1970's. Additional presentations are being prepared for inclusion in a variety of professional journals and popular magazines as a basis for increasing public awareness of the contemporary nature and contribution of home economics to society.

---

[59] Ibid., p. 99.

[*] Written for this volume. Dr. Flossie M. Byrd is Dean of the School of Home Economics at Prairie View Agricultural and Mechanical College of Texas. Her degrees are from Florida Agricultural and Mechanical University, Pennsylvania State University, and Cornell University. Her experiences include teaching homemaking in high school in Florida and positions as teacher educator at Florida A and M University and at Prairie View A and M College. She has held offices in national home economics organizations, served on numerous state and national home economics committees, and was co-chairman of the NASULGC Home Economics Commission during 1967–1969.

Amendments to the National School Lunch Act and the Child Nutrition Act of 1970 and 1971 provided authority to increase federal financial aid for free and reduced-price lunches and also to introduce nutrition education into schools.

Other federal legislation is pending that, if passed, will affect the resources available to the home economist; the needed funding for all of these programs, or deflection of funds from them will affect the training, services, and research in many areas. Home economics educators, particularly, should have available the *Catalog of Federal Domestic Assistance,* published yearly and available from the Superintendent of Documents.

Two noteworthy takeoff points for all home economists of the present and future came early in the 1970–1980 decade, preceded by years of hard but rewarding work. The first of these was the realization of the new national headquarters building mentioned earlier. The second was the official notification by the National Commission on accrediting giving recognition to the American Home Economics Association for accrediting programs in the field of home economics at the undergraduate level in colleges and universities of the United States; this action was taken by the Board of Commissioners of the National Commission on accrediting at its annual meeting on March 26, 1971. Both of these are really means by which home economists may more effectively work toward helping to solve current problems such as new directions for the family, nutrition, child-care centers, rehabilitation, consumer education and consumer protection, environmental problems, the problems of the disadvantaged, *and* the education of all—babies, youth, and adults—including parents. All of these current problems are of vital importance but, perhaps, none more so than new directions for the family indicating a need for in-depth study of the nuclear family and its alternatives, men and women in isolation, changing sex roles, differing life styles, and so on. Also, see pages 14, 21, 22, 42, 43, 47, 48, 53, 54, 55 for additional ideas on this subject.

The women's liberation movement, although not new, must also be considered by home economists as a current problem.

When a comprehensive history of the American feminist movement is written it will be clear that the first phase of that movement—the struggle for women's rights—took form during the same years of the nineteenth century that home economics was emerging, and in response to many of the same needs of the society of that day. Both sprang, in part, from that great egalitarian surge that coincided with our population's westward movement. While the women's rights movement in the early years was concentrating on women's suffrage and obtaining equal rights for women, home economics was developing new professions for women and opportunities for educational courses and curricula in the colleges and universities that would be as useful to women as the new education in engineering and agriculture was for men. One of the objectives of the early programs in home economics was to free the homemaker from household drudgery so that she might spend her energies on more creative endeavors.

The current women's liberation movement might be classified as phase II of the American feminist movement.

. . . .

It is appropriate that we examine our responsibilities as professional home economists in relation to liberation. Our predecessors contributed in significant ways years ago, when women were seeking equal rights. Now there are new goals and new responsibilities.[60]

It is clear that much of the decision making relating to the needs of family members is now being made by public agencies. The homemakers, both men and women, need to be educated or reeducated to participate effectively in many educational decisions, including those concerning the public schools, child-care centers, and the school lunch program, and in the decisions that affect health being made through law makers, as in laws relating to product safety, sanitation, and other pollution problems. The homemaker who wants to protect individuals and the family from crime needs education that he can use effectively to influence the adequacy of police protection, street lighting, and the fulfillment of justice.

Mary C. Eagan, in her article, "The Expanding Service Arena in Home Economics," succinctly summarizes the changes that are affecting the education and the working roles of the home economist.

Changing sphere of influence of parent and home. Dramatic changes have been occurring in the role of the family in meeting the needs of its individual members, with various social institutions gradually assuming more of the responsibilities formerly carried by the family. . . .

Interchange and sharing of family roles. Men are accepting responsibility for home making and child care activities, and women are increasingly involved with wage earning. . . .

Increasing use of "team approach" to meet the complexity of changes affecting individuals and families. . . . Those in home economics must learn to work with those employed at many levels in their own profession as well as in other professions.

Greater awareness of the need to improve delivery of human services, while simultaneously improving use of human resources. This is the basic concept in much of the recent legislation that focuses on improving services

[60] Helen LeBaron Hilton, "Now That Women Are Liberated," *Journal of Home Economics,* 64 (April 1972), pp. 2–5.

to the poor and disadvantaged and at the same time providing opportunities for involving and employing the community in the program and giving them a chance to use their skills and to develop new ones in a situation where they can advance.

Increasing emphasis on the responsibility of the education system to make provision for every student to acquire the skills that will allow him to earn a livelihood for himself and for his future family and to prepare him for total living, no matter at what level of the educational system he leaves. . . .

More citizen participation and consumer involvement in the planning and implementation of programs and services will help put an end to citizens being only on the "receiving" end. . . . All professional workers will need to know how to work with citizens as aides, volunteers, cooperative planners, etc.[61]

In paragraph four of Ms. Eagan's quoted article, we find a very positive and hopeful statement in relation to recent legislation. The writer feels that it is vital that professionals and students in home economics keep up-to-date through current literature on pending and passed legislation that affect the lives of individuals and families. It is the responsibility of the professional and future professional to take positive action through their legislators on pending legislation *and* to find ways of implementing legislation that can be made to work to benefit individuals and families with whom they work. Examples of this follow.

BUDGET

The 1974 budget request for the Department of Health, Education, and Welfare (HEW) reveals major changes proposed by the Administration in several programs. The changes reflect a basic philosophical disagreement with the programs of the Great Society. The Democrat controlled Congress will not agree with all Administration proposals but some changes in programs are expected as the Senate and House "work their will."

OEO

The poverty program, for example, is slated to be dismantled and to cease operations as an organizational entity as of July 1, 1973. . . .

The program on community economic development, directed toward providing economic and community development in rural and urban areas with concentrations of low-income persons, will be transferred to the Office of Minority Business Enterprise.

Programs related to economic upgrading, farmworker housing, high school equivalency programs, and day care for migrant farm workers will be transferred to the Department of Labor. . . .

[61] Mary C. Eagan, "The Expanding Service Arena in Home Economics," *Journal of Home Economics,* Vol. 64 (February 1972), pp. 49–75.

EDUCATION

Legislation is again recommended to the Congress to authorize a program of special revenue sharing in elementary and secondary education. The proposed effective date is July 1, 1973. The new program would consolidate over 30 existing program authorities into a single formula grant to the states with five earmarks: disadvantaged, handicapped, vocational education, impact aid, and support services. According to the Administration, the "earmarks for the handicapped and vocational education will insure a minimum level of funding in these priority areas but give state and local school officials much greater flexibility in targeting and programming the funds." It is doubtful that the earmarking would extend to categories such as consumer and homemaking education.

Sharp cutbacks are proposed for the training programs of the Social and Rehabilitation Service. . . .

WELFARE

Approximately one-half of the $30 billion appropriations for HEW from general revenues in 1974 is accounted for by public assistance payments and the new Supplemental Security Income (SSI) program for the aged, blind, and disabled. The SSI program, which becomes effective January 1, 1974, will be administered by the Social Security Administration as a Federal rather than a Federal/State welfare program with uniform national eligibility standards.

The Aid to Families with Dependent Children program will continue as a Federal/State program in the Social and Rehabilitation Service. . . .

Only $2 billion of the $2.5 billion authorized for social services is requested in the 1974 budget. These social services funds finance day care, foster care for children, and aid to the elderly and mentally retarded.

The work incentive (WIN) program would increase from $291 million in 1973 to $534 million in 1974. Funds for day care are included and will more than double.

CONSUMER AFFAIRS

Executive Order 11702 transferred the Office of Consumer Affairs from the Executive Office of the President to HEW. The director of the Office of Consumer Affairs continues as the special assistant to the President for consumer affairs. . . .

CONSUMER AGENCY

Once again legislation has been introduced to establish a Council of Consumer Advisers in the Executive Office of the President and an independent Consumer Protection Agency. . . .

Legislation to establish an independent consumer protection agency was approved by the Senate during the 91st Congress but not by the House. In the 92d Congress such legislation was approved by the House but not by the Senate. Proponents of the measure are hopeful that both bodies will reach agreement during the 93d Congress.

SCHOOL FOOD

The legislation proposing special revenue sharing in education would also include some funds currently appropriated for child feeding programs of the Department of Agriculture. According to the 1974 HEW budget, $244 million in school lunch foods, but not those for free or reduced-price lunches, would be transferred to the block grant to the states.

USDA regulations modify Federal prohibitions against "competitive food service." State and local school authorities would have sole responsibility to regulate the foods sold in competition with school lunches so long as the profits from the sale of such foods go to the school or school-approved student organizations.[62]

Some of the long-range predictions of significance to the home economist were outlined by Dr. Flossie M. Byrd in her article in the June 1970, *Journal of Home Economics;* these are a doubling of world population, increased physical and mental stress, mounting environmental pollution, a soaring gross national productivity, a move to ocean farming and the use of synthetic proteins; a dilemma of "people problems," a profamily shift, added momentum to the knowledge explosion, shortened work hours, unemployment, scarcity of natural resources, and the prolongation of life. Certainly the *education of the home economics professional must be different* if we are to function effectively in helping to solve the problems of now and of the not-so-distant future; certainly, too, both the national headquarters and the home economics accredited programs must implement the meeting of our responsibilities in these areas.

The home economics profession honors its history as do other organized groups. The role of women, the increasingly valued education of women, and the awakening of science affected the realization of homemaking education. Count Rumford, born in the eighteenth century, has been said to be the first to apply science to the kitchen. Shortly, classes in sewing were introduced to the elementary grades. Catherine E. Beecher's *A Treatise on Domestic Economy* and *Domestic Receipt Book,* written in the 1840's, became guides for teaching domestic science.

The Federal Land-Grant Act, or Morrill Act, gave federal funds to state universities to promote the teaching of agriculture and the mechanic arts. Land-grant colleges developed in the West, while private schools remained the place of domestic education in the East.

[62] Editorial Staff of *Journal of Home Economics,* "Washington News," *Journal of Home Economics,* Vol. 65, No. 4 (April 1973), p. 4.

Various cooking schools and kitchens promoted nutrition and sanitation in the East; examples are the New York Cooking School, the Boston Cooking School, the Boston Normal School of Cookery, the New England Kitchen, and the Rumford Kitchen.

Other enterprises that had a great influence on the profession were the Kitchen Garden Association, the National Household Economics Association, the Federation of Women's Clubs, and the nutritional investigations of the United States Department of Agriculture and the agriculture experiment stations.

The noted leaders of the field include Mrs. Ellen H. Richards, through whose leadership and scientific understanding the American Home Economics Association was founded; Wilbur O. Atwater, the father of American nutrition and the organizer of the experiment stations of the Department of Agriculture; Mr. and Mrs. Melvil Dewey, whose guidance, encouragement, and patronage at the Lake Placid Conferences gave impetus to the new profession; Caroline Hunt, a follower of Mrs. Richards and the author of her biography, as well as an essential member of the conferences; Mary Hinman Abel, who served as the first editor of the *Journal of Home Economics;* Keturah E. Baldwin, who edited the *Journal of Home Economics* for some forty years; and Isabel Bevier, the author of *Home Economics in Education* as well as other notable books on the profession.

In the twentieth century home economics received considerable advancement through the federal government. The Smith-Lever Act in 1914 brought home economics to rural areas through cooperative extension. The Smith-Hughes Act in 1917 promoted vocational education by supplying funds for secondary public schools. After succeeding vocational acts that supplied further funds, the Vocational Education Act of 1963 redefined home economics education to include training for wage earning. Large appropriations were made for this new purpose and home economics is seeking to utilize this opportunity for the advancement of professional objectives. The 1968 amendment to the Vocational Education Act of 1963 authorized allotments of funds on a matching basis to states for "Consumer and Homemaking Education." In the twentieth century, too, we find two outstanding achievements by the AHEA: the new national headquarters building and recognition by the association for accrediting programs in the field of home economics at the undergraduate level in colleges and universities of the United States. Other federal legislation, passed and pending, is supportive of our family-oriented program.

The American Home Economics Association and American home

economists have made a strong contribution to home and families throughout the world. They are working with Home Economics Associations of many other countries for the same purposes that concerned the American pioneers of the profession.

The next pages in the history of home economics will be determined by you, the student and future professional. The major current careers in home economics are described in the next chapter. It is to be hoped that you will find there an avenue, in line with your own objectives, whereby you can make significant contributions to solving the present and future problems of our world; or, perhaps, with vision and idealism—tempered with realism—you can help in carving out new careers that will uphold a history of which you, too, can be proud.

3

Careers for Men and Women in Home Economics

As you, the student, have studied the objectives of the profession of home economics and of the American Home Economics Association, *the* overall professional organization, you alone can tell whether these objectives align with your own and are such that you feel a personal commitment. The career opportunities in home economics for both men and women are manifold and unique; the salaries compare favorably with those in other professions.

The abstruse opinion that home economics careers are for women alone is one that is changing. Men have been actively interested and often involved in promoting the objectives of home economics as indicated, for example, in the founding of the American Home Economics Association and in the support of federal legislation nurturing home economics. More recently men have become aware of the contributions they can make by pursuing an active and rewarding career in home economics.

While deploring the shortage of men in home economics professions, the author also deplores the factitious values expressed by some in the "women's liberation movement" that might cause many women to have a "guilt feeling" unless they worked outside the home for money, regardless of need and regardless of other kinds of contributions that they might make for the good of society. For the latter reason homemaking as a career is discussed first because it may well be the profession in which many women will find their most rewards and opportunities for contributions.

Homemaking

When Ellen H. Richards led the movement resulting in the organization of home economics, it was with the sincere belief that science could be applied in the home to the advantage of the family. The President's Commission on Higher Education included in its goals for general education as an imperative need in our society: "To acquire the knowledge and attitudes basic to a satisfying family life."[1] A publication of the American Home Economics Association stated:

> The Committee on Criteria for Evaluating College Departments of Home Economics . . . believes that education for home and family life should be the first objective of a program of home economics in higher education. It believes that such education strengthens rather than weakens the professional preparation of students at the undergraduate level and that it gives meaningful focus to the total program of college education for home economics students.[2]

Grace M. Henderson later stated that home economics has "the responsibility of integrating the contributions for all the sciences, arts, and philosophy into one functional whole for service to families. . . . [The] integrating function for improving family life . . . is the unique purpose of Home Economics."[3]

Thus, education in home economics is centered on home and family life. It has been so since its historical beginning and basically continues to be so today. Historically, too, homemaking is the oldest occupation, for wherever there have been families we find accounts of homemakers who have looked to the feeding, shelter, clothing, and care of the young in the family. The roles of men and women in homemaking vary both in period of time and in different cultures. In the United States, the homemaker has usually been thought of as the woman, who is primarily responsible for the managerial aspects of feeding, clothing, and sheltering the family and of taking care of the young. Yet in the United States today we are inclined to consider marriage as the entering into

---

[1] *Report of the President's Commission on Higher Education* (Washington, D.C.: U.S. Government Printing Office, 1947), p. 56.

[2] American Home Economics Association, *Home Economics in Higher Education* (Washington, D.C.: The Association, 1949), p. 32.

[3] Grace M. Henderson, *Development of Home Economics in the United States* (University Park, Pa.: College of Home Economics, Pennsylvania State University, 1954), pp. 14–16.

a partnership with shared responsibilities. This sharing of responsibilities and the division of labor are largely dependent upon the home background and the kinds of education that the husband and wife have had.

Most professional home economists are well aware of the fact that there are at least two schools of thought on the major objectives and purposes of home economics in higher education. An examination of college and university catalogues will no doubt indicate more. However, some contend that the major *raison d'être* is to train professionals who will then be of service to families. Others believe that it is possible to educate a highly competent professional *and* at the same time educate this person so that he will function effectively as an individual, a homemaker, and a citizen. The latter group maintains that this applies to men as well as to women although the education for each will be different. In the writer's studied opinion, home economics has the unique opportunity *and* responsibility to offer the kind of educational programs that will prepare young people for their multiple roles. The following quotation from Sigmund Nosow seems pertinent for the potential home economist as well as for those professionals currently in higher education.

The changing social order has created intellectual and social problems which must be faced. The needs for general education at all levels in home and family living become more pronounced daily. Home economics has the longest tradition of interest and service in this area. The services it has so admirably continued to perform within the rural communities and has extended to urban communities must be broadened. Those who are highly oriented to research and the unique specialties which still are found within home economics might do well to recognize that the history and success of home economics has rested upon public support and the belief that what home economics does is valuable.[4]

In the United States more than 90 per cent of the people marry and have homes. More women college graduates are in the profession of homemaking than in any other single occupation. So you have already made the choice of homemaking as a profession or our society has made it for you. Today more and more parents are realizing the values in a college education for their daughters and more colleges and universities are recognizing the importance of education for home and family life for both men and women either through the home eco-

[4] Sigmund Nosow, "The Nature of a Profession: Home Economics, a Particular Case," *The Field of Home Economics—What It Is* (Washington, D.C.: American Home Economics Association, 1965), pp. 48–49.

nomics curricula and/or through general education courses directed toward education for home and family life. No other educational program can so clearly show that its curriculum offers education (1) that can be used for a lifetime and (2) that is preparation for the profession of homemaking *and* a wage-earning profession.

Nature of the Homemaking Profession

Professional or amateur? Most definitions of profession include a contrast with amateur. Many professional organizations have established standards or criteria for their professions. The following statements have been adapted from the National Commission on Teacher Education and Professional Standards, *The Teacher and Professional Organizations.*[5] Although they do not include all of the criteria for the teacher, the ones selected do seem to identify homemaking as a profession.

Homemaking is a profession in that it affords a life career; involves intellectual activities and responsibilities; demands a body of specialized knowledge, skills, and attitudes; has a well-defined function; exalts service above personal gain; and demands continual growth.

Sigmund Nosow in discussing home economics as a profession indicates that there are certain attitudes as well as basic characteristics that determine professionalism. The attitudes include those toward work, pay, self-esteem, colleagues, clients, employers, and the general public. The basic characteristics include a coherent body of ideas and principles that are learned through education and that are based on research and form the basis for practice; "authority over a given body of knowledge emphasizing the layman's comparative ignorance"; community approval of the profession; and a set of values and attitudes upon which the person bases his work and way of interacting with others. A significant characteristic of the professional is the idea that this is a career and implies an attitude toward work that is professional in nature. Professor Nosow also points out that no profession in "the real world" contains all the characteristics in any definition or description of a profession.[6]

Most people are familiar with the many responsibilities and contributions of the homemaker. A hard look at some of these may clearly

---

[5] National Commission on Teacher Education and Professional Standards, *The Teacher and Professional Organizations* (Washington, D.C.: National Education Association, 1956), pp. 4–7.

[6] Nosow, op. cit., pp. 37–38.

indicate the differentiation between amateur and professional standing. Also, it cannot be emphasized too strongly that housekeeping and homemaking are not the same.

The home economist in homemaking understands and applies scientific principles in the management of the home; this implies efficiency in planning and in performance. The education and training should provide for efficiency at both levels whether the homemaker directs or performs at one or both. The education and training should develop the ability to weigh values and make sound decisions. Goodyear and Klohr have stated, "Creative management puts routine tasks in their place by providing for the achievement of goals through the intelligent and responsible use of human and material resources. It places emphasis on values that provide for optimum self-development and that promote satisfactory human relations."[7]

The homemaker should be skilled in methods of guiding the family members to an understanding of their values and goals and in directing them toward the achievement of these. This skill involves an understanding of human relations inasmuch as effective management involves democratic decision-making. The homemaker finds understanding of human relations particularly, though not exclusively, keyed to good family relations for effective family living. It is important in the courtship days and in the establishment of the home and continues as long as the family exists. The professional has an understanding of and is skilled in the arts and sciences of child development as well as in family relations.

The consumer is very much the center of a great deal of debate, printed material, and proposed legislation today. Most people mean the homemaker when they speak or write of the consumer because it is the homemaker who is responsible for the purchase of the major portion of consumer goods. The professional homemaker is trained and skilled in family economics.

Most people are aware of the involvement of the homemaker in the preparation and service of food for the family; the selection and construction of clothing for family members; and the selection, use, and care of housing, furnishings, and equipment. Fewer are aware of the scientific and artistic principles involved for the best performance in these areas of the homemaker's responsibilities.

However community is defined, few today would absolve the homemaker from responsibilities in the community. The professional home-

---

[7] Margaret R. Goodyear and Mildred C. Klohr, *Managing for Effective Living* (New York: John Wiley, 1965), p. 41.

maker has an appreciation of his role in community and governmental affairs and actively participates in these affairs. The degree of participation may vary with the family developmental stage. The type of participation may vary with the specific needs of the community and the particular training and interests of the homemaker. The professional homemaker is aware of the fact that local, national, and international affairs do impinge upon the family and is alert to their interrelationships.

SPECIAL REQUIREMENTS

For the amateur homemaker age and/or consent of parents are the standard legal requirements and it is assumed that the young homemaker has learned from her mother and/or that it does not take much, if any, special education to manage and carry out the responsibilities in the home. However, statistics on juvenile delinquency, divorce rate, and consumer problems, for example, show clearly that something needs to be done in relation to these; special education should help.

The professional homemaker should have broad training in home management, family relations, child development, food, nutrition, clothing, textiles, housing, interior design, equipment, art, psychology, sociology, political science, economics, and consumer economics.

ADVANTAGES

Many of the other professions in home economics include the majority of the foregoing requirements. It is comparatively easy for the student to prepare for the profession of homemaking and a wage-earning profession at the same time. Thus the student may follow a wage-earning profession for a few years until marriage, to return to wage-earning when the need arises or she so desires. If the span of time is long between the original preparation and the return to work, refresher courses should be taken. Homemaking combines well with part-time wage-earning professions. More and more employers are hiring dietitians, teachers, social workers, and home economists for business on a part-time basis. Many home economists carry on an independent business of their own.

Much has been written in the past few years concerning the boredom and frustrations of the American homemaker. People who do things poorly are often bored and/or frustrated. The homemaker who is educated for homemaking is able to use her knowledge in a creative way for the attainment of a personally satisfying happy life and for the achievement of the social, economic, aesthetic, and scientific values in successful family life. The rewards can be greater than those found in the pay envelope: many people work outside the home in order to make a living; the educated homemaker works to make living worthwhile. The homemaker is eligible for membership in the American Home Economics Association.

POSSIBLE DISADVANTAGES

The attitude of society, or a portion of society, toward being "just a homemaker" may cause some women to lose perspective and to become dissatisfied. The hours spent in the home may lack stimulation and the woman may neglect her appearance and cultural interests. Fatigue, long hours, and emotional strain are sometimes listed by homemakers as disadvantages.

THE HOME ECONOMIST IN HOMEMAKING*

by Mary Ellen McFarland

The graduate home economist who is a full-time homemaker, by choice or circumstance, has an important role to play in her own home and family, in the community, and in the profession. Her influence on all fronts, as a professionally trained woman in one of the fields of home economics can not be underestimated. She does not claim to be an expert in every aspect of the broad scope of home economics but adequate in her own area of specialization. Many homemakers have had post college employment as teachers, dietitians, in business fields of home economics, and so on before becoming full-time homemakers. Some are employed on a part-time basis, as this fits well with homemaking in certain family situations.

Personally, I don't subscribe to the theory of dire boredom in the role of

---

* Written for this volume. Mrs. Mary Ellen McFarland is a home economist in homemaking who received her home economics training at the University of Minnesota. She has been a home economics teacher in secondary schools and adult evening school classes. She is an active member of the Minnesota and American Home Economics Associations and the Twin City Home Economists in Homemaking.

Mrs. McFarland has served as the national chairman of the Home Economists in Homemaking and as a member of the board of directors of the American Home Economics Association. She was a member of the Minnesota Governor's Commission on the Status of Women. She has also served as a board member on two different school boards. Mrs. McFarland is a member and contributes actively to the Arden Hills League of Women Voters, the Minnesota Citizen's Committee on Public Education, the Minnesota Consumers League, and the Minnesota Council on Family Relations. While her children were in school she was an active member of four different parent-teacher associations.

FIGURE 3-1. *Mrs. Mary Ellen McFarland, home economist in homemaking, in one of many homemaking activities.*

homemaker but do feel that some outside interests and activities are vital for most women to keep in touch with the world beyond their families' walls. For some, community volunteer services may be the answer, but for others combining homemaking with paid employment may be a more rewarding choice. For some, homemaking may be a completely satisfying fulfillment of their goals, but others may desire to pursue a more professional course. "It is important for a woman with a profession or specialized skill to keep in touch with her academic field during the years when homemaking and motherhood take most of her time. It is realized, of course, that frequently it is not easy to do this if home responsibilities are demanding. However, there are various ways a woman can try to maintain her professional skills during the years when her primary responsibilities are to family and home. For example: 'She can retain her membership in professional association, subscribe to technical journals, and perhaps occasionally attend annual conferences of her professional association.' "[8] The American Home Economics Association is unique in having organized a professional section in its structure, Home Economists in Homemaking, for the unemployed home economics graduates who are full-time homemakers.

[8] *Job Horizons for College Women* (Washington, D.C.: U.S. Department of Labor, 1967), p. 67.

This section brings together on national, state, and local levels members who have a desire to retain professional affiliation with home economics, to receive the *Journal of Home Economics,* and to participate in programs designed to up-date information and skills.

"She can take occasional courses. The increase in the number of localities served by university extension departments and development of more community colleges make this possibility more feasible than ever before.

"She can attend lectures or institutes. Her attendance will not only help refresh her memory about certain subject matter but will also put her in touch with others in her profession.

"She can find some way to practice her skills."[9] As a homemaker she does practice many of her professional skills in her daily homemaking activities plus in her volunteer services within the community. Home economist homemakers are very active as volunteers in their communities. In a membership survey of the Home Economist in Homemaking section of AHEA it was proved that the HEIH member serves her community in a great number of volunteer capacities relating to her professional field, e.g., in state legislative actions on day-care centers, consumer problems, college and university building needs for home economics, welfare programs, education, and so on; she serves on nutrition councils and works in nutrition programs for Head Start, nursing homes, senior citizens, and day-care centers, and with hospital patients preparing for dismissal. She teaches classes for unwed mothers, cooking and sewing to the blind, and food-stamp education programs; serves on consumer councils, home safety councils, family life consultative committees, and school curriculum committees. She has gained considerable experience in working with groups; in federal, state and local governmental units and programs; in using human resources; in expanding her communication skills; and in using time, financial, and home management practices to allow her to participate so actively outside her home. Each individual homemaker may not have such a wide range of volunteer experiences, but she will undoubtedly participate in school, church, and community activities as they relate to her family. Today there is a need "for a corps of well organized, professionally prepared and up-to-date home economists mobilized for community action in each city and town of this country with a special program of work aimed at improving home and family living through specifically tailored plans of action."[10]

The home economist homemaker is an interpreter of home economics and its specialized programs to the community and also serves as recruiter for home economics at secondary school and college levels. Her influence is felt on her family, neighborhood, community, and profession. Her values and skills in family living are instilled in her children and communicated by informal means to others in her community. Her leadership skills are used in professional groups and in community activities. To date, the potential of homemakers to serve as resource persons or as research data collectors for home economics has not been explored. Homemakers constitute a pool of trained home economists for both part-time and full-time employment. Home

[9] Ibid., p. 68.
[10] Doris E. Hanson, "Professional Power Through Volunteer Service," American Home Economics Association Annual Meeting, Boston, Massachusetts, June 24, 1969.

economists as homemakers stand as an asset, not a loss or liability, to the profession and to the community at large.

Apparel Design

Nature of the Work

"Designing is a process by which something new is created."[11] The apparel designer will observe the latest styles, develop new ideas, and see the ideas carried out in the pattern making, draping, and sewing of original models. Major positions in this field are as designers and as fashion illustrators.

A designer may work for a garment industry, a custom-made shop, a pattern company, or an accessory or millinery house. He might work as a free-lance designer or he may design apparel for the stage, motion pictures, or television. A designer may design one type of garment or work with several related types of garments. The geographic area in which he works will be determined by the location of fashion centers and textile and garment industries. In the United States, most designers are currently employed by garment and pattern industries. In Europe, a designer usually operates as a small business, making complete wardrobes for a limited clientele.

A fashion illustrator portrays the clothing in careful detail so as to interest people in buying. If this work is with a pattern company, stress is placed on seams and other sewing details with the purpose of selling patterns and giving the sewer an idea of the problems he might face. With fashion magazines, the illustrator may emphasize the trends being discussed in the fashion world or add unusual touches aimed toward selling clothing and accessories.[12] Fashion illustrators also work with retailers, newspapers, and garment industries.

QUALIFICATIONS

Creative imagination and ability are musts in the field of apparel design. Artistic ability and skills as well as vision are implied here. The designer must have knowledge of and skills in sketching, pattern

[11] Mildred Thurow Tate, *Home Economics as a Profession* (New York: McGraw-Hill Book Company, 1961), p. 145.
[12] Olive A. Hall, *Home Economics Careers and Homemaking* (New York: John Wiley, 1958), p. 185.

making, grading, and garment construction. A sense of style and flexibility are important. Subtle discriminations must be developed and maintained in relation to the shifting variations in patterns of living; to do this one must be sensitive to what is happening in the arts; in the sports world; and in social, political, and economic areas, as well as in family life. In relation to the last grouping it might be noted that some are now designing for such groups as the handicapped and the elderly.

A designer must have a knowledge of fabrics and textiles, including the names, characteristics, cost, and available colors of fabrics suitable for the types of garments to be created.[13] A knowledge of clothing construction and body structure is also necessary. Designers must design clothing the consumer will buy. To do this he must develop a sense of merchandising, must anticipate people's needs and interests, and must be able to design styles in fabrics that will sell.[14]

Other aptitudes and abilities needed in the area of apparel design are practical judgment, initiative, adaptability, perseverance, the ability to accept suggestions and criticisms, the ability to work under pressure, good grooming, poise, self-assurance, confidence, good health, and stamina. All of these add to the probabilities of success in this profession.

ADVANTAGES

The field of apparel design can be an extremely interesting, exciting, and challenging field. A designer has the opportunity to work creatively with beautiful fabrics and has inside information on trends in grooming and fashions.[15] He may have opportunity to travel to the great fashion centers. Promotion is rapid if he is creative, capable, and a hard worker. Designing is among the highest paid kinds of work in the clothing field. The apparel designer is eligible for membership in the American Home Economics Association and in Home Economists in Business.

POSSIBLE DISADVANTAGES

Lack of talent and training contributes most often to failures in the field. In addition, designing is a highly competitive field and there is constant pressure to produce. As a rule, a designer must start at the

---

[13] Tate, op. cit., p. 147.
[14] Ibid., pp. 147–148.
[15] Hall, op. cit., p. 191.

bottom as designing-room assistant, sketcher, or pattern maker, or he may even start in some phase of merchandising. Beginning salaries are low. Routine work and tension are also characteristics of this work. However, a person who has unusually high artistic aptitude may find it profitable and pleasurable to combine art and home economics training in preparation for becoming an apparel designer.

Clothing and Textile Merchandising

Nature of the Work

Merchandising and retailing are concerned with the buying and selling of merchandise in its distribution to the consumer and the activities necessary to carry on these functions. Merchandising in clothing and textiles may be carried on through small stores, large department stores, specialty shops, and mail-order houses.[16]

A person entering a career in merchandising might start as a sales person, working directly with the customers; or he might be employed as a personal shopper, taking care of phone and mail orders or shopping with customers who ask for such help; or he might be employed as a comparison shopper, checking on the offerings of competitors; or he might work in the adjustment office, handling returned goods and complaints. These jobs give selling and service experience in all departments and furnish an excellent background in department store business and problems.[17]

Other positions are available as one gains experience. A home economist working in the training department may be responsible for setting up training programs and teaching employees. He may also help provide useful merchandise information. A style training-supervisor may organize classes in textiles, color, line, design, and display; in interior decoration; and in fashion information. Those involved in promotion must watch the fashion trends and keep the staff informed on styles, fashion, and fabrics. Advertising and writing copy for textiles and accessories are also a part of promotion.

The buyer selects the merchandise that the store sells. One may

16 Tate, op. cit., p. 152.
17 Institute of Women's Professional Relations, Chase Going Woodhouse, Director, *Business Opportunities for the Home Economist* (New York: McGraw-Hill Book Company, 1938), Chapter V.

64

become head of stock and assistant buyer before he is promoted to the position of buyer. A buyer is usually in charge of a major division in a large department store. His responsibilities include going to market, analyzing merchandise for quality, predicting whether or not it will appeal to the customers, and placing orders within the store's budget. He must be prepared to follow through to see if the merchandise is delivered and ready for selling within a reasonable length of time. The buyer advises on the special points of the merchandise that should be promoted through advertising or display. He also informs the sales people of selling features and techniques and in turn the sales people keep the buyer informed on the types of merchandise that appeal to the customer. The buyer must know how much markup is necessary to help the department meet operating expenses and be alert in recognizing when to mark down merchandise in order to sell it. Inventory records help him to know when to reorder stock and discontinue ordering merchandise that is not selling.[18]

The fashion coordinator works with the buyers from all of the fashion departments. It is his responsibility to coordinate the store's merchandise. This enables a customer to purchase an item of apparel and to be able to purchase accessories, lingerie, and other articles in a similar price range and of a suitable color and style. The fashion coordinator plans fashion shows and is involved in personal appearances and publicity for fashion designers. He might also be involved in promotion outside the store, such as appearing on a television program.[19]

QUALIFICATIONS

The home economist interested in a career in merchandising must have a strong interest in clothing and textiles and in business promotion and must enjoy working with all kinds of people. He must be able to plan, organize, and follow through with assignments. He will need the ability to predict the consumer's wants. He must be able to work under pressure and think quickly using common sense and good judgment. He should ask himself: Do I have the ability to assume responsibility, a business sense, an artistic appreciation, good taste, a forceful and tactful manner, an agreeable voice, and personal leadership qualities? Self-confidence in personal appearance, control of emotions, flexibility, open-mindedness, good health, and stamina are also necessary.[20]

[18] Hall, op. cit., Chapter IX, p. 195.
[19] Ibid., p. 198.
[20] Ibid., pp. 195–196.

SPECIAL REQUIREMENTS

Although many people working in the retailing business have not been specifically educated for this work, home economists entering executive training programs and similar merchandising programs are required to have a bachelor's degree in home economics with specialization in clothing and textiles. Courses in accounting, marketing, clothing selection and construction, textiles, fashion, home furnishings, management, journalism, public speaking, advertising, psychology, photography, and salesmanship as well as experience in selling are vital.

ADVANTAGES

Retailing or merchandising is a big field for ambitious and capable women as well as men. Executive positions are available for those with the determination and the ability to advance.[21] Positions are stimulating and challenging. Opportunity is provided to use one's own ideas and judgment and to be recognized for them. Working with people, being alerted to the latest fashion trend, and being able to see and handle the unusual are other advantages in retailing. Good salaries, discounts on purchases, travel expenses, and employee insurance as well as commissions are among the remunerative benefits in this field.

Women hold 46 per cent of the executive positions in over 1,700,000 department stores, high fashion shops, specialty stores, and other retail firms in the United States.

Large turnover of personnel through promotions and marriages creates many openings.[22]

Another advantage is eligibility for membership in the American Home Economics Association, in Home Economists in Business, and in the National Retail Merchant's Association.

POSSIBLE DISADVANTAGES

Working in retailing or merchandising and with the fashion world is not all glamour. Most often one must start at the bottom as a salesperson or in another position requiring no merchandising experience.

[21] Ibid., p. 193.
[22] *Home Economics Has a Career for You in Textiles and Clothing* (Washington, D.C.: American Home Economics Association, 1966), p. 9.

The competition is keen and the hours are long and irregular. Saturday is usually the busiest day and evening work is often required. Buying trips are interesting but they are hard work. Examining merchandise all day, writing orders in the evening, and being away from home are not easy if one is married. The buyer is under constant pressure to make a profit. The solution of problems such as customer or staff complaints rests with the buyer.

THE FUTURE IN THE CLOTHING AND TEXTILES PROFESSION*

by Lura M. Odland

Textiles, clothing, and related industries continue to grow at unprecedented rates. This is the result not only of the fact that more and more

FIGURE 3-2. *Students test fabric sample for tensile strength and elongation on the Instron Testing Instrument. (Courtesy of the College of Home Economics, University of Tennessee.)*

* Written for this volume. Dr. Lura M. Odland is Professor of Nutrition and Dean of the College of Home Economics of the University of Tennessee. Dr. Odland is a nationally and internationally recognized authority on programs of higher education for women. She is active in the promotion of research programs and curricula planning, most recently in relation to continuing education for women.

women are working outside the home but also because of ever-expanding consumer demands for greater quantities of and more quality in textile and apparel items. In these fields, unlimited opportunities exist for creative and imaginative young women and men who have the initiative and are able to meet the challenges of the ever-changing forces—growth of science and technology; communications speed-up; urbanization; increasing mobility; and changing values, attitudes, and goals—that have and will continue to have important implications for these industries.

Ours is the Age of Consumerism! More than ever before the consumer is aware of his rights and more responsive to the protection of them. Today's consumers are more educated, sophisticated, affluent, and diverse and are greater in numbers than ever before.

The more educated consumer expects more information about the products he purchases; permanent labeling and a standardized care vocabulary will be only the beginnings. Because of our expanding and complex society, man has come to desire more individuality. Low-cost, disposable dresses made from new synthetic fabrics could enable women never to be seen more than once in the same outfit. "Cake-mix" fashions (partly finished products to which the buyer can add his own personal touches), a greater variety of offerings, and the boutique concept are forecast as possible developments.

Concern for product safety continues to increase, especially product flammability. New products that are more serviceable, durable, and time-saving are being predicted: low-cost disposable products, metal fibers, quick-freeze fabrics, elimination of the disadvantages of man-mades with

FIGURE 3-3. *Display is only one of the responsibilities of a textile and clothing-merchandising field trainee. (Courtesy of the College of Home Economics, University of Tennessee.)*

68

the addition of some of the comfort and wearability properties inherent in natural fibers, new and better variants, new finishes that will protect against dirt and disease, standardization of garment sizes, and performance standards for durable press. Increased growth of the knit and synthetic industries is foreseen. The accompanying effects of these forecasts on the economy of our nation and the world cannot be overlooked.

More careful study of consumer motivations is needed in order to help predict what the buyer will purchase and to help him make wiser choices. Such studies concerning the social and psychological aspects of textiles and clothing will be of continuing benefit and importance to the consumer, teacher, home economist, retailer, manufacturer, advertiser, and so on.

Quite importantly, it is realized that different age and minority groups, such as the economically disadvantaged, the physically handicapped, and the elderly, have varying needs, attitudes, and preferences concerning the textiles and clothing they wear. The informing and teaching of some of these groups have begun, a phase that must be expanded if basic research and development are to be of value.

Governmental agencies have begun to assist in these various areas. With this assistance and the continued interest of well-educated young women and men, the textile and clothing professions will grow beyond the horizons we can visualize at this point.

Interior Design

According to the definition officially approved by the American Institute of Interior Designers, the "Interior designer is a person qualified by training and experience, to plan and supervise the design and execution of interiors and their furnishings, and to organize the various arts and crafts essential to their completion."[23]

The two main divisions in the interior designing profession are commercial, or contract, and residential. Commercial or contract interior designing is concerned with public spaces, such as offices, hotels, motels, restaurants, factories, clubs, hospitals, ships, banks, shopping centers, school and university buildings, and so on. The residential interior designer is concerned with the home, whether it be an apartment or a separate entity; here his job may range from a single room in a private residence to the entire residence or to the designing and coordinating of the interior of a large apartment complex. In residential interior design it is particularly important for the designer to consider functional needs and use as well as the personal tastes and habits of the client.

[23] American Institute of Interior Designers, "Student Affiliates, Student Chapters, Education and Career Information" (New York, 1970), p. 1.

The interior designer may work from blueprints, making detailed floor plans and elevations, drawing furniture to scale. His presentation to the client may include scaled floor plans; color charts; samples of materials suggested for wall coverings, draperies, upholstering; pictures of furniture; and, usually, renderings. His final proposal includes an estimate of cost—including furnishings, labor, transportation, and all incidentals necessary to completion. Once the contract is accepted, the designer is responsible for assembling the furnishings, including any custom-made merchandise and for contracting the services of any needed craftsmen.

A growing profession, interior designing offers a number of different types of positions. Large department stores that carry home furnishings employ interior designers, as do many furniture stores. The person trained specifically for home designing most often starts work in one of these. Other opportunities exist with private decorating firms, architectural firms, extension service, colleges and universities, magazines, hotels, chain restaurants and motels, and museums. Manufacturers of floor coverings, wall coverings, furniture, lighting fixtures, and drapery and upholstery fabrics also employ interior designers. The ultimate aim of many interior designers is to establish their own interior design business.[24]

QUALIFICATIONS

Artistic ability and aesthetic appreciation as well as a flair for creative ideas and discriminating taste are very important in the area of interior design. The interior designer must have a feel for interior fashion; skill in creating, manufacturing, and promoting a design; and a workable knowledge of furnishings, architecture, textiles, and related fields. He must be a businessman with an awareness of cost control and an ability to think in terms of the mass market. He must practice psychology in working with people, understand their likes and dislikes, and be able to design interiors that will satisfy the needs and desires of the prospective users.

Other personal qualifications of the successful interior designer are imagination and enthusiasm, patience and perseverance, and poise and self-assurance. He must have a tactful and pleasing manner, the ability to assume responsibility, sound judgment, and a willingness to take and apply criticism. Integrity, good health, and stamina are vital to the maintenance of almost all the characteristics previously mentioned.

[24] Ibid., p. 1.

SPECIAL REQUIREMENTS

"Good taste" and a "love of lovely things" are not enough.[25] A career in the field of interior design requires training and experience. A bachelor's degree in home economics or a related field offering courses in interior design is necessary. Programs should include the history and theory of art, architecture and interiors, mechanical and free-hand drawing, watercolor, rendering and presentation, two-dimensional and three-dimensional design, furniture design, color scheming, floor planning, structural design and mechanical equipment, textiles, accessories, management, marketing, psychology, economics, sociology, and professional practice. The student considering a career in interior design should study the recommended requirements as outlined by the American Institute of Interior Designers' National Committee on Education in their pamphlet entitled "Student Affiliates, Student Chapters, Education and Career Information." Active membership in the professional organizations—The American Institute of Interior Designers and the National Society of Interior Designers—is dependent upon academic and technical training and experience. Since the summer of 1970 the American Institute of Interior Designers has required that applicants take, and pass, a comprehensive examination.

ADVANTAGES

Interior design can be a satisfying career for talented, persistent, and qualified people. It is an extremely stimulating and challenging field with excellent outlets for creative abilities. Opportunity is presented to work with a variety of people and materials. Advancement and excellent salaries are available for qualified persons. The interior designer is also eligible for membership in the American Home Economics Association if he meets the membership requirements as stated on page 35.

POSSIBLE DISADVANTAGES

The beginners in the field of interior design may experience difficulty in immediately locating a job in the field and may begin as a salesperson or a secretary. Beginning at the bottom and working one's

25 Woodhouse, op. cit., p. 223.

71

way up is the usual procedure. Starting salaries may be low and competition is great. The hours of work are long and irregular, inasmuch as appointments must be made at the convenience of the customer, often during the weekend. The work involved in measuring, estimating, and trying samples may be physically tiring. Attention must be given to a great many details, such as writing orders, figuring estimates, and checking inventories. Customers may be indecisive, changeable, or unjustly critical, but they must be treated with courtesy.

MAN DESIGNS FOR MAN°

by Naomi G. Albanese

Questions have been raised about design education. Is it wise for the interior design student to become a specialist? The best arguments for this point of view are based on an awareness of the varied roles the interior designer must assume in the practicalities of the profession today. The designer's specialty lies in integrating the skills of many others; and his education, training, and experience must prepare him for doing this.

The four-year curriculum at UNC–G is unique in that it is based in the humanities and sciences as well as art and designing. It has as its focal point the individual and the setting in which he finds himself. Sixty-six per cent of the 122 semester hours required for a bachelor's degree is in liberal arts, for training and education only for an occupation is illiberal, narrowing, and crippling to the inquiring and inquistive mind. The remainder of course requirments is concentrated in housing and design within the School of Home Economics.

The design majors are learning to be designers for people and their specific personalities, problems, and budgets. The major's being offered in home economics is an advantage. One of the strengths of the program is the background material in home and family living, for one can provide for people only if one knows people and how they live.

The broad scope of study required includes such diverse courses as lighting and wiring, textiles, and household equipment and laboratory courses that provide in-depth study and actual participation in the refinishing, upholstering, and tailoring of furniture. The course offerings also provide opportunities for exploration in the physio-psycho-sociological areas. For example, students come face to face with cold reality as they visit housing projects in which every apartment is alike and in which every kitchen is alike. These apartments are occupied by people from different ethnic groups, socioeconomic strata, and cultural backgrounds. By studying

° Written for this volume. Dr. Naomi G. Albanese is Dean of the School of Home Economics of the University of North Carolina at Greensboro. She has served as vice-president and as president of the American Home Economics Association. She has held many committee memberships in the Association and in the Home Economics Division of the Association of State Universities and Land-Grant Colleges. A unique program in interior design is carried on at UNC–G in the heart of Furnitureland, U.S.A.

FIGURE 3-4. *Students work with many commercial firms in planning interiors. Here we see Dianne Taylor and John Vriner (center) winners of the competition to design the office interiors for the Alton Box Company's new building, the architectural plans for which were prepared by Smith-Entzeroth, Inc., in St. Louis. Also in the illustration are representatives of these companies: Mr. Walter Moran, chairman of the Department of Interior Design and professor of the class in interior design, and Dr. Thomas Brooks, Dean of the School of Home Economics. All-Steel Equipment, Inc., furnished the prize money for this competition. (Courtesy of the Department of Interior Design, School of Home Economics, Southern Illinois University, Carbondale.)*

how these people make use of the space and how they furnish their surroundings, the students begin to sense that interior design extends far beyond the physical surroundings in that it permeates the thoughts and feelings of the occupants.

Field trips to various industries are an integral part of the student's program to develop a sensitivity for and some knowledge of the many facets of the home furnishing industry located in the South. Seminars scheduled each week are planned with cooperating industries and are held at the basic resource plant location, whether the product be rugs, textiles, or furniture. Because industries themselves have been so enthusiastic in their response, the program has been enriched by a continual source of classroom materials, guest lecturers, and instructional tours.

73

Design majors gain much from supervised work experiences with practicing designers, manufacturers, photographers, and architects. In these experiences theory and reality come into focus; the exercise of skills, the knowledge of facts, and the inculcation of activities and ideals are blended to meet individual and social needs sufficient for our time. This experience may also become the launching vehicle for exciting adventures into a design career.

Upon graduation, career opportunities exist at the manufacturing, the wholesale, and the retail sales levels; with architects, contractors, or independent decorators; on the staffs of periodicals; and with consultants of home-planning centers. Interior design graduates of the University of North Carolina at Greensboro have found a niche in the profession from New York to California.

Careers in Food and Nutrition

Dietetics*

Dietetics is a profession concerned with the science and art of human nutritional care, an essential component of the health sciences. It includes the extending and imparting of knowledge concerning foods that will provide nutrients sufficient for health and during disease through the life cycle and concerning the management of group feedings for these purposes.[26] The dietitian is a specialist educated for a profession responsible for the nutritional care of individuals and groups.

NATURE OF THE WORK

The dietitian is employed chiefly in hospitals, college and university food services, school food services, industrial plants, related health facilities, public health and welfare organizations, commercial organizations, and the armed services. Over 50 per cent of all employed dietitians work in hospitals. Public health nutritionists and university teachers are the next largest group. Several hundred dietitians hold the rank of ensign, lieutenant, major, or colonel in the Armed Services Medical Specialist Corps or the Navy Medical Service Corps.

* The American Dietetic Association Headquarters staff revised a large portion of this section and reviewed the whole.

[26] Committee on Goals of Education for Dietetics, Dietetic Internship Council, The American Dietetic Association, "Goals of the Lifetime Education of the Dietitian," *Journal of the American Dietetic Association*, 54:2 (February 1969), p. 92.

HOSPITAL DIETETICS

A hospital dietitian's duties depend upon the size and type of institution. In a large hospital the work may be very specialized, whereas in a small hospital the dietitian may be required to carry on all phases of dietetics.

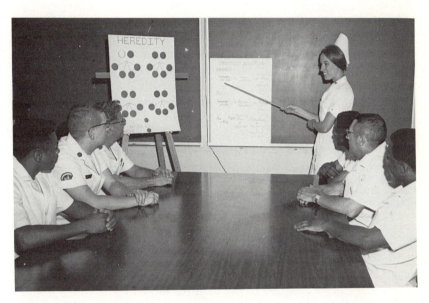

FIGURE 3-5. *Teaching is an important part of the work of a dietetic intern. In-service training programs for food service employees are taught by the interns. Here 2nd Lt. Mary Popp teaches a class to the medical diet aids on carbohydrate utilization. (Courtesy of Fitzsimons General Hospital, Denver.)*

A hospital administrative dietitian applies the principles of nutrition and management to planning and directing food service systems. This includes responsibility for assessment and use of equipment, food, manpower, and supplies; supervision of the total food service; establishment and analysis of food cost controls; instruction of supportive personnel; records; and maintaining and improving all standards related to food preparation and service.

A clinical dietitian is concerned with meeting the nutritional needs of patients. Duties include consultation with the physician regarding

75

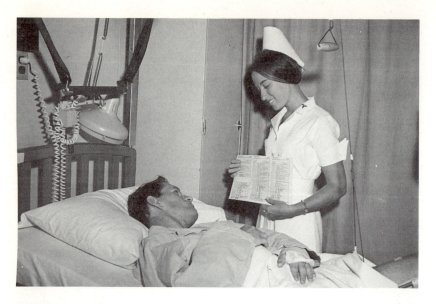

FIGURE 3-6. *Visits are made to the patient daily by a dietitian or a dietetic intern. 2nd Lt. Mary Popp is reviewing with him this patient's menu for the next day. (Courtesy of Fitzsimons General Hospital, Denver.)*

the nutritional needs of the patient, including the modification of diets; and the instruction of patients and their families on the requirements and importance of diet and ways in which the food needs of the patient can be adapted to the food for the family.

The dietitian whose specialization is education may be a member of a university faculty or, if employed in a medical center, may teach nursing, medical, and dental students, as well as medical and dental interns and residents. Where there is a dietetic internship, the dietitian educator is responsible for the dietetic curriculum of the dietetic interns.

The research dietitian is a member of the clinical research team. The research dietitian participates in planning the nutrition aspects of the study and is concerned with the physiological and psychological effects of the prescribed diet.

QUALIFICATIONS

The future dietitian should be aware that the approach to dietetics is based on the sciences of nutrition and management. A person in dietetics works daily with all kinds of people, so it is necessary for him to demonstrate a warm but objective attitude and to be an excellent communicator. Adaptability, resourcefulness, dependability, tactfulness, accuracy, integrity, and poise are important. A willingness to be helpful to others, emotional control, the ability to analyze, demonstrate, direct, and encourage along with the ability to write and speak simply and clearly are especially important in dietetics. Because dietetics is the application of food to meet the nutritional needs of individuals, the dietitian must have a keen interest in and knowledge of food, its composition, its effect on individuals, its quality, and the ways it can be adapted to meet the needs of the individual.

SPECIAL REQUIREMENTS

A dietitian must have completed a baccalaureate degree. The major subjects are usually in dietetics, food and nutrition, and management, as well as a broad cultural education. Academic requirements for membership in the American Dietetic Association include courses in food preparation in both large and small quantities, meal planning, nutrition, diet therapy, institutional management, chemistry, bacteriology, business, and the social sciences. Courses in marketing, institutional equipment, and research procedures are also desirable.

The professional education of the dietitian is strengthened in an internship program approved by the American Dietetic Association. Various types of institutions offer internships, such as hospitals, university food services, business, and commercial enterprises. Internships offer classroom study and clinical experiences related to the practice of the profession of dietetics. If the organization is a university, often graduate credit may be earned.

Because specialized internships will be more available in the future than in the past, the following excerpt from a letter written by Mary Popp, an intern in a specialized program, gives an excellent description, perhaps typical.

The Dietetic Internship Program is structured to facilitate progressive learning. Each intern progresses as rapidly as his capabilities allow from the basic skills to responsibilities similar to those assumed by staff dietitians.

Following a week of general orientation, we began basic learning experiences. During this phase, principles were reviewed or learned and basic skills were developed in each of the food service branches—Diet Therapy and Production and Service.

We are now in our second phase, *intensive* learning experiences based on staff review of all the resources available within the hospital and other resources in the community. Our assignments stimulate us to analyze, evaluate and to think creatively. While in diet therapy we have been assigned wards on which we are responsible for asking the patients about their food comments, finding medical diagnosis, instructing and writing modified diets, and attending staff meetings. The time goes by much too quickly each day.

Six weeks later we shall undertake our intensive learning phase in production and service during which time we shall observe and supervise in the preparation of food and loading of carts; we shall be conducting sanitary and safety inspections and testing and standardizing recipes among other things.

Throughout the year each of us interns will be working on projects such as seminars, holiday dinners, cycle menu write-ups and the like. We shall be participating in community nutrition and will spend some time affiliating with the hospitals.

Coordinated undergraduate educational programs in dietetics are offered by some accredited colleges and universities. The curriculum is planned so that the clinical experience supplements the educational program and is approved to meet the requirements for membership in the American Dietetic Association. Graduates of these programs in dietetics are eligible for membership in the Association immediately after graduation, without the internship.

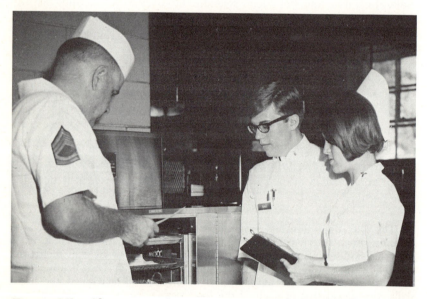

FIGURE 3-7. *Observing in the pastry section are 2nd Lts. Elena Wong and Richard Cass. During the year, each dietetic intern will test and standardize for the patients four pastry products. (Courtesy of Fitzsimons General Hospital, Denver.)*

FIGURE 3-8.   *Dietetic interns participate in the requisitioning, receiving, storage, and issuing of food and supplies. 2nd Lts. Mary Stewart and Mary Popp are checking the quality of a delivery of vegetables just received. (Courtesy of Fitzsimons General Hospital, Denver.)*

REGISTERED DIETITIAN

A member of the American Dietetic Association may apply to take a national registration examination and if he satisfactorily completes it can be registered upon payment of the fees. To maintain registration he must meet continuing education requirements. *R.D.* is the designation for the Registered Dietitian and indicates to the public the competency of the individual.

ADVANTAGES

Satisfaction in the field of dietetics goes beyond material benefits. One is rewarded from knowing he is contributing to the maintenance, restoration, and rehabilitation of an individual's health.

The dietitian can find part-time positions that combine with homemaking. Salaries are comparable to those of other health professionals and are determined by the level of responsibility of the position and the capability of the dietitian. Paid vacations, holidays, and health and retirement benefits are usually received. The demand continues to be

79

MINIMUM ACADEMIC REQUIREMENTS FOR ADA MEMBERSHIP

The Core plus ONE Emphasis, plus ONE Concentration constitute the requirements for membership or internship, as designated for the specialties.
Credit for a course may be used only once.

CORE SUBJECTS

22 semester hours* — Basic Minimum
All core subjects required

Natural Sciences—14 s. h.
human physiology } 6 s. h.
and bacteriology
chemistry—8 s. h.

Food—6 s. h.
selection, preparation,
meal planning
Nutrition—2 s. h.

Plus one of the following:

EMPHASES

Choice of one Emphasis — 9 semester hours — Basic Minimum
Underlined subject areas required

I
FOOD SERVICE MANAGEMENT
organization and management
quantity food production and service
advanced food production management
equipment selection, maintenance, and layout
principles of accounting
purchasing

or

II
EDUCATION (Business and Industry, Clinic,
College, Extension, School, and Public Health)
educational principles and techniques
educational psychology
anthropology
child psychology
sociology

or

III
FOODS—EXPERIMENTAL AND
DEVELOPMENTAL
experimental foods
advanced bacteriology
consumer economics
cultural aspects of food
food styling
quantity food production and service
psychology of advertising
technology of food
theory and technique of communication

Plus one of the following:

CONCENTRATIONS

Choice of one Concentration — 15 semester hours — Basic Minimum
Underlined subject areas required

A
THERAPEUTIC AND ADMINISTRATIVE
DIETETICS
advanced nutrition 2 s.h.
*biochemistry***†*
personnel management or industrial psychology
principles of learning or educational psychology
Remainder of credit:
diet therapy****
advanced food production management, equipment selection, maintenance, and layout***
foods: cultural, experimental or technological
principles of accounting***
purchasing***

or

B
BUSINESS ADMINISTRATION
advanced accounting
*advanced food production management***
equipment selection, maintenance, and layout***
personnel management
*purchasing***
Remainder of credit:
business law
communication
human relations
industrial psychology
labor economics

or

C
SCIENCE—FOODS AND NUTRITION
advanced nutrition 6 s.h.
*biochemistry***
foods: cultural, experimental or technological
Remainder of credit:
child growth and nutrition
community nutrition
diet therapy****
principles of learning
or educational psychology
statistics
food processing and preservation

1. Applicants for Internship and Membership
a. Clinic Interns: Core + Emphasis I or II + Concentration A or C
b. College, Business, or Industry Interns: Core + Emphasis I + Concentration A or B
c. Hospital Interns: Core + Emphasis I + Concentration A or C

2. Experience applicants for membership:
a: Bachelor's degree: Hospital: Core + Emphasis I + Concentration A or C.
a: Food Service Administration: Core + Emphasis I + Concentration A or B.
b. Master's degree: Core + Emphasis I, II, or III + Concentration A, B, or C.

LEGEND: *Social and behavioral sciences are considered to be essential and assumed to be included in college degree requirements.
†Food Chem. may be used by College or Industrial Interns   **If not used in Core   ***If not used in Emphasis I   ****Required for hospital and clinic interns

Adopted November 1, 1958   **Revised August 1967**

80

greater than the supply. In addition to the ADA, dietitians are eligible for membership in the American Home Economics Association and the American Public Health Association, among other professional associations.

POSSIBLE DISADVANTAGES

Most dietitians are employed on a weekly work schedule of forty or less hours. However, dietitians in hospitals may sometimes work on weekends and those in commercial food services may have somewhat irregular hours.

DIETETICS—THE PROFESSION AND THE LONG VIEW[*]

by Katherine Hart

Dietetics as an organized profession dates from the founding of the American Dietetic Association during World War I. From the beginning, the members of the profession were involved in diverse activities for both civilian and government services: as clinical dietitians, as administrative dietitians, and as public health nutritionists.

Dietitians are specialists in the analysis and interpretation of the nutritional needs of human beings, individually or in groups, sick or well, in terms of the physical, psychological, and social nature of man. One may say that the speciality of the dietitian is food—how people respond to food; its use in meeting nutritive needs; its planning, purchase, preparation, service, and acceptance. The dietitian has always been concerned with people, with nutrition and man, with management and performance.

Dietitian is a generic term covering both dietitians and nutritionists and implies competence in human nutrition. The clinical dietitian with the doctor, the nurse, and the medcal social worker serves as a member of the health team in the hospital milieu, plus participating in research and in counseling patients on their food needs. The administrative dietitian, as a manager in a food service system, contributes to formulating management policies; trains and supervises personnel; and is responsible for the technical operations involved in the procurement, production, distribution, sanitation, and control of quality food in educational institutions and business and industry, as well as in hospitals. The public health nutritionist is the member of the health team who assesses community nutrition needs and plans, directs, coordinates, and evaluates the nutrition component of health services for the maintenance and improvement of the health of all groups in the society. Public health nutritionists work in hospitals and clinics, health and welfare agencies, food industries, and educational institutions.

Four subject-matter or knowledge areas—physical and biological sci-

[*] Written for this volume. Katherine Hart is Professor, Department of Food Science and Human Nutrition, Michigan State University. Active for a number of years in the profession of dietetics, she was national president of the American Dietetic Association in 1965–1966.

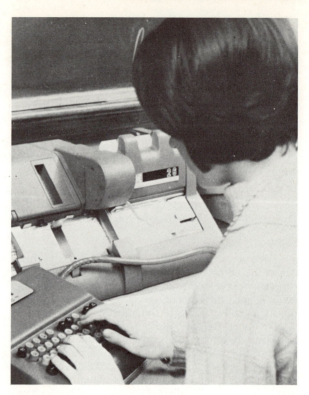

FIGURE 3-9.
Quantity Food Research Laboratory—working with the computer. (Courtesy of Michigan State University.)

ences; behavioral and social sciences; professional sciences; and communication sciences—are considered essential to anyone functioning in the profession of dietetics in the present and immediate future.

The profession of dietetics will continue to be more exacting in demands for specialization—specialization at the undergraduate level as well as in postgraduate training. The future dietetic specialist will need education commensurate with his responsibilities—education as a scholar in the science of nutrition for his role as teacher and consultant and as a research team member, education to improve his managerial skills, and education for future community-centered health organizations in line with current medical trends. Inherent in a program for the more highly educated specialist is graduate education tailored to acquiring more background in the physical and biological sciences; in the behavioral and social sciences; and in the nutritional, food, and management sciences—graduate education that also serves as preparation for future positions of leadership in health and nutritional planning.

The need for manpower in the profession of dietetics is impressive. For the medical and health services industry, the U.S. Department of Labor has projected the need for the next decade to be 17,000 more dietitions

82

than the 30,000 currently employed. Career opportunities for the well-qualified dietitian with professional drive and imagination are unlimited.

Institution Management

NATURE OF THE WORK

Institution management is an area that demands the services of men and women in a variety of positions in food service in institutions such as tea rooms, restaurants, hotels, motels, airlines, college food services, school food services, retirement and convalescent homes, mental institutions, child-care institutions, and industrial food services. A home economist working as a food service manager plans nutritious and attractive meals for large groups of people. The purchasing of the food, supplies, and equipment related to its preparation are also his responsibility. The food service manager supervises the storage, preparation, and service of food. He must keep records of the number of

FIGURE 3-10. *Quantity Foods Laboratory, Bevier Hall, University of Illinois at Champaign-Urbana. Men and women enrolled in hospital dietetics, institution management, and restaurant management programs use the laboratory in preparation for a profession in food management service.*

meals served, cost of serving, quantities of food to be purchased, employees' hours and wages, and possible cost of utilities. Building and maintaining good relationships with staff, clientele, employer, and salesmen are important to the food service manager. He employs, trains, and directs food service workers, studies the patrons' likes and dislikes, develops new recipes, and works to maintain quality of flavor in the large quantities of food.

School food service is one of the really great fields for the institution management person. As state or county supervisors or university food service supervisors, we find this is big business with big salaries. Too often such positions are held by people untrained in the science of food and nutrition and the needs of children and/or young people.

The National Restaurant Association, in its pamphlet "Opportunities for College Graduates in the Quantity Food Service Industry," has classified the titles of positions:

Institutions need college graduates as:
food service supervisors, managers, and directors in college and university residence halls
dietitians in hospitals
managers and directors of school lunch programs
supervisors and managers of industrial food services
food service managers and directors of other types of institutions wherever people are housed and fed away from home

Commercial restaurants offer such positions as the following to graduates of four-year programs:
assistant manager
manager
food production supervisor
purchasing agent
food cost accountant
food service director
director of recipe development
personnel director
sales manager
banquet manager

The chart is from the *Vocational Guidance Manual—Careers in the Quantity Food Service Industry,* produced for the National Restaurant Association by the H. J. Heinz Company.

Restaurant Organization

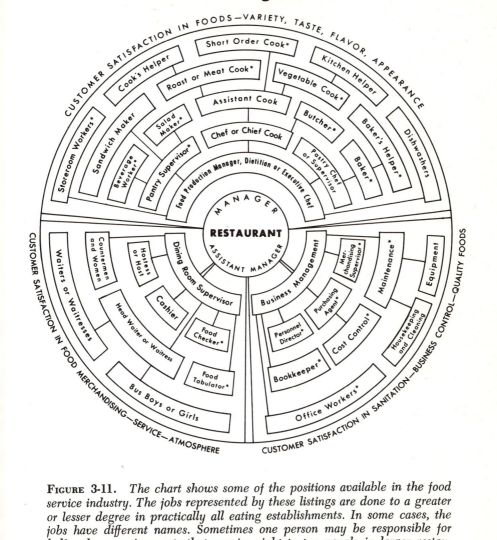

FIGURE 3-11. *The chart shows some of the positions available in the food service industry. The jobs represented by these listings are done to a greater or lesser degree in practically all eating establishments. In some cases, the jobs have different names. Sometimes one person may be responsible for half a dozen assignments that require eight to ten people in larger restaurants. This chart also illustrates the interdependence of all restaurant positions and demonstrates how the ultimate goal of each one is the pleasing of the customer. (Courtesy of the National Restaurant Association.)*

QUALIFICATIONS

For young people who wish to enter the field of institution management, a scientific and artistic interest in good-quality food, an interest in working with and serving people, and an interest in the food industry are necessary. Knowledge and abilities in business and administration are important to the success of food service institutions. The ability to teach people, create interest, and delegate responsibilities is an essential part of working with people. Other necessary personal qualifications include a sense of humor, an eagerness to learn, a willingness to work hard, cleanliness and accuracy in handling food, originality, self-confidence, a pleasing appearance, good health, stamina, the ability to maintain emotional control under pressure, and the ability to meet emergencies calmly.

SPECIAL REQUIREMENTS

A bachelor's degree with a major in institution management or foods and nutrition is the basic educational requirement as preparation for work in the field of institution management. Either a hospital or administrative internship program, approved by the American Dietetic Association, may be taken. Relatively few administrative internships are approved by the American Dietetic Association. Information about the programs may be obtained directly from your university or from the American Dietetic Association. Internships consist of experience in food purchasing, preparation, service, and merchandising. Training stresses the development of standards and techniques of food preparation and recipe experimentation. Experience in administration, personnel management, and food cost control is also included. Emphasis is given to all areas of management. Classes, seminars, projects, and field trips add to the experiences.[27] Computer programming should be included if at all possible.

Most young men and women interested in a food service career have as their ultimate objective an administrative position in commercial food service. With this in mind most college programs in institution management have included the requirements outlined by the National Restaurant Association for entrance into an executive apprenticeship, which they sponsor. These include:

[27] Hall, op. cit., p. 213.

1. Food planning, preparation and service. Food selection and preparation, fundamentals of nutrition, dietetics, quanity cookery, and experimental cookery.
2. Special food courses. Menu planning and service; food purchasing; meat selection, purchasing and cutting; and catering and banquet service.
3. Fundamental science. General chemistry and/or food chemistry, bacteriology, and biology. Human physiology and food sanitation are recommended.
4. Personnel and human relations. Psychology and principles of education. Recommended also are employee interviewing and personnel management.
5. Organization and management. Principles of business administration, economics, and accounting. Recommended also are business management, principles of marketing, business law, labor economics, interior decoration, food service, layout and equipment, and business English.[28]

ADVANTAGES

Opportunities for advancement are available for those who are qualified. One may begin in the internship position and progress to assistant food service manager. With experience he may become service manager-director-administrator.

The work is interesting, challenging, and diversified. There is much satisfaction in knowing that one is contributing to the physical well-being of those whom he is serving. The demand for qualified people in food service is great, positions are available in all regions, and salaries are high. There is freedom of operation and a chance for initiative and growth. National organizations lending support to this field are the American Home Economics Association, the American Dietetic Association, and the National Restaurant Association.

POSSIBLE DISADVANTAGES

Successful operations take constant vigilance. Public and personnel relations require constant attention. There is a great deal of pressure to meet production schedules, so careful management of time is essential. Moreover, there is pressure to show profit if one is a food service manager for a commercial concern; even if one works for a governmental or other nonprofit organization, there is pressure at least to break even.

Although many opportunities exist, failures may occur, especially

[28] National Restaurant Association, *Executive Apprenticeship—Restaurant and Food Service Careers* (Chicago: National Restaurant Association, 1954), p. 10.

among small, newly established firms. Competition in this field is strong.

The Nutritionist

The nutritionist is one who knows the relationship between food and health and interprets it to others. The two most important areas of the nutritionist's professional work are research and interpretation. Research work is treated in a separate section; only the interpretative aspects will be discussed here.

The nutritionist may be employed by a social welfare or public health agency, by a college or university, by a trade association, or in the home economics division of a food, utility, or equipment company. Newspapers and magazines, advertising agencies, and manufacturing, distributing, and processing companies also employ nutritionists. Indicative of the growing awareness of the importance of good nutrition are the employment opportunities available for nutritionists in such organizations as the Food and Agricultural Organization of the United Nations, the technical assistance program of the World Health Organization, and in many federal programs, such as the Peace Corps and VISTA.

NATURE OF THE WORK

In general, the nutritionist works with groups rather than individuals. Advice is given to these people and/or agency administrators on the application of the principles of nutrition. If the nutritionist is working for a commercial concern, the nutritional information is related to the company's products. Diet studies may be carried on; educational materials prepared; radio, television, and public lectures given; and magazine and newspaper articles written. Cooperation with other agencies in solving nutritional problems is often a part of the responsibilities.[29]

Because of the increasing demand for nutritionists in public or community welfare organizations, the major duties for the nutritionist in these agencies are outlined here:

Advises agency administrators and staff on nutrition as it relates to the services of the agency.

[29] Hall, op. cit., pp. 227–232.

Works as a member of a medical team in planning to meet specific health needs of individuals and families.

Interprets to staff members nutrition research as it relates to the services of the agency.

Co-operates with government and voluntary agencies and community groups in the nutrition aspects of a community program.

Advises school nurses, teachers, and other professional people on nutrition phases of their programs.

Advises food service administrators on nutrition problems in hospitals, nursing homes, and child care institutions.

Assists public health nurses in the dietary aspects of patient care through conferences and home visits.

Conducts dietary surveys; develops nutrition phase of community health studies.

Prepares or evaluates publications, films, posters, exhibits, and other nutrition education materials.[30]

New avenues of work are opening up for the nutritionist and the importance of such work is being increasingly recognized:

TO EAT AND ENJOY

The two guiding principles followed in the space nutrition program are to provide food that is nutritious and which will also reinforce the astronauts' daily eating habits. We see it as our duty to feed the man exploring in space with meals he will relish and enjoy. In the latter, formulas and synthetics have no place. . . . Nutrition is not important as a goal of space flight. It is only important as an indispensable condition to the achievement of these goals. . . . This is the reason, sufficiently persuasive to us, that prepared mixes or formula feedings are not used in the space program. . . . The object of the NASA nutrition program is to provide meals, not feedings. . . . The fact that astronauts took their earthly eating and sleeping habits with them has led us to examine just how important it is for men in a strange environment to eat together. This has brought us face to face with the problems of the whole area of acceptance of food. This plays, or at least should play, an important role in meal planning and diet scheduling by every dietitian and physician. Yet we all seem to be bereft of facts to substantiate any conclusions. We have been asking ourselves just how much of a role does the sociability aspect of dining play in allaying stress. It must be remembered we are supporting men who day in, day out, are in one of the most stressful situations at least psychologically, ever devised. It is also one in which even the slightest error is not forgiven. Anything that reduces stress—no matter how little—takes on enormous importance.[31]

[30] *Home Economics Careers in Health and Welfare* (Washington, D.C.: American Home Economics Association, 1965), p. 4.

[31] Paul A. LaChance, Ph.D., and Charles A. Berry, M.D., "Luncheon in Space," *Nutrition Today* (Wilton, Conn.: Cortez F. Enloe, Inc., June 1967), pp. 6–8.

FIGURE 3-12. *The problems of providing astronauts with meals that are satisfying and nutritionally adequate are unlike any others nutrition scientists have tackled. From their solution will come much new knowledge and some very unusual foods. (Courtesy of the National Aeronautics and Space Administration.)*

QUALIFICATIONS

The student interested in a career as a nutritionist must have a strong interest in science and in social service. The ability to speak and write simply, clearly, and effectively must be developed. Social consciousness, a well-balanced personality, good health, good grooming, the ability to work well with all kinds of people, patience, adaptability, ingenuity, and executive ability are other attributes that are important for the nutritionist.

SPECIAL REQUIREMENTS

A bachelor of science degree in home economics with specialization in food and nutrition is the minimal requirement. Courses at the undergraduate level should include nutrition—normal and therapeutic; foods—nutritive values, menu planning, purchasing, and service with consideration of individual, family, and institutional needs; other sciences—chemistry, physiology, biology, microbiology, sociology, psychology, child development, and family relations; consumer education and home management; education and communication techniques—methods of teaching, group dynamics, public speaking, and journalism; and personal and community health.

Today many young people are finding it advantageous to go directly into graduate school after completing the bachelor of science degree. A master's degree is considered a necessity. If one wishes to be a public health nutritionist, a master's degree in nutrition is usually required. The graduate program should include public health areas, social welfare, education, and the behavioral sciences.

ADVANTAGES

The demand for nutritionists is far greater than the supply and will probably continue to be so as science develops an ever-increasing awareness of the values inherent in good nutrition. Positions offer interesting and stimulating contacts. Other advantages include variety in the daily and weekly work, opportunity for advancement, and satisfaction in doing work that is basic to the welfare of people everywhere. Nutritionists are eligible for membership in the American Home Economics Association and in the American Dietetics Association.

POSSIBLE DISADVANTAGES

The nutritionist must be an expert in the field, requiring intensive study at the beginning level and continuing study to keep up with the advancements of science and new methods of communication. Some travel is likely to be required and this may or may not be considered a disadvantage. The nutritionist needs a rare amount of tact and above-average ability in writing and speaking. It is difficult to measure achievements and this may be discouraging.

91

Home Economics Teaching

A home economics teacher is in the largest field of paid employment in the home economics profession. He works with both young people and adults, helping others to discover the "whys" of homemaking. Students are helped to become better family members and to be prepared to establish more successful homes. The home economics teacher is not only a director of learning but also a counselor, in that he helps to solve the personal problems of students. He is also a professional member of associations, a citizen, and a community member.

Perhaps the following quotation may interest the potential teacher and challenge the student's thinking. It is a student's brief opinion of what she envisages in this profession. This material was written by Judy McIntyre, a junior student in the Department of Home Economics Education, School of Home Economics, Southern Illinois University, in answer to a final examination question of the course "Home Economics Education 309a, Methods and Philosophy of Teaching Home Economics." The course was taught by Dr. Anna Carol Fults, Professor and Chairman of the Department of Home Economics Education.

How Would You Describe the Personal Change Experienced as a Result of this Class

If I were to describe the growth that I have experienced during the last three months I would have to relate it in terms of my philosophy. However, immediately I must make a distinction between the academic philosophy and the personal philosophy that I have acquired. Before entering this methods class three months ago, I had studied different educational philosophies so that I had formulated my own theory of education. I had combined some aspects of experimentalism along with aspects of existentialism so that I had a philosophy of education which seemed suitable for me. This philosophy, however, was suitable only in academic terms. At this point even though I had internalized the ideas of this academic philosophy (and in that respect had made it a personal thing) I had not yet achieved that personal philosophy which allows one that peace of mind from knowing how he is going to adjust to life in order to make it the most meaningful for him.

During these last three months, because of intense introspection, a few unique experiences, the weekly logs, and the help from such people as Bel Kaufman (Up the Down Staircase), Bruce and Holden (The Teacher's Personal Development), Louise Sharp (Why Teach?), Hall and Paolucci (Teaching Home Economics), and, of course, my father and the faculty in the Home Economics Education Department, I have at last developed a personal philosophy that will direct me toward realizing my fullest capabilities. Needless to say, these last three months have been a most crucial period in my personal development.

The formalizing of my personal philosophy began with a clearer realization of myself. Through a "biased objectivity" and with the guidance of others came a greater understanding of myself; along with understanding came confidence; and with confidence—acceptance. I don't suppose I've ever realized more keenly how one can never accept others until he has accepted himself. Until one can be honest with himself his perception of reality will be distorted; how then can he be clearly aware of others? The author of *The Teacher's Personal Development,* in quoting Erich Fromm, says that objectivity requires not only seeing the object as it is but also seeing oneself as one is. . . . Thus we can observe our pupils with interest and respect provided we see ourselves as we are. The realization of oneself is not always the most pleasant of experiences, which I painfully discovered. Admitting one's limitations is something most people try to avoid. But after realizing some of my limitations I have been able to accept myself and hence develop self-confidence. I am no longer afraid to openly express many of the things I have kept repressed for I realize that despite my limitations, my worth and value as an individual are unaltered. And here lies the key to my personal philosophy. Now I realize that I, along with everyone else in the world, am a beautiful creature—who possesses great potential and who deserves every opportunity of realizing this potential. My old perception of life was somewhat negative. But now I believe that man, in his search for a meaningful life has great possibilities. Furthermore, I realize that my efforts are needed to help others. And even more important I want to help! While riding on the train in Chicago I looked out my window and I saw the Negro children leaning over the rails in their tenement houses. On their faces was a stare—a blank stare. They seemed to be waiting, wondering . . . but not hoping. As I walked in the streets I saw hungry people. All around me I saw a need; I saw people that I know I can help. I don't expect to see immediate and spectacular changes. The type of help I hope to give will be expressed subtly and the results will be expressed subtly. But I know that as a teacher I will affect the lives of many, and I'll never know where my influence will stop.

During these last three months I have realized this: I am a part of a complex society—a society that is not perfect, for it is made up of imperfect people. I, along with every other member of this society, have a responsibility to myself and to others to try and overcome the imperfection that exists. And I know that I, in a very small way, can help. But what's more important is that I want to help and I will help. This, then, will give meaning to my life; for in helping others to realize their potential I will be realizing mine.

Nature of the Work

Opportunities for teaching are found in elementary and secondary schools, in adult education, and in colleges and universities.

Homemaking teachers in junior and senior high schools teach homemaking subjects, such as child development and family living; clothing selection, care, and construction; food selection, preparation, and service; home furnishings, home management, and family economics; guide students' home experiences; confer with parents on homemaking programs; sponsor a chapter of the Future Homemakers of America; cooperate with other teachers in course planning and school activities; and offer classes in marketable skills in home-economics-related jobs at the eleventh- and twelfth-grade levels.

Teachers in adult programs plan programs to meet the needs of homemakers in the community; help adults become more understanding parents; and teach homemakers new and efficient methods of homemaking.

The faculty in colleges and universities help young people acquire basic knowledge and prepare for a useful career; contribute to the growth of home economics through research; write textbooks and magazine articles; and attend and take part in professional meetings.

Supervision—city, county, regional, state, and national levels: supervision of student teachers in a local school or in a college or university home economics teacher education department; give supervision to home economics teachers in public schools; provide coordination of home economics programs; serve in an administrative capacity. Requires master's or doctor's degree.

Peace Corps volunteer: opportunities in developing countries for those qualified to teach home economics; interesting and challenging experience for those with a social service worldwide interest.

The breadth or depth of teaching will depend upon the size of the school, the age of the pupils, the number of home economics teachers, and the type of program. A secondary school may be under a vocational or nonvocational program. The vocational home economics teacher makes home visits in order to give parents an opportunity to participate in planning and gain an understanding of programs, in order to get an idea of what the pupil has been able to put into practice at home. The vocational teacher meets other requirements of the state office, such as requiring home projects, keeping records, guiding a Future Homemakers of America club chapter, and following suggested curricular approaches.

A new program being instituted in secondary schools is in wage-earning or marketable skills. Training students to prepare for jobs related to home economics upon completion of high school is a new role of the home economics teacher. Workshops are being held in colleges and universities to prepare home economics teachers to accept this new responsibility. As we look at the predictions of the future we find that it is estimated that unemployment will be a major problem for the unskilled. This places the responsibility squarely upon the shoulders of those preparing high school teachers of home economics and equally so upon the high school teacher. The home economics teacher must know how to initiate marketable skills programs, be able to encourage students to participate in such programs, and be adept in carrying on such programs within the community or area. The home economics high school teacher needs to be aware, too, of the Upward Bound and ACTION programs for those who have the potential for college work so that this group will not fall into the unskilled and employed category. See pp. 112–113 for a brief summary of the Upward Bound program.

The home economist interested in education should have considerable patience, a pleasing personality, and a thorough knowledge of subject matter. He should have the ability to work well with others, to understand people and their needs, to adapt to new situations, to be resourceful, and to make friends while maintaining respect. A home economics teacher needs good judgment and a well-grounded sense of values. He should enjoy people, be interested in their welfare, show enthusiasm with poise, maintain a pleasing and clear voice, have a pleasing appearence, and dress appropriately. He must have a strong interest and belief in the importance of education for home and family life.

SPECIAL REQUIREMENTS

The requirements of this profession vary with the state and community, but generally they include a bachelor of science degree from an accredited college or university with a major in home economics and specialization in home economics education. To teach in a vocational program that is reimbursed by the state and federal governments, a home economist should have a degree from a school that offers a vocational certificate. A teacher certification curriculum includes general education, professional education, and specialized education (or home economics subject-matter) courses. For college teaching a home economist usually will specialize in one of the home economics subject-matter areas and receive a master of science degree and possibly a doctoral degree. All of these imply skills and theoretical knowledge.

ADVANTAGES

The turnover is rapid in home economics. About one third[32] of all home economics teachers are replaced yearly. The demand, therefore, has been great. The salary, too, is an advantage of the profession. A home economist in education receives a salary equal to, or better than, people in similar professional fields. Often a home economics teacher is employed on a ten- or twelve-month basis, rather than the usual nine of other teaching areas. Home economics teaching is a challenging and rewarding field for one who enjoys helping people in their day-to-day lives. The free time in the summer contributes readily to travel and study. This is a field with which homemaking can be combined easily and to the advantage of one's profession through actual experience. The home economics teacher is eligible for membership in the American Home Economics Association, the National Educational Association, and the American Vocational Association.

POSSIBLE DISADVANTAGES

There is routine work in grading papers and keeping records, but some routine is expected in most professions. The home economics teacher requires continual study and preparation in order to keep abreast of new knowledge and methods. There are often extra-curricular responsibilities and some work after school. None of these disadvantages are restrictions limited to the teaching profession. They are found in many businesses.

THE FUTURE IN HOME ECONOMICS TEACHING*

by Marjorie East

Most home economists are in some sense teachers because they help people learn how to live better. A great many of them are teachers in the more customary sense: they teach in schools or colleges. Practically every public secondary school employs one or more home economists, and there

---

[32] Tate, op. cit., p. 89.

* Written for this volume. Dr. Marjorie East is Professor and Head of the Department of Home Economics Education, Pennsylvania State University, University Park. She has served as president of the American Home Economics Association. She has made valuable contributions to the profession of home economics, including holding many offices and chairmanships of major committees, such as the AHEA Committee on Accreditation.

are some 350 four-year colleges and some 400 two-year colleges that teach home economics. About a quarter of the school teachers leave their jobs each year to spend more time with their own families, so there are many teaching positions waiting for new college graduates.

School teaching is appropriate for the beginning home economist. The girl who enjoyed her own junior and senior high school days will like returning to the cheerful, busy atmosphere of adolescence. The students will admire her youth, poise, and confidence. She will be stimulated to do her best by often hearing herself quoted: "My home ec teacher says. . . ."

School teaching is also appropriate for the woman whose children are in school. Her mature wisdom and her experience of testing the home economics concepts in her own home have made her valuable to students and to the school. And she enjoys helping other people's children as well as her own.

There are many college teaching positions available for both men and women who study one of the special areas of home economics beyond the bachelor's level. Junior college and other postsecondary positions usually require a master's degree, and four-year college positions usually require a doctor's degree.

Both schools and colleges are exciting places to work. The students are in the process of becoming adults and are making many important decisions about their future: whom to marry, what career to prepare for, what to believe and to stand for, what kind of a person to become. Answers to questions like these change for each generation. Teachers have the chance to keep in tune with each one of the new generations as they grow up.

Our country is changing rapidly, too. New professions develop, like that of the consumer adviser. New social concerns arise, such as for improved health, safety, and nutrition. Moral values change, such as those related to sexual permissiveness. New attitudes toward old ideas develop, such as the new roles for women and men in the modern world. New economic problems arise, such as inflation, depression, and unemployment. Schools and colleges are always right in the center of social change because parents want the best for their children and the young people want to get ready for tomorrow's world, not yesterday's.

Home economics is especially sensitive to social changes, and school programs are different now from what they once were. Home economics classes now emphasize consumer decisions rather than the home production of goods from the raw materials. How to buy intelligently in the marketplace, how to plan ahead and use credit wisely, how to decide when not to spend, these are the new skills being taught. Another major emphasis is on human development: how to understand one's own physical and emotional development and that of infants and small children, how to select delicious foods that are also safe and healthy, how to dress in fashion so as to fit in with the chosen group. Some schools teach special job skills for such careers as those in the hospitality industry in hotels, motels, and restaurants, or as those in day-care centers for young children. Many schools also teach the old-fashioned useful arts of cooking and canning, sewing, and baby sitting.

As new changes come into our lives, home economics classes will be

Figure 3-13.
Home economics teachers know that transportation is the third largest item in the average family's budget and that decisions about used cars must be made by both men and women. (Courtesy of the AHEA.)

changing too. If the country changes over to the metric system of weights and measures, home ec will teach how to translate clothing sizes, recipe proportions, and new measuring procedures. If science shows how to control and choose the sex of a planned-for baby, home ec will be teaching not only how it is done but how to decide which sex to choose. If our society decides that zero population growth is desirable, home ec will be instructing on conception control. If society values highly the few children it allows to be born, then home ec will be devoting even more of its energy to transmitting the best of child development knowledge to present and future parents.

Teaching skills are changing, too. Tomorrow's teacher will use even more electronic aids. Cassettes for TV, and computer analysis and instructional systems are two of the most promising. As we learn more about identifying learning levels and diagnosing learning troubles, teaching may come to be more of a specialized profession. Each learner can have an individually planned curriculum that will help him learn what he needs to know in the way he learns most easily. The teacher may become less of a performer standing in the spotlight of attention before a group of students, more of a special learning adviser to a number of individual students.

Teaching is now and certainly will continue to be a challenging, changing profession.

The Home Economist in Extension Work

The extension home economist or home economics agent or home demonstration agent is employed by the land-grant university, the U.S. Department of Agriculture, and the county government. Thus we have a national system supported jointly by the federal government, the states, and the counties, one that has been in effect since 1914, when Congress passed the Smith-Lever Act.

Nature of the Work

The extension home economist helps homemakers and boys and girls in the community to be better homemakers, family members, and citizens. The extension home economist, working with other county agents and volunteer leaders, develops programs based on family wants and needs; provides information from research related to child care and family life, foods and clothing, home management and housing; works with people from the many agencies and organizations that have a concern for the family; presents radio and television programs; writes newspaper articles; answers inquiries by letter or telephone; provides information for the consumer; may be responsible for or help to plan and carry out youth development programs; may help to train professionals from other agencies; and may train and supervise professionals to work with disadvantaged families.

The extension home economist is a staff member of the land-grant college and holds a federal appointment in the U.S. Department of Agriculture. He usually works for and throughout a county, traveling extensively. His office is usually in the county seat, where he generally has a secretary and possibly assistants. If the county is large and finances permit, an assistant may share in the total program or be in charge of the educational programs for young people.

Although extension work had its beginning because of the desire to help rural people, it has more recently included urban areas in its sphere of work. Many metropolitan areas, such as Cook County in Illinois, may employ more than one extension home economist, so that the actual area of work is less than the entire county. The needs and wants of urban people may vary considerably from those of rural people.

Extension workers in many states are increasing efforts to develop methods, materials, and means to help the economically deprived. Lack of funding for these programs has been a handicap. With national interest in, and financial support for, work with these two groups, extension workers can and will make responsible contributions toward improvement in the lives of the economically deprived. The expanded nutrition program is a major thrust in the education of this group of disadvantaged.

The trend in extention work also seems to be toward the employment of subject-matter specialists who may live in one county and serve several counties. A cluster of different subject-matter specialists living and working in one region permits multicounty programming. These specialists would, of course, have done graduate work in their area of specialization.

Other trends in extension work are toward more emphasis on research and on publications. The research may be subject-matter or sociologically oriented. The researcher must be located where facilities are available for the study. Publications may be written for other extension workers, although more probably for the general public. Research and publishing require special techniques and skills that are usually acquired at the graduate level of study. It should be realized that not all home advisers will research and/or publish. The majority will still interpret research findings.

A home economist entering extension needs to have a deep interest in the welfare of people, in social service, and in education for the home and family. He should desire to be a leader and to train others to be leaders. The characteristics needed for this career include the ability to work well with others and an understanding of people and their problems. An extension home economist should have an unpretentious and friendly manner; be forceful but not dominant; be patient, tactful, and sincere; have a keen sense of responsibility; and have a sense of humor, a pleasing appearance, good health, and abundant energy.

SPECIAL REQUIREMENTS

A bachelor's degree with a major in home economics or a related area is required. Specialization in extension service training is most desirable; this usually includes, or should include, field experience in a county between the junior and senior year. Because of the shortage in the profession, many people are employed as extension home economists when their specialization has been in home economics education. Positions of advancement, such as subject-matter specialist or regional supervisor or senior extension adviser, usually require further study on the graduate level or a master's degree. College courses in the principles and history of extension work, sociology, economics, pyschology, public speaking, journalism, and demonstration techniques will be helpful along with experience in group work, such as scouting, church work, camp counseling, and field experience.

ADVANTAGES

The advantages of the career lie in its experiences. The breadth of the programs is stimulating and offers opportunity for cooperation and creativity. The amount of travel can be an advantage when one enjoys it. Also one meets many people who have confidence in and respect and affection for him as a county agent. There is personal satisfaction in one's freedom to exercise his talents and resources with opportunity to use initiative and creativity. Positions are available almost everywhere, with good opportunities for advancement; the number of extension positions available is second only to those in teaching; positions are also available internationally. Salaries compare favorably with those in other home economics professions; fringe benefits make the positions attractive. The in-service training that is provided for extension personnel is a real asset in keeping up-to-date. This, too, is a career that combines well with homemaking. Eligibility for membership in the American Home Economics Association and in the National Association of Extension Home Economists also enhances this profession.

POSSIBLE DISADVANTAGES

The long and irregular hours with some night work may prove a disadvantage to the extension career as now known. Also such a position usually requires constant adherence to community conventions.

THE FUTURE IN THE EXTENSION AND
CONTINUING EDUCATION PROFESSIONS*

by Mary Nell Greenwood

Our country's concern for the education of youth and continuing education for adults enhances the opportunities for home economists. With the

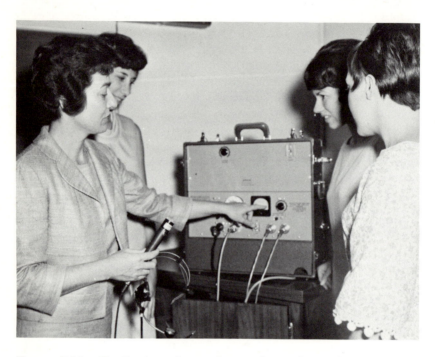

FIGURE 3-14.   *Dr. Greenwood is explaining the newly installed tele-lecture equipment at the University of Missouri to three extension home economists with the University's Extension Division. These new employees have the opportunity of participating in a three-month training program in order to acquaint them with the University, its extension organization, and its adult education programs.*

* Written for this volume. Dr. Mary Nell Greenwood is Director, Quality of Living Programs, University of Missouri Extension. Her bachelor of science degree in vocational home economics is from Central Missouri State College, Warrensburg. She holds master of science and doctoral degrees in extension administration from the University of Wisconsin, Madison. She has been an extension worker since 1951, when she was appointed county home agent at large. She has also served as county home agent, extension consumer information agent, district home economist, associate professor of extension education, assistant director in charge of home economics programs, and Director of Continuing Education for Women and Professor of Extension Education. She has recently served as Vice-President for Cooperative Relations in the American Home Economics Association.

reservoir of knowledge expected to double between 1970 and 1975, kindling the desire among adults for the conscious, continuous pursuit of new knowledge is imperative. Recent legislation has provided resources for expanding educational opportunities for adults from every walk of life. The growing complexity of problems evolving from social and economic changes means that continuing information is required by decision-making units—individuals, families, and communities. Without question, the responsibilities and adjustments of the family are greater than ever before in an increasingly complex society. Therefore, education for family and community living has come to the forefront among educational needs in America.

Home economists concerned with the continuing education of adults face these challenges:

- Designing dynamic programs directly related to the significant concerns of families and communities. Among the broad national concerns to which home economists uniquely contribute include family stability, consumer competence, family health, housing, and community resource development.
- Developing programs in conjunction with other disciplines, such as sociology, medicine, and engineering.
- Formulating creative educational approaches that utilize the latest research, institutional media, and auxiliary personnel.
- Acquiring and maintaining a high level of competence within home economics in order to accommodate to specialization, simultaneously

FIGURE 3-15. *Extension home economists in the field: from food surplus distribution points to the migrant camps. (Courtesy of the University Extension, the University of Wisconsin.)*

FIGURE 3-16. *This family is learning about the four basic food groups from program aide Carrie Howard. She is working with the Expanded Foods and Nutrition Education Program in Beloit, Wisconsin. (Courtesy of the University Extension, the University of Wisconsin.)*

keeping abreast with the ever-changing economic, social, and cultural conditions.

Increasing numbers of home economists will be needed to work in continuing or adult education. With the continuing emphasis on developing human resources, new and challenging programs utilizing the competencies of home economists will evolve.

Careers in Child Development and Family Relations

Few, if any, areas are developing more rapidly than are child development and family relations. Home economics has from its conception placed primary emphasis upon family welfare and is the only field of study that has this primary focus. Recent federal legislation has given such impetus to programs for children and families that the opportunities are almost staggering. Thus, although the need is not new, the opportunities to work in the field are greater than ever before. If one is interested in working with children, youth, or families, preparation for a career in child development and family relations may now present the best opportunities.

The Specialist in Child Development

NATURE OF THE WORK

Positions in child care are available in public and private nursery schools, kindergartens, and elementary schools; in mental health departments and state departments of health; in programs for exceptional and handicapped children; in extension work as 4-H or youth directors; in hospitals, orphanages, and child welfare agencies; in organizations such as Girl Scouts, Boy Scouts, Girl Guides, and Camp Fire Girls; in Project Head Start, Upward Bound, and community action programs. Advanced positions for those who have additional study include child center director, camp director, or child care specialist, and positions in research.

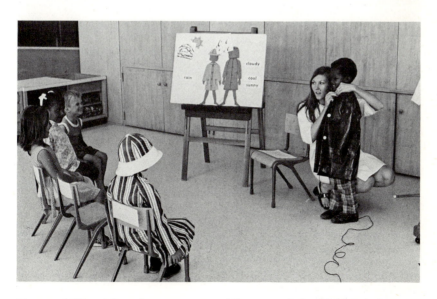

FIGURE 3-17. *A learning experience. (Courtesy of the Child Development Laboratory, Southern Illinois University.)*

Nursery school teaching may be the career in child care with the most workers. A nursery school often operates from three to four hours a day. If there are two sessions, the school may be open from nine to four. Phillips explains the role of the nursery school teacher in the following excerpt.

. . . The nursery school teacher must set up the kind of environment in which children can play creatively and constructively. She develops understanding of children as individuals and skill in guiding them through all kinds of experiences, whether in the area of music, art, science, or getting along with others. She learns to plan for each child as an individual and for the group as a whole. She is frequently called upon to serve as consultant on children's toys, equipment, and supplies, and on marriage and family relations; she may write for magazines and newspapers, or appear on radio and television.[33]

Project Head Start. With the passage of the Economic Opportunity Act of 1964 we find, for the first time in our history, the "whole" child included in a nationwide endeavor. Sargent Shriver, formerly Director

FIGURE 3-18. *Project Head Start.* (*Courtesy of the U.S. Department of Health, Education, and Welfare.*)

[33] Velma Phillips, *Home Economics Careers for You* (New York: Harper & Row, 1962), p. 139.

of the Office of Economic Opportunity, appointed a planning committee including leaders in child development, education, medicine, nursing, psychology, public health, and social work. The Head Start Child Development Centers were started in the summer of 1965 and provided a six- to eight-week educational experience for approximately 561,000 children. The children were in the age group that would begin school in the fall of 1965. The goals were as follows:

To improve the child's health

To help the child's emotional and social development by encouraging self-confidence, self-expression, self-discipline, and curiosity

To improve and expand the child's mental processes, aiming at expanding ability to think, reason, and speak clearly

To help children to get wider and more varied experiences which would broaden their horizons, increase their ease of conversation, and improve their understanding of the world in which they live

To give the child frequent chances to succeed. Such chances might erase patterns of frustration and failure and especially the fear of failure

To develop a climate of confidence for the child which would make him want to learn

To increase the child's ability to get along with others in his family and, at the same time, help the family to understand him and his problems, thus strengthening family ties

To develop in the child and his family a responsible attitude toward society and foster feelings of belonging to a community

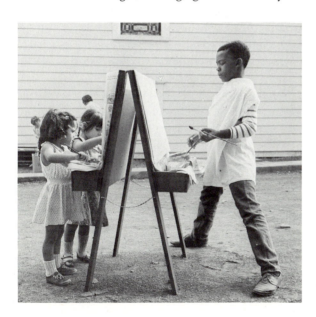

FIGURE 3-19. *Project Head Start. (Courtesy of the U.S. Department of Health, Education, and Welfare; the Children's Bureau; and Esther Bubley, photographer.)*

107

To plan activities which would allow groups from every social, ethnic, and economic level in a community to join together with the poor in solving problems

To offer a chance for the child to meet and see teachers, policemen, health and welfare officers, all figures of authority, in situations which would bring respect and not fear

To give the child a chance to meet older children, teen-agers, and adults who would serve as "models" in manners, behavior, speech, and the like

To help both the child and his family to greater confidence, self-respect and dignity.[34]

To work with parents, helping them help their children and to become more useful citizens in the community was another goal of the Head Start program.

The philosophy of childhood education in the United States has been one in which there is respect for the child's manner of reacting and learning; consideration for his personal development; and interest in working closely with parents. Yet until Project Head Start, childhood education had received less than fervent interest. The first kindergarten in the United States was opened in Watertown, Wisconsin, in 1855. The first public nursery school was opened in 1919 in New York. In 1935, more than 65,000 needy children were enrolled in nursery schools under the Federal Emergency Education Program, but these schools were phased out as unemployment became less. Day-care centers were provided in World War II; these were primarily for children of mothers who were employed outside of the home. These, too, were largely phased out after the war. In 1950, only 51 per cent of all five-year-olds were enrolled in kindergarten or first grade.

In 1969, Head Start joined other child-and-parent programs in the newly established Office of Child Development, U.S. Department of Health, Education, and Welfare. Head Start contains the following components:

1. Health—a child who is in poor health will function at a lower level than if he were a well child. Head Start Centers provide a complete medical examination and follow-through for the correction of defects.
2. Nutrition—Head Start children are often malnourished. The nutrition program, then, normally provides at least one hot meal and

[34] Milly Cowles, "One Front in the War on Poverty: Early Childhood Education," *AAUW Journal*, 59:1 (October 1965), p. 15.

FIGURE 3-20.
*Project Head
Start. (Courtesy
of the U.S. De-
partment of
Health, Educa-
tion, and Wel-
fare.)*

snack each day for the child *and also* gives parents an opportunity
to learn how to plan and prepare well-balanced meals and how to
use this knowledge in their own homes.

3. Education—the methods of teaching used are designed to fit the
   needs of each specific group of children.
4. Parental involvement—Head Start requires a parent advisory committee, selected by the parents themselves, that serves at the administrative level. Frequently, home economics classes are held for
   parents and often parents serve in nonprofessional positions, on
   either a volunteer or a paid basis.
5. Social services—the social service worker strives to lead the family,

the community, and the Head Start Center into a relationship that is mutually useful.

6. Psychological services—the psychologist or psychiatrist provides specialized information as a member of the Head Start team; he works with teachers, aides, and the children.

By the fall of 1972, more than 4 million children have taken part in Head Start, over 400,000 people have worked as volunteers in the program, and the families have begun participating more fully in the life of the community.

Parent-and-child centers are being organized to reach children under the age of three and to reach deficiencies at an age earlier than that reached by Head Start.[35]

Project Head Start, then, represents the first national effort initiated in the interest of the economically disadvantaged child. There are indications that, in general, the project is successful in achieving its basic purposes. There are also indications that the project has an impact on family living, through family involvement, that is beneficial to all members of the family, including the Head Start child. Few national programs so typify our American ideal of equality of opportunity.

The home economist interested in working in the field of child care should have sincere respect and affection for children, should be well adjusted personally, and should be well poised, friendly, sympathetic, and flexible. The child care worker should be interested in music, art, and literature, as well as science, and should have enthusiasm, initiative, resourcefulness, and a willingness to work hard.

SPECIAL REQUIREMENTS

This home economist should have a strong college background in nutrition, family relationships, home management, child psychology, childhood education, physical care of the child, and supervised experiences with children. A bachelor's degree in home economics with emphasis upon education and child development is generally a minimum requirement. Nursery schools at the college level will require a master's degree and possibly work toward a doctoral degree.

[35] *Head Start—A Child Development Program,* N 23 C (Washington, D.C.: Office of Child Development, U.S. Department of Health, Education, and Welfare, 1970), pp. 1–11.

ADVANTAGES

A home economist in child care, whether working in a private nursery school or a Head Start program, can enjoy the rewarding experience of watching the development of children through their social, emotional, physical, and intellectual growth. The experiences will help to prepare the home economist for parenthood and life in general. The working environment is generally sunny and attractive; the hours are not long. Beginning salaries are comparable to those for other teachers, and the demand for persons trained in child care and development is great and will probably remain so. The home economist in child care is eligible for membership in the American Home Economics Association, the American Association for Childhood Development, and the National Association for Young Children.

POSSIBLE DISADVANTAGES

The disadvantages of the profession include the concern when a child is ill and the physical demands, which may be fairly strenuous.

The Specialist in Family Relations

A specialist in family relations has had thorough background training in home economics. The family is at the core of all home economics study and it is believed that the most lasting behavior patterns of individuals are set in the home. The expression that "As is the home, so is the state, nation, and world" may be trite but nonetheless true. Thus, training in child care and family relations helps one to live more effectively in the family and to help others to achieve more satisfying, effective family living.

As indicated earlier, many of the career opportunities in this area may entail both child care and family relations. The person who is primarily interested in the area of family relations will find many opportunities for teaching in secondary schools, junior colleges, and in universities; the university level may also include research. There are also more opportunities for teaching at the adult level than ever before. Adults are seeking help on problems from prenatal to the senior citizens categories. The adult work may be carried on through extension services, schools, churches, or civic groups.

Family relations specialists are also needed in community action programs, in Upward Bound programs, in training Foster Grand-parents, in working with migrants, in VISTA, in the Peace Corps, and in the Neighborhood Youth Corps. Because these programs are comparatively new, thumbnail descriptions are given.

Upward Bound. Upward Bound, a program originally in the Office of Economic Opportunity, has been sponsored by the Office of Education, Department of Health, Education, and Welfare since July 1, 1969. Upward Bound has as its major aims the discovery of capable boys and girls who would not be likely to attend college and their motivation and preparation for college work. It is a precollege program for high school students from low-income families, who may have the potential to pursue college studies if given adequate preparation and if properly motivated.

Begun on a national scale in the summer of 1966, Upward Bound programs were sponsored at almost three hundred colleges, universities, and secondary schools in 1969. Approximately twenty-three thousand young people were resident students for the six-to-eight-week summer session in 1969.

During the academic year following the resident summer session, representatives from the Upward Bound institutions continue to meet the students in classes on Saturdays, through study sessions with college undergraduate tutor-counselors, or through cultural enrichment programs while the student continues his secondary education. The Upward Bound institutions must make every effort to involve the parents in the educational efforts of their young people.

The vast majority of these students come from families with incomes below the federally established poverty lines or from families that receive welfare or live in public housing. In 1969, 49 per cent of the students were male, 51 per cent female; 38 per cent were white, 54 per cent were black, 6 per cent American Indian, 1 per cent Oriental, and 1 per cent other.

Two thirds of all Upward Bound students who graduated from high school from 1967 through 1969 enrolled in college. The benefits of such a program cannot be measured solely in dollar terms; they include the value of a college education to both the individual and society. It is hoped that such education would also result in more effective citizen participation, greater family stability, lowered crime rates, better child rearing, and economic benefits that presumably will accrue to future generations. These are important considerations, as

FIGURE 3-21. *There is enthusiasm in the stride of Upward Bound students en route to summer classes. These students are on the campus of Ripon College, in Ripon, Wisconsin. (Courtesy of the Office of Economic Opportunity.)*

a successful Upward Bound program would include the breaking of the intergenerational poverty cycle.[36]

There is a new program similar to Upward Bound in Action. This new program may eventually replace the Upward Bound program. Anyone interested in participation in or in helping to develop this new program may write to *Action,* Washington, D.C., 20525.

VISTA. The Volunteers in Service to America program, first authorized by Congress in 1964, gives adults eighteen years old and over the opportunity to join the fight on poverty for at least a year. Some 4,600 volunteers are living and working in urban ghettos, small towns, rural poverty areas, and migrant streams, on Indian reservations, in institutions for the mentally handicapped, and in Job Corps centers. All volunteers must have the desire to serve, the willingness to learn, the patience to persist through frustrations, and the ability to define prob-

[36] Office of Economic Opportunity, *An Evaluation of Upward Bound* (Washington, D.C.: U.S. Government Printing Office, 1969).

lems in terms of possible solutions. The VISTA volunteer is actually the catalyst who recognizes and helps local neighborhood leaders, helps develop other leaders, and in this way helps to ensure continuing action. On July 1, 1971, VISTA became a part of ACTION, an agency created to administer six government voluntary programs in an effort to coordinate forces to attack poverty-related social and economic problems in the United States *and* in the developing countries abroad. Other programs in ACTION are the Peace Corps (See pp. 115–162), the Service Corps, the Active Corps of Executives, the Retired Senior Volunteer Program, and the Foster Grandparent Program.

Neighborhood Youth Corps. The Neighborhood Youth Corps is administered by the U.S. Department of Labor. NYC provides full- or part-time work experience and training for boys and girls fourteen years of age or older, enabling them to stay in or return to school or to increase their employability if they are out of school. In-school youth work twelve to fifteen hours a week; out-of-school youth work up to thirty-two hours and receive eight hours of counseling, remedial education, and job-related training each week. State or local governments, private and nonprofit agencies provide jobs in hospitals, schools, playgrounds, settlement houses, and so on, for nurses' aides, hospital orderlies, teachers' aides, librarians' aides and assistants, auto-mechanic helpers, filing clerks, and typists.

Counseling. Counseling has long been the major career opportunity for the family relations specialist. The counselor may find his career opportunity in the programs just outlined. The counselor helps people to understand themselves, interpret their needs and desires, make plans for meeting their needs and desires, and adjust effectively to family or other group living. It could be stated that his objective is to help others to live more successfully.

A family relations consultant needs first to have worked toward adjustment in his own personal life in order to meet the needs of the people with whom he will work. He needs a sincere interest in, understanding of, and sympathy for people; an open, friendly personality; and the ability to be objective about situations. When a counselor can empathize with his clients, he can help them to express freely their real feelings and to come closer to accepting reality and adjusting to it. Besides these basic abilities, a bachelor's degree and probably graduate work will be needed. A home economics major with a specialization in family relations will be a strong background. Courses in marriage and family life, psychology, sociology, and guidance will add to one's preparation for the profession of family relations consultant.

ADVANTAGES

A home economist working in a family relations position receives benefits both personally and financially. The personal satisfaction of helping others and the remunerative gains can be very rewarding. Membership eligibility includes the American Home Economics Association and the National Council on Family Relations.

POSSIBLE DISADVANTAGES

The primary disadvantage of family life work generally lies in becoming too involved with the problems of others. This will be avoided if one is able to remain objective.

As an outstanding professional worker in these areas sees the future:

THE FUTURE IN CHILD DEVELOPMENT AND FAMILY RELATIONS PROFESSIONS[*]

by Glenn R. Hawkes

American family living patterns and child-rearing philosophies are undergoing constant revision. At no time in the history of man has this change been so rapid and so spirited. From these changes and changes in the social order a series of new "helping" professions is emerging. These professions are exciting, challenging, stimulating, and shifting in emphasis from day to day.

We no longer live in an agrarian society in which the extended-family-type clan was available for help and support and in which advice was freely given. To replace these services society has developed new professions for people who are interested in education and service as it relates to family living. New and developing families are increasingly urged to obtain this professional help as they set down their lifetime patterns. Opportunity is on the increase.

The critical nature of the family as the cradle of personality development is beyond question. And as we attempt to better the situation of our minority and disadvantaged groups it is apparent that those who are equipped to work with and research about minority and disadvantaged families are in a most enviable position. They will be on the edge of change. Their role in

[*] Written for this volume. Dr. Glenn R. Hawkes is Associate Dean, Family and Consumer Sciences, University of California at Davis.

society will be enhanced. The work is exciting and stimulating, and it calls for maturity in commitment on the part of people who want to participate.

It is impossible to keep up with the demand for children's workers. They are needed in education, welfare, social services, and recreation. Furthermore, they work in a wide variety of settings—the school, the day-care center, the settlement house, and so on. Our society claims to be interested in providing increased opportunities for children. As new opportunities develop we will see wide application of the skills of the professional child-serving person. New teaching programs are emerging as the age of school entrance becomes lower. Many states have adopted legislation that requires certification and credentials for working with young children. The student would be well advised to explore these laws.

Welfare "reform" is pointing in the direction of increased day-care openings for children. The cornerstone of this new thinking is intervention at increasingly younger ages. The child development and family relations profession appears to be a likely spot for recruiting for these programs.

For those who are interested in the excitement of modern family living and for those who are interested in professions that are constantly changing and developing, nothing can be much more satisfying than working in family relations and child development. There must be a strong commitment to people, to service, and to change. Land-grant colleges and universities generally provide education in child development—sometimes under home economics and sometimes as a separate major. The programs in this area are growing at such a fast pace that only yearly inspection of catalogues will give the student current information. Certainly one should look at programs in education or psychology to ascertain their contribution.

The satisfaction that comes from serving, as well as the application that can be made to one's own family, is an abundant reward. Those who serve children and families are serving the future.

The Home Economist in Business

The home economist in business is one who holds a degree in home economics or a degree with a major in home economics from an accredited college or university and is engaged in a home economics capacity in:

1. a business organization created for profit, or
2. a municipally owned utility created for profit, or
3. an association supported by a business organization for profit, or
4. a free-lance or consultant service to which is given 50 per cent of the average working year.[37]

[37] Martha Easter, Directory 1971 Home Economists in Business Section of the American Home Economics Association (Corning, N.Y., 1971), pp. 7–8.

The classification of the positions of home economists in business, as outlined in the 1971 Directory are Communications; Consumer Marketing—Equipment and Housing; Consumer Marketing—Family Services; Consumer Marketing—Food and Nutrition; Consumer Marketing —Household Products; Consumer Marketing—Textiles and Clothing; Home Service; and Institution Management.[38] Because these do represent variety in positions as well as in the actual work done, a variety in personal interests and characteristics, and a range in requirements, the author asked professionals in business who are particularly successful to write résumés describing some or all of these. Some of these fall into the same HEIB category but portray different facets within the category. Not all HEIB categories have been included. One category, interior design, has been added by the author. Professional organizations for all of these include the American Home Economics Association and Home Economists in Business.

THE HOME ECONOMIST IN BUSINESS—FOODS[*]

by Helen Wolcott Horton

Fresh, canned, frozen, dried, refrigerated, and dehydro-frozen are only a few of the forms in which today's homemaker finds food products in the grocery store. Behind each of these products are the home economists with the food industry who have helped develop and perfect them. This increased variety in food products, although providing a greater selection for the consumer, requires more decision making as well, and the home economist has the responsibility of making the company's product stand out competitively as well as clearly communicating the content, net weight, yield, and preparation needed through information provided on the label and in advertising.

The creation of new food products is of major importance to the economic growth of a food company, and ideas for these new products come

[38] Ibid., p. 3.

[*] Written for this volume by Helen Wolcott Horton. Mrs. Horton is a food consultant operating her own company, Consumer Food Marketing and Communications. Prior to this, she served as director of the Ann Pillsbury Consumer Service Kitchens, where her experiences provided the basis for this material. The examples used, although typical of those of other companies, were based on actual practice while Mrs. Horton was Consumer Service Director of the Pillsbury Company. Mrs. Horton previously served as an account executive and director of home economics with McCann-Erickson, Inc., an advertising agency, and as associate director of home economics with the National Live Stock and Meat Board. She is a graduate of the University of Illinois. Mrs. Horton is a member of the American Home Economics Association, a member and former national chairman of the Home Economists in Business. She is a member and former officer of the Illinois Home Economics Association as well as the Chicago HEIB group. She also holds memberships in American Women in Radio and Television, Phi Upsilon Omicron, Mortar Board, and Connoisseurs, International.

FIGURE 3-22. *Grant W. Law, Director, New Product Planning (left), and Ed Gustafson, Product Manager, review a recipe brochure prepared by Helen Wolcott Horton for a new consumer product developed for the Household Products Division, Miles Laboratories, Inc.*

from many sources. The development of the product is largely a matter of teamwork and in many companies the home economists on the consumer service staff develop ideas for products based mainly on home recipe models. In doing this they work closely with research and development scientists for their technological information and for formulating the recipe into a commercial product—dry mix, refrigerated, or frozen. At the same time, the home economist works with marketing and commercial research in developing a concept for the product and, through consumer testing, in determining the homemaker's acceptance of the product, as well as identifying the feasibility of introducing it. If and when the decision is made to produce the product, she then writes the label directions, prepares the food for the package illustration, and works with the advertising agency to develop advertising for the product.

The home economist with the food industry may be required to do a good deal of traveling. She must meet with representative consumer groups in various parts of the country to learn their reaction to the product and make trips to plants producing the products for production approvals.

Photography for the label, print ads, or television commercials may be done in studios from New York to California. Introduction of the product to the trade, press, consumers, and educators may require trips to major cities across the country and television appearances, radio interviews, product demonstrations, or convention exhibits. It may even involve extensive trips outside the country to introduce products in foreign markets.

Figure 3-23. *A tasting panel of home economists and other staff evaluate an entree: Is it (1) attractive to the eye; (2) easy or time-consuming to prepare; (3) appealing to the taste? (Courtesy of the National Live Stock and Meat Board.)*

Publicity releases for the product require unusual recipe ideas, photographs, and a flair for writing to capture the attention of food editors. The sales force needs recipe leaflets and photographs for use in grocery stores. Educators make use of materials prepared for classroom use.

Even then work with the product is not completed. The home economist searches for new service ideas for the product to feature in cook books or advertising, works with other members of this team constantly to improve the product, weighing new technological data and raw ingredients as well as evaluating competitive products in doing this. Work is done with extensions of the product line, applying the basic technology developed in furthering new product ideas. It is a continually challenging role, demanding creativity and decision making yet providing a high degree of satisfaction to

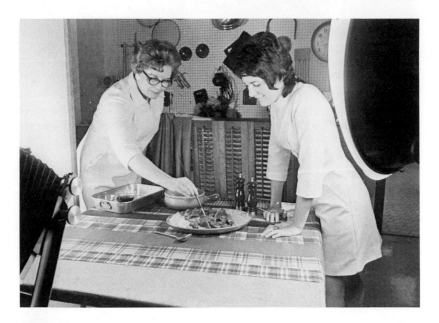

Figure 3-24. *Food photography requires skill to make a subject appear as it is! Brushing sauce on a meat entree gives it a just-off-the-range look. (Courtesy of the National Live Stock and Meat Board.)*

the home economist as the product is seen being served in homes across the country.

What are the requirements for a home economist contemplating such a position? First of all, a genuine creative interest in food. A survey of all the major food companies listed these criteria for the home economists they employ:

1. A home economics degree with a major in foods and nutrition (or the equivalent) with emphasis on experimental foods, nutrition, chemistry, and meal management.

2. As many business-oriented courses as possible in the following areas:
   Economics
   Marketing
   Advertising and Journalism
     Copy and Layout
     Radio
     Television
     Feature Writing
   Public Speaking
   Statistics

3. Good grooming, a pleasing personality and appearance, and ability to work with others, as well as maturity and some decision-making ability.

120

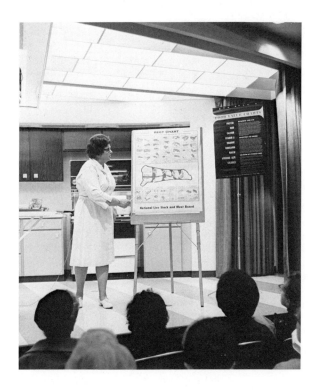

FIGURE 3-25. *Meat identification and the nutritive value of meat are two subjects of interest to homemakers who want to learn more about meat buying and how to feed their families adequately. (Courtesy of the National Live Stock and Meat Board.)*

The financial rewards and opportunities for professional growth are unlimited. Home economists recognized as executives with their companies are gaining in number. Salaries even at beginning levels are among the highest paid to women in the country.

Concomitant with the economic and sociological growth of the American consumer and his unsatiable demand for new products with greater convenience is a fertile field for the home economist to explore with the food industry in the future.

THE HOME ECONOMIST IN BUSINESS—EQUIPMENT [*]

by Max E. Fuller

A college graduate with a baccalaureate degree in home economics who enjoys working with people, who likes to travel, and who finds it challenging to explain rather complex ideas to a group of interested people may wish to explore the career opportunities open in the appliance industry. Although

[*] Written for this volume by Dr. Max E. Fuller, Director of Field Education for the Maytag Company, Newton, Iowa. Active as an educator and college administrator for twenty years, Dr. Fuller left the campus to join Maytag in 1954. Under his supervision, the program of training and the pattern of field activities were developed for the Home Service Department as described in this article.

121

it is impossible for one associated with a particular manufacturer to provide detailed descriptions on all the career possibilities within an industry, perhaps this discussion of the role of the home economics graduate within the Marketing Division of the Maytag Company may offer an adequate overview.

When the Maytag Company seeks a home economist for a staff position within the Marketing Division, we are concerned primarily with three sets of qualifications.

First, we insist upon a professional degree in home economics. We believe it is vitally important that the home economist employed by our company be fully qualified to participate actively in the professional affairs of the American Home Economics Association, that they be eligible for membership in the Home Economics in Business groups, and that they have the academic background to meet on common ground with professional home economists in educational institutions, in editorial positions on various magazines and newspapers, and in business and industry.

We should not attempt to specify the academic background other than the degree requirement. Although it might seem especially appropriate for an appliance manufacturer to seek only those persons with majors in household equipment, we have had many highly competent employees in this area of our Marketing Division who have come to us with majors in textiles and clothing, in interior design, and even some with no major at all in the field. Our experience over the past two decades would lead us to suggest that although the professional degree in home economics is vitally important, the particular area of concentration in the field is not a governing factor.

Second, we are very much concerned with the personal characteristics of the young home economics graduate. We seek an individual who is mentally alert, is eager to learn, is willing to work hard, and gives promise of having the kind of inquiring mind and self-starting characteristics that indicate active and creative participation in all departmental activities. We look for someone with a flair for creative ideas in the presentation of information: academic experience in the field of communications is highly valuable; extracurricular participation in theater, radio, television, debate, or other speech activities provides an excellent indication of ability to communicate effectively.

We look for someone who is neat, pleasant, and attractive in appearance, and someone whom we believe to be sufficiently self-reliant to cope with all the unpredictable situations that develop when traveling for extended periods in the United States or Canada.

Third, and this is very important, we evaluate all applicants for positions within the Marketing Division—including home economists—in terms of the image we believe they will create when dealing with the public either individually or in groups. Like all who produce consumer goods, we are necessarily continually conscious of consumer attitudes and opinions. We have a very real concern for public opinion about our products, about our people, and about our policies. The Maytag home economists, like all other staff members within the Marketing Division, personify the Maytag Company for all the various and diversified groups of the public with whom they come in direct personal contact. Therefore, we would evaluate the applicant

122

FIGURE 3-26. *Maytag staff home economist Deedee Miller, a 1968 gradu-ate of Kansas State University, Manhattan, discusses fabric care with Sylvia Scott in a half-hour television program. "The Woman's Angle" is seen in the Baltimore, Maryland, area on channel 2.*

Maytag home economists are frequently interviewed during their travel on local radio or television stations.

in terms of the kind of image we believe would be reflected by that individual. We must insist upon the type of young person who under all circumstances would act in accordance with the high standards that we as a company seek to maintain.

Once the home economist has joined our company, the first consideration is training. Incidentally, the Maytag Company prefers to hire home economists directly from the college campus upon graduation: we do not insist upon previous experience. We believe that recent college graduates bring a freshness and enthusiasm to our organization that is sometimes—but not always—lacking in one who has been in the business for many, many years. The first thing we do in our training program is to expose our home economics trainees to the activities of each of the departments within our Marketing Division; they even attend one of the schools regularly con-

FIGURE. 3-27. *Maytag senior staff home economist Carolyn Rodgers speaks to a group of kitchen specialists from Save Supply Company, Charleston, West Virginia. The advantages of owning a dishwasher and the sales features of dishwashers were presented during a sales training meeting for men who specialize in planning kitchens for new and remodeled homes.*

Carolyn earned a Bachelor of Science degree in home economics from Baylor University, Waco, Texas, in 1967.

ducted for the men who service and repair Maytag appliances. They spend a month or two in our Product Testing Laboratory participating in the testing program we maintain within the Marketing Division both for our own products and for the products of our competitors. They must learn all about our products and the best ways to demonstrate the important features of each. They must become familiar with and proficient in the various presentations that have been developed to fit specific program requirements for group meetings with schools, with representatives of utilities, with dealers, with salesmen, with service men, and with groups of the general public. The home economics trainee is given ample opportunity to practice all of these presentations both before groups of other marketing trainees and before the television camera as well—for the videotape recording provides a most valuable opportunity for self-evaluation. Although individual differences may account for slight variations in the actual length of the training period, on an average it is about six months from the time the individual joins the Maytag Company before assignments are made for independent activities in the field.

Figure 3-28. *Staff home economist Jan Campbell explains laundry procedures while washable garments are modeled at an open house held by Peoples Natural Gas in Bemidji, Minnesota. "The Maytag Fashion Show" is a consumer education program that highlights current fabrics and their care, including information concerning laundry procedures, laundry additives, and current features of laundry appliances.*

Jan is a 1969 graduate of the University of Southern Mississippi, Hattiesburg, Mississippi, where she received a Bachelor of Science degree in home economics in equipment.

Once the training period has ended, the responsibilities of a Maytag home economist lie in three areas.

First, approximately three fourths of the time is spent working with the Maytag field organization in the United States and Canada. This work may involve giving formal presentations to groups of consumers or to groups of students in high school or college; it may involve conducting informal training sessions for utility home economists or for extension home economists; it may involve the presentation and demonstration of specific information about our products or about recommended procedures for their effective use to retail sales personnel; it may involve meetings with dealers' service personnel to discuss the best ways for solving certain customer problems; it may also involve direct person-to-person discussions with dealers or

Figure 3-29. *In her duties as a staff home economist for the Maytag Company, Barb Kennon, a 1969 graduate of Iowa State University, Ames, trains utility home economists in the Hialeah Sunshine Kitchen of the Florida Power and Light Company, Miami. At the utility's annual workshop, Barb uses knowledge of fabric performance gained from both her training at Maytag and her bachelor's degree in textiles and clothing. Barb gives a demonstration of laundering in her new portable laundry equipment...*

utility representatives about the development and scheduling of programs of the types mentioned.

But whatever the type of program or the size or type of meeting, the Maytag home economist must communicate effectively. The programs presented must be educational and entertaining rather than strongly sales oriented. Through programs relating to laundry equipment, consumers are informed of current developments in washable fabrics and current trends in the laundering-aids industry and have an opportunity to learn how modern home laundry equipment can best be used to utilize all this information. Similarly, programs relating to kitchen appliances will provide the consumer with suggestions for the effective use of these appliances in terms of good home management procedures, as well as bringing them up to date on information on fine china, silverware, place-setting ideas, and the like. The specific goal of all these programs is that the consumer be better qualified to choose intelligently the appliance model best suited for his needs and that he be better informed on proper operating procedures for the various appliances. The job of the staff home economist is to provide accurate information—to educate; this is an important aspect of the total marketing process, even though the staff home economist is seldom involved in the actual closing of a retail sale.

The remaining one quarter of the time of a staff home economist is spent at the company home office in two specific areas.

First, the staff member will participate in the handling of customer correspondence that relates to the care and use of the appliance. The questions and problems raised by consumers can at times become quite complex; therefore, in meeting this responsibility the staff home economist may find it necessary to consult with other departments within the Marketing Division, including Service, Product Testing, Product Planning, and the like. Professional training in home economics is particularly useful here, as it enables the staff member to understand more completely the customer's point of view, as well as to explain more effectively the suggested solutions. The manner in which this segment of customer correspondence is handled is extremely important, for it can easily make the difference between a satisfied customer and one who is bitterly antagonistic toward the company and its products. It would seem likely that the increased emphasis being placed upon customer relations in many industries might well provide a wide range of opportunities for the home economics graduate who has developed particular skill in this form of communication.

Second, the staff home economist must necessarily devote some time to the development of new programs and presentations and to continuing study to remain current in all closely related fields—textiles, fashions, laundering aids for the home laundry appliances, and dishes, utensils, silverware, home management practices, and the like for the kitchen appliances.

Although the vagaries of schedules with groups will not always permit, we try to arrange travel schedules so that the staff member will spend about one week of each month in the office. Further, we arrange the work assignments so that each individual is responsible for a certain geographic area for one quarter of the year; this geographic assignment changes every three months, so that the home economist has an opportunity to work in all sectors of the United States and Canada and to become acquainted with a wide variety of different marketing situations.

I see several distinct advantages accruing to the individual who selects this particular career opportunity upon graduation. For one thing, it offers the young, relatively inexperienced graduate a chance to become directly and personally involved in what is perhaps the most exciting segment of the consumer goods industry—marketing. It offers an opportunity for the assumption of responsibilities within the Marketing Division not usually assigned to one so soon after college graduation. The extensive travel, the varied activities, and the constant opportunities to work with people result in relatively rapid development of poise, of self-assurance, and of the ability to exert strong leadership influences. Skill in effective communication is developed at an accelerated rate because of the nature of the various work assignments. And with the rather large portion of time spent in traveling— all companies pay travel expenses—it is relatively easy for a single person to accumulate attractive savings over a two- or three-year period.

Disadvantages—certainly there are a few in any job situation. After three or four years, the extensive travel demanded by this kind of a professional position in marketing would be considered a distinct disadvantage by many. Extensive travel can be glamorous and exciting—and educational— for a few years after graduation; to continue it indefinitely may become tiresome. If one is married, being away from home three fourths of the time may place severe strains upon family relationships.

Quite frankly, another long-range disadvantage inherent in this type of position is that opportunities for advancement to more responsible positions within the company organization are relatively few, even though the salary ranges are as good if not better than those for most jobs open to home economists with similar qualifications and experience. In general it is true that the individual with a degree in business may move in many directions within an organization, whereas the individual with highly specialized professional background is pretty much limited to staff positions. The majority of home economists who have held staff positions in our Marketing Division within the last two decades have resigned when they discovered that marriage and extensive travel were not compatible. Many have left our employ to put their experience and training to work in related fields—with utilities, with educational institutions, with radio or television stations, with magazines, and occasionally with advertising agencies. A few have left to return to school to earn advanced degrees; generally after the advanced degree has been granted, these persons enter teaching or research.

It might be fair to say that although there are not unlimited opportunities for promotion, nonetheless the opportunity to qualify immediately upon graduation without previous experience would make this kind of job opportunity a very valuable one for the new graduate. The opportunities for varied experiences, the opportunities to travel widely, and the opportunity to observe a wide variety of markets and marketing situations add up to an excellent background for advancement to greater responsibilities, if not with the appliance manufacturer, then in related areas for which this experience might qualify the home economist.

THE HOME ECONOMIST IN BUSINESS—EQUIPMENT*

by Rosemary Archibald

The role of the home economist in equipment will change focus as equipment changes, but her place in the marketing structure of her company will be even more important than it is today.

---

* Written for this volume. Miss Rosemary Archibald received her home economics training at the University of Illinois. She has served as district home economist for the International Harvester Company, Home Service Adviser and Kitchen Planning Supervisor for the Milwaukee Gas Light Company, and has been with Harper-Wyman since August 1960. Originally their Home Service Director, she now also supervises Harper's Advertising and Field Service Departments, with the title of Marketing Communications Manager. Miss Archibald has served as national HEIB chairman and has served on many committees in the Chicago HEIB group and in the Illinois Home Economics Association.

FIGURE 3-30. *The equipment field has a bright future for home economists. Two developments will make their job at once more difficult and more challenging; technological innovation and the consumer or marketing orientation of many corporations. A deeper knowledge of materials, electronics, psychology, group dynamics, sociology, marketing, and statistics will be required of the equipment home economist. She will be testing more exotic components. She will be expected to find out what the consumer wants instead of just informing the consumer about what the company has to sell. In sort, she will be a communication bridge between manufacturer and consumer. Rosemary Archibald, Home Service Director of Harper-Wyman Company, a manufacturer of range components, typifies the future equipment home economist, surrounded by some of the old and new tools of the trade.*

Designing and manufacturing gas range and grill controls and components sounds like a man's business—and it is. But it is usually a woman who selects and uses the gas range that incorporates these controls and components. To bridge what could be a wide gap between the technically oriented manufacturer and the nontechnical homemaker, Harper-Wyman Company relies heavily on its home economists.

Most homemakers are not very knowledgeable about burners, valves, venturi, and oven and top burner thermostats—some of the gas range components. They are, however, very interested in how these components perform when installed in a range or gas grill.

At Harper-Wyman, the Home Service Department serves as the homemaker's spokesman. From the idea stage, when a handmade sample is brought to the department for testing, to the marketing and promotion of the final product, Harper's home economists make sure the user's—Mrs. Homemaker's—point of view is an important factor in every decision.

The concern for the homemaker goes beyond the testing and evaluation of new Harper-Wyman products. Food products and utensils are also tested because of their relation to range components.

Recipe development is another homemaker service of this Home Service Department. Family-type foods are used in testing and evaluating products and many of these recipes are later included in the cooking guides that are furnished for gas ranges using Harper-Wyman components. These booklets contain more than recipes and instructions for "getting your money's worth" from new range controls. They also provide valuable information on the art of cooking with today's new foods, techniques, and utensils. All the booklets give the homemaker information that will help her save nutrients, cooking time, and food dollars.

What will happen to equipment in years to come? Just as today, it will be designed to suit the foods, homes, and family life patterns of the era. However, some of the limitations we now know will be nonexistent because of advancements in material and manufacturing technology. There will be literally no limitation to what kind of appliance can be designed—anything will be possible.

Here the home economist's role in product design will be vital. She must be the one to help sort out—from all that is possible—what is practical for the living pattern of the day. She will be the generalist with the interdisciplinary knowledge to guide the increasingly specialized appliance designer or engineer. The home economist will also have a more important role in the selling of a product. Appliances change today in more or less evolutionary fashion. Tomorrow's changes will come more quickly and will be more radical.

The advertising and promotion of such new products will need guidance from the person who understands both the equipment and the user—the home economist. The training of sales personnel will become increasingly important as choice and change in appliances multiply.

After the sale has been made, the user will still need the home economist's help in using the equipment. Yes, appliances may be simpler to operate, with more push-button convenience, but this only changes the focus of the help needed. New appliances forced into old management practices are not always a success, and this will be even more true of sophisticated future equipment. Engineers may assume that the user will automatically use new products correctly, but the home economist will recognize the need and provide help in making the transition.

There is a bright future for the skilled home economist in the equipment field. She will perhaps need more technical skills, but her understanding of the homemaker and her role will remain her forte. As the liaison between her company and the user, she is a key person in the marketing chain. Without her, equipment of the future could fail to live up to the promise it offers.

130

THE HOME ECONOMIST IN HOME SERVICE WITH
A UTILITY COMPANY*

by Sheila A. Castellarin

The home economist in business working in the field of home service is a link between the company and the community in bonds of service and goodwill. Home service is a vital tool for making the personal contacts that build sound customer and community relationships.

The responsibilities in home service work also encompass being an integral and contributing part of the company marketing and sales promotion activities. Responsibilities in the marketing and sales promotion efforts include understanding, interpreting, and analyzing consumer wants and needs; working with dealers, builders, advertising personnel, and others to help in increasing consumer purchases of the company products; developing

FIGURE 3-31. *The home-service adviser presenting a talk before a television camera. (Courtesy of Columbia Gas of Ohio, Inc.)*

* Written for this volume. Miss Sheila A. Castellarin is General Home Service Director for Columbia Gas of Ohio, Inc. She is responsible for supervising a staff of forty home economists. Her particular responsibilities involve the recruiting and training of new home economists as well as general supervision and coordination of the entire home-service program for the company.

promotions and projects both to train others to sell the product properly and to encourage consumers to want the product.

The work is attractive because the variety of activities encourages enthusiasm for promotion, sales, and service. It is not a routine job and there are many opportunities to work with different age groups. Flexibility and versatility are a must in home service to meet the varied and numerous requests that may come in quick succession. These varied activities may include answering customer inquiries about nutrition, menu planning, fabric care, or kitchen planning; calling on homemakers to discuss the use and care of appliances; presenting programs for school and club groups; organizing and teaching youth and adult classes on the use of equipment; conducting sales-training lessons for appliance sales people; appearing on radio and television; and writing booklets, newspaper articles, and program scripts. There are many opportunities for initiative, imagination, and creativity to develop activities and programs that would add to this partial list.

A degree in home economics and the background this course provides are the basic requirement for home-service work. Emphasis in household equipment, public speaking, journalism, experimental and quantity cookery, demonstration methods, psychology, and physics is valuable. Some knowledge of business administration and sales promotion is also helpful.

The personal qualifications for home-service work are as important as

FIGURE 3-32. *The home-service adviser making a call to show a home-maker the various controls on the range. (Courtesy of Columbia Gas of Ohio, Inc.)*

Figure 3-33. *A demonstration presented before a group. (Courtesy of Columbia Gas of Ohio, Inc.)*

Figure 3-34. *The home-service adviser demonstrating outdoor appliances. (Courtesy of Columbia Gas of Ohio, Inc.)*

the basic training. As a representative and spokeswoman for the company, a person in home-service work must have an attractive and appropriate appearance, a pleasant speaking voice, poise, a courteous manner, and enthusiasm for the work. An ability to adjust to changing conditions and emergencies as they arise and sound physical health are essential to meet the requirements of the work.

Working conditions are pleasant and possibilities for advancement are great. A position in home service qualifies individuals for membership in important professional, community, and trade organizations. A great deal of personal prestige accompanies the job. Many contributions to company progress have been made by home service. Because of the effectiveness of the program, its future appears limitless.

THE HOME ECONOMIST IN BUSINESS—ADVERTISING AND PROMOTION°

by Wilma M. Sim

This area of constant change is one filled with challenge. The home economist working in advertising and promotion may be associated with an

FIGURE 3-35.
Miss Wilma M. Sim, Director of Farm Journal Family Test Group, working with reports to be filed.

° Written for this volume. Wilma M. Sim, or "Mary Sheldon," Director of Farm Journal/Countryside Family Test Group, Philadelphia, Pennsylvania, keeps her finger on the consumer pulse through contact with one thousand Test Group members all across the country. Under her direction, the group is a sounding board for *Farm Journal/Countryside* editors. They also test products for manufacturers on their farms or country acreage or in their homes and report their reactions to Mary Sheldon.

advertising agency; a public relations firm; a manufacturer of food, textiles, household equipment, home furnishings, or health and grooming products; a trade association; or one of the communications media—radio, TV, newspapers, or magazines.

Activities will be varied. Some home economists will supervise photography and provide directions for using new products or newly designed packages for products. Others will be responsible for preparing a variety of pamphlets and film or slide presentations. Often they will be asked to give lectures, demonstrations, or presentations to their own company members, client representatives, or consumer groups. And sometimes these home economists will be responsible for setting up exhibits at which they will talk with hundreds of consumer visitors.

Inasmuch as the efforts of home economists in this field are usually ultimately directed toward consumers, an interest in people, knowing how to work with all types of people, and the ability to communicate verbally and/or by the written word are important. Valuable also is an ability to obtain from consumers reactions to ideas and products through personal

FIGURE 3-36. *Miss Gertrude Kiekin, Creative Director of Farm Journal's Countryside Enterprises Division, and Robert C. Chapin, Marketing Director, go over a project with Miss Sim.*

Prior to holding this position, Miss Sim had a daily "Homemaking with KSD-TV" show in St. Louis, traveled parts of twenty states for Swift and Company, and was a 4-H Club agent in Minnesota. She has served as chairman of the Home Economics in Business group in St. Louis and is past president of both the Missouri Home Economics Association and the Philadelphia Club of Advertising Women. In 1970 she was chosen Philadelphia Advertising Woman of the year. She is active in the American Advertising Federation, having served as chairman of their 1970 national ADDY Award competition.

interviews, telephone conversations, or information they willingly supply on written questionnaires following the development of an informal rapport.

In addition to good basic home economics training in college, courses in public speaking, journalism, merchandising, photography, marketing, advertising, economics, and psychology will help provide the broad preparation needed for work in this field. Also, work experience in retail selling, camp counseling, extension, or teaching will make the home economist a valuable asset to the organization. This job not only requires recognition of consumer needs and help to meet those needs, it also calls for relaying consumer reaction and opinion to management.

Home economics jobs in advertising and promotion are a natural for the creative person. Introducing new products that are developed every year to consumers is always fun for the inventive person. Also developing new ways to promote a well-established product can be exciting for one clever enough to come up with fresh, original ideas.

Although creativity is a must, a home economist in this area also needs to pay attention to detail—be meticulous and thorough. The ability to see a project from the first germ of an idea to the final presentation and follow-up often requires many hours of plain hard work. However when the project is completed, the results are satisfying and well worth the required time and effort.

Advertising and promotion is truly a challenging field for home economists. They're expected to keep up-to-date on all that is going on in the world, to keep their finger on the pulse of the consumer, to work for

FIGURE 3-37.
Miss Sim discusses the final test report with her secretary, Linda Brenner.

improvements in products, family living, and community and national affairs. By these challenges creative home economists can, through advertising and promotion, best serve the interests of the society they're helping to shape.

HOME ECONOMISTS IN JOURNALISM*

by Willie Mae Rogers

Most women's magazines and most newspapers have service departments and service editors. These departments, in varying patterns, present a program in adult education in their pages—the purpose of which is to help the homemaker with her complex job of managing a house and caring for a family. In most cases such departments are staffed by graduate home economists.

It is almost impossible to describe the satisfaction such editors derive from their work. To have an audience of millions of women who inspire one with a constant desire to provide the best possible material, to experience the fun and joy (and sometimes heartbreak) that comes from reader mail, to know the thrill of seeing one's name on a byline—these are true satisfactions.

The desirable personal qualifications and preparatory background of the home economist who chooses magazine work are similar to those required for other kinds of work in the home economics field. She should have a good basic education, broad cultural interests, the ability to do the work, and an open, inquisitive mind—a desire to experiment, to reach out and explore. She also must have a respect for truth and accuracy and be dedicated to the pursuit of these qualities. Good health is, of course, of supreme importance as is good grooming and a fair share of the social graces.

She should have basic training in chemistry, physics, and biology, and if possible psychology, economics, and sociology, on which she should

* Written for this volume. Miss Willie Mae Rogers, Director of Good Housekeeping's Institute, has had wide experience in the field of home economics, both as a teacher and as a businesswoman. A graduate of Union University, Tennessee, she first taught home economics in a Tennessee high school, and later the Insular Board of Education of Puerto Rico asked her to conduct special courses for the Board. Miss Rogers then joined the staff of the Union Electric Company in St. Louis, Missouri, as assistant director of Home Economics. Eight years later she organized, developed, and directed the Home Economics Department for the Admiral Corporation in Chicago.

In 1953, Miss Rogers accepted the directorship of Good Housekeepings Institute. Her work includes the direction of all Institute activities and the coordination of all service departments of the magazine. In 1966 Miss Rogers was elected a vice-president of Good Housekeeping Magazine. In May, 1967, Union University conferred upon her the honorary degree Doctor of Humanics.

She is a member of the board of directors of the United States of America Standards Institute and currently serves on the Institute's Advisory Committee on Consumer Council Procedures.

build more specialized training, together with practical experience. Any experience that narrows the gap between college and the job is invaluable.

In interior decorating and furnishing she usually works with graduates of specialized schools who often lack knowledge of wearing qualities and the care of furnishings. This she should be able to supply.

Fashion experts on magazine staffs usually come from special schools or have had fashion experience in retailing. Home economists with specialized training in textiles should be able to work with these fashion experts to relate fashion to the practical problems of the care of clothing and household textiles; she should know what services dry cleaners and the commercial laundry offer, up-to-date laundry methods, and how to use modern home laundry equipment and supplies, detergents, and water conditioners. She should understand textile chemistry so that she is able to interpret to readers significant developments in textile chemistry and so that she can work the more effectively with textile chemists.

In preparation for work in any service department of a home magazine or a newspaper's women's page, the home economist should study the problems faced by homemakers: living standards, family finances and budgeting, work schedules in housekeeping, and the best use of time to cope with the many facets of a homemaker's life.

Obviously the ability to write well is a valuable asset in magazine and newspaper work. Courses in journalism with special application to the home economics field are extremely helpful, though they do not necessarily develop good writers. Graduates in home economics should know how to organize material and write good letters and clear reports, but they may have to turn to a talented journalist for the writing of articles. The home economist should be able to supply these writers with organized, up-to-date information. A course in speech and public speaking is important, also some instruction in business practice and procedures.

At Good Housekeeping Institute graduate home economists work in five different (but related) areas: textiles, needlework and sewing, foods and nutrition, foods and cookery, and appliances and home care. Their work covers both laboratory and editorial activities. They work closely with engineers, chemists, beauticians, fashion editors, decorating editors, and various technicians.

Institute home economists also must work with manufacturers, advertising agencies, and industry associations as well as with the all-important reader.

Home economics in journalism offers jobs that are stimulating and influential and that are within the reach of those with broad experience who have given ample evidence of their ability to do creative work, to work effectively with other people, and to carry responsibility. The demands this work makes on the individual are by no means light. Like any other important work, it requires capacity for sustained effort and genuine interest, enthusiasm, and vision.

Most home economists working in this field agree that the rewards are truly great.

THE HOME ECONOMIST IN RADIO AND TELEVISION°

by Jayne Whalen

During the late 1940's and early 1950's when television was brand-new, speech and drama majors rushed straight from graduation to the nearest television station. But it was the magic Bachelor of Science in Home Economics that opened the door to the local (WHIO-TV) TV station for me—the degree, plus four years of college, part-time modeling, fashion coordination, and activity in the Dayton Advertising Club. At that time, no one quite knew what television demanded, and so, from day to day, we felt our way—made our own rules and discarded them as we pleased. Home economists who were used to careful, exacting, test-kitchen, classroom methods of demonstration were insulted when TV producers asked them to perform a thiry-minute demonstration in six to eight minutes. These home economists insisted on clinging to their field as they knew it, not realizing that this new medium demanded a reshaping of ideas. And why not? The purpose of commercial TV is to entertain, to inform and to sell—never to "teach" as such.

Audiences (then and now) resent being treated as a high school foods class; they want to enjoy themselves. Consequently, a home economist in television must have an entirely different approach to the profession. A fair background in foods and food handling is necessary, but basically, the TV home economist is a reporter or liaison, as it were, between every facet of the food industry and the consumer and the kitchen. A TV home economist must keep the homemaker aware of what's new, using food demonstrations and guests (i.e., home economists doing public relations work for food and equipment companies, university extension service home economists, restaurateurs, famous chefs, celebrities, and others).

At WTMJ-TV in Milwaukee, Wisconsin (each market probably has a different method of handling this), I am responsible for programming and presenting the food segment of a daily women's show and for the production, which includes shopping for the food and preparing it. I also write food commercial copy and am involved in the preparation and production of these commercials. Both editorial and commercial content is written and presented with service to the homemaker in mind, and with the integrity any home economist brings to the job.

Those seeking positions in this field should realize that the "TV personality" or commentator jobs are not plentiful. However, food and equipment companies and their advertising and public relations agencies employ many young home economists who spend part of their time devising recipes and writing releases for TV demonstration and part of their time traveling, visiting newspaper foods editors, and making appearances on local TV shows across the country.

° Written for this volume. Mrs. Jayne Whalen started her television career doing food commercials while still a student at the University of Dayton in Ohio. She came to WTMJ-TV, the Milwaukee Journal Station, in 1959, when her husband was transferred to Milwaukee. With a husband and four children, Mrs. Whalen serves as an example of that happy combination of homemaking and a career.

FIGURE 3-38. Mrs. Whalen, in the circular studio's new kitchen, demonstrates a new product as part of the station's "Today for Women" show. (Courtesy of WTMJ–TV.)

Educational requirements would, of course, be a Bachelor of Science in Home Economics with a major in foods (perhaps a general home economics background would do) AND a minor (or many extra courses) in the humanities, English, composition, and literature. The small details or how-to of radio and television should certainly *not* be covered in course after useless course, although one or two electives would be helpful.

The future? Probably with the growth of UHF stations, there will be more need than ever for competent food writers and for home economists able to prepare food for TV cameras—primarily for commercials. Interest in food in all its forms and in food preparation is common to everyone. No matter how easy and automated cooking becomes, the subject of food will never become outdated, which, of course, means that the future for home economists in TV and radio is most promising.

THE HOME ECONOMIST IN BUSINESS—CONSULTATION*

by Carol A. Sellew

Communicating with others is the work of the consultant home economist in business. Helping people help themselves through personal consultation, newspaper feature stories, or radio and television interviews is usually one of the consultant's major job responsibilities.

A consultant has a bachelor's degree with a major in one of the fields of home economics. There should be ability in at least one and preferably more of the following: writing creatively and/or factually; public speaking in giving reports, speeches, interviews, and dramatic presentation; a knowledge of finance related to family budgeting; meeting people well, using good judgment, and accepting responsibility; and analyzing and acting constructively in all situations.

Companies find the work of a consultant valuable in expanding markets for new or existing products and services, especially because of a consultant's ability to provide company oriented information services and promotion techniques. This may involve a consultant in researching, creating, testing, writing, and producing materials for distribution in all types of media.

A company may employ a consultant full time for such activities as answering the hundreds of questions asked each week by consumers, contributing to the company advertising, developing and testing new ideas for products, and preparing exhibits and/or educational materials.

* Written for this volume. Mrs. Carol A. Sellew is "Bette Malone," moving consultant for United Van Lines, Inc. She has served as a home economist with the Philadelphia Electric Co., the Boston Gas Company, and the Union Electric Company in St. Louis, Missouri. She is a member of the American Home Economics Association, the Missouri Home Economics Association, and the St. Louis HEIB Group. Her services to these professional organizations include many committee positions and chairmanships at national and local levels. She was the recipient of the Laura McCall Award—Electric Industry in 1959–1960 and the Laura McCall Award—Gas Industry in 1961–1962. Mrs. Sellew is a graduate of Iowa State University.

FIGURE 3-39. *The image of Bette Malone. The image represents:*
—*A married woman twenty-eight to thirty-five years of age with several children: she is able to understand the needs of a family on the move.*
—*A woman with education.*
—*A woman with a warm personality who can speak with authority.*
—*A woman who is oriented to the realities of moving families and provides help in the smooth transfer of household goods, as well as the transfer of people's lives. (Courtesy of United Van Lines, Inc.)*

With several years' work experience and special talents, some home economists find they can and like to work independently, either selling their services part time or creating their own businesses. Remuneration for a free-lance or independent consultant may be on an hourly basis, a project basis plus expenses, a packaged job estimate, or a regular salary rate. Experience and earned reputation for ability are important factors in becoming an independent consultant.

FIGURE 3-40. *Bringing to life some of the moving tips described in the preplanning guide developed by Bette Malone for anyone who is moving. Shown here are Kathryn Wise, interviewer; Bette Malone (Carol Sellew); and Len Sampson. interviewer on the "Good Morning Show," KOMO-(ABC)–TV, Seattle, Washington.*

THE HOME ECONOMIST IN BUSINESS— PUBLIC RELATIONS*

by Gwen Lam

In its broadest sense, public relations is a part of the job of all home economists in business. However, more and more opportunities are becoming available for home economists to devote full time to public relations, an important facet of industry. Positions are found in food, textile,

*Written for this volume. Miss Gwen Lam is a free-lance writer dealing primarily with industry-sponsored educational programs for schools. She was vice-president of Glick & Lorwin, Inc., New York, a public relations firm that specializes in the development and implementation of industry-sponsored educational programs. Miss Lam owned her own firm in Chicago, the Educational Materials Corporation, which was later incorporated into Glick & Lorwin. She has degrees from Texas Technological College, Lubbock, and Iowa State University, Ames. Miss Lam has taught in high school and has served as editorial director of the Wheat Flour Institute, Chicago. She has held various offices in local, state, and national home economics associations, including the vice-presidency of the American Home Economics Association.

and equipment companies, retail firms, trade associations, and advertising and public relations agencies.

An underlying goal of public relations is to build goodwill for a product or service. Typically, the home economist in public relations serves as a member of a team that plans and implements programs to build goodwill, understanding, and acceptance. Other members of the team might be marketing and advertising specialists, product managers, research workers, art directors, and others involved with a product or service.

The activities of home economists specializing in public relations include:

1. Writing product stories for use in newspapers and other printed media.
2. Writing scripts for use on radio or television.
3. Participating in radio or television programs.
4. Presenting talks (or preparing them for others to present) before varied groups representing highly technical or professional audiences or consumers.
5. Planning industry-sponsored educational programs for schools, professional groups, of the community in general.
6. Producing booklets and filmstrips, films, and other visual aids about a product or service.
7. Translating pertinent results of research for consumers.
8. Transmitting consumer needs to management.
9. Preparing displays and exhibits for special meetings.
10. Attending professional or industry meetings.

Because communications in its varied forms is so basic to the public relations practitioner, the young home economist interested in public relations needs to develop proficiency in creating and expressing ideas—written, spoken, and visual. He should have a good background in subject matter, should keep up with what's going on in the field, and know where to turn for information. In addition, he must be attuned to the needs of various groups that frequently serve as liaison between industry and the public: for example, newspaper and magazine editors, radio and television broadcasters, teachers, extension agents, and other community leaders.

Developing new and unusual ways to tell a story and then seeing those ideas executed are some of the most satisfying aspects of a job in public relations. The home economist works hard and frequently has inconvenient travel schedules, yet usually considers the accomplishments satisfying reward for the efforts. Salaries are in line with those of other home economics positions in business. Remuneration to experienced home economists who are successful in public relations can be impressive. Truly creative people who can originate and execute imaginative projects are rare and valuable assets to industry.

The Home Economist in Business—Finance*

by Shari G. Bryant

Just what career opportunities are available to home economists in the money world?

* Written for this volume. Mrs. Shari G. Bryant is director of the Money Management Institute of the Household Finance Corporation. Mrs. Bryant began

FIGURE 3-41. *Money Management Institute staff layout and page proof for soon-to-be-released Money Management Institute publication. (Courtesy of the Money Management Institute of Household Finance Corporation.)*

You might be a financial columnist for a newspaper or magazine, a money management consultant for a financial institution, or a family finance specialist who prepares print materials and audiovisual aids used for consumer education. Other possibilities include employment with a financial or credit counseling service or working with low-income and socially disadvantaged groups.

What all these "money" positions have in common is providing expert financial guidance to individuals and families, so that they will be assisted to make wise use of their resources and also to understand and fulfill their role better as consumers and citizens in our economy. This involves the home economist's understanding and ability to communicate objectively the basics of wise management of money and consumer credit as well as how to shop for goods and services intelligently.

her home economics career with Smith-Bucklin Trade Association Management Firm as a staff home economist. Subsequent professional experience included work with the Rural Gravure Service of Chicago, Illinois, and Madison, Wisconsin, and serving as manager of the Home Service Department of the Food Merchandising Division of Wilson and Company, Inc. Mrs. Bryant is a member of the Chicago HEIB group, the American and Illinois Home Economics Associations, and American Women in Radio and Television. She has served on the Consumer Service Committees for both the Grocery Manufacturers of America and the American Meat Institute. She is a graduate of Northern Illinois University, DeKalb.

What kind of preparation will you need for a position like this? What subject areas should you emphasize?

A well-rounded home economics background is extremely helpful because money management is applicable to all areas—food, clothing, equipment, and family living. In addition, courses in journalism, economics, consumer affairs, education, marketing, advertising, sociology, radio, television, and public speaking are useful. General business courses are especially beneficial to give you knowledge of how companies function. Other business courses covering such subjects as investments, insurance, taxes, law, and real estate will be a definite asset, too, when you are helping families develop effective spending plans. Later on, advanced degrees, relevant work experience, and being able to keep up to date are highly desirable also.

Careers in money management are challenging and exciting because the work is interesting and varied. Like other business positions held by home economists, jobs in the money world offer such diverse activities as writing articles, news releases, and booklets, engaging in research, giving speeches, attending conventions, appearing on radio and television, editing bulletins and publications, planning and developing educational programs, and working with other professionals both inside and outside the corporation.

Recent graduates can learn about money management job openings by seeking employment where established programs already exist. Some examples are public relations and consumer-service-oriented departments of financial institutions, their trade associations, and agencies.

What's in store for the future? Long-range-planning experts tell us that people will be spending and shopping differently in the years ahead. Additional computerized services, more shopping by telephone, and increased financial counseling are just three of the possibilities. Therefore, tomorrow's home economist in the money world should find many new doors open. Be ready with the skills, initiative, interest, creativity, and personality to take advantage of the opportunities!

THE HOME ECONOMIST IN BUSINESS—DETERGENTS*

NATURE OF WORK   *by Jane Creel*

The home economist working for detergent companies finds the work especially varied and stimulating because the concern is not only with the company's own products but with all of the other things with which the products will be used—either "in, or on, or with." Additionally, because the

---

* Written for this volume. Jane Creel has been home economics director of Lever Brothers Company since 1960 with responsibility for the Lever Homemaking Center and home economics activities related to the Company's consumer products, including soaps, detergents, foods, dentrifices, and toiletries. Her prior experience included positions as manager of the Home Economics Department of the Monsanto Company in St. Louis, Service Manager of the General Merchandising Division of R. H. Macy, Inc., in San Francisco, and two years overseas with the American Red Cross. Her B.S. degree in home economics is from the University of Nevada.

Miss Creel is a member of the American Home Economics Association and its legislative committee and is past chairman of the New York chapter of HEIB.

Figure 3-42. *Utility home economists at a training seminar on soaps, detergents, and laundry equipment sponsored by Lever Brothers. (Courtesy of Lever Brothers.)*

kinds of products worked with are used and purchased daily by almost every homemaker, this home economist must understand how and why women use these products and be sensitive to changing family living patterns. This means that no matter what the specific job assignment may be, the home economist must be up-to-date on:

> Appliance developments, including new washing machines, dishwashers, dry-cleaning equipment, ranges, small appliances, floor waxers, vacuum cleaners, air conditioners, and even hair dryers and other beauty aids.

She is first vice-president of the Advertising Women of New York, home economics chairman of the National Council of Women, and a former national board member of the Electrical Women's Round Table. She is also a member of the New York Women's Council of the New York State Department of Commerce, the Advisory Council of the New York State College of Human Ecology at Cornell University, the American Home Economics Association's representative on the miscellaneous standards board of the American National Standards Institute, Inc., a member of the Consumer Advisory Council of Underwriters Laboratory, Inc., the consumer services committee of the Grocery Manufacturers of America, the home economics committee of the Soap and Detergent Association, and the consumer education committee of the Association of Home Appliance Manufacturers, and a member of the Committee on Women in Public Relations.

FIGURE 3-43. *Miss Creel discusses detergents with a few of the many visitors to the department. (Courtesy of Lever Brothers.)*

Textile developments, including new fibers, blends, finishes such as permanent press, and new dyeing and stability processes. Textiles include those used in home furnishings and clothing.

Changes in household materials, including china, tableware, and cooking utensils.

Changes in surfaces to be cleaned, ranging from Teflon cookware and self-cleaning ovens to floor and carpet coverings.

Depending upon the department in which the detergent home economist works, this information is applied to product planning, product testing, writing package copy, writing instruction books, consumer correspondence, advertising, promotion, or sales. Because the work requires that thinking be done in terms of the homemaker's viewpoint, information from other fields is combined with knowledge of the company's own products. This is correlated in terms of homemaker needs, attitudes, convenience, safety, and intrinsic values.

Additionally, because there is a time lag in educating the homemakers to the many new technological breakthroughs, a considerable portion of the home economist's work is involved in consumer and educational materials.

PERSONAL QUALIFICATIONS

The personal qualifications for success in this field are thoroughness, persistence, persuasiveness, independent thinking, creativity, and flexibility. The ability to translate technical language into laymanlike terms for homemakers and the ability to work constructively with other people are essential.

148

SPECIAL EDUCATION REQUIREMENTS

In addition to her home economics courses, the home economist in the detergent field should have a strong background in chemistry and at least one basic course in statistics. This home economist should be knowledgeable about electronic data-processing (EDP) because it so directly affects, increasingly, so many of the activities. Because she serves as a communicator between business and the homemaker, the home economist should have better than average ability to express herself in both writing and speaking.

ADVANTAGES

Because of the necessity to keep abreast of so many other associated fields (e.g., equipment and textiles), the home economist in detergents becomes both informed and involved with many aspects of changing living and family patterns. The daily use of detergent products by every family keeps the home economist constantly in touch with people's attitudes. Additionally, this home economist's service and contribution have an immediate effect on countless homemakers throughout the country.

THE HOME ECONOMIST IN INTERIOR DESIGN*

by Jill Siwicki Smith,
N.S.I.D., I.B.D.

Vast possibilities and opportunities are available to the graduate who selects commercial interior designing as his profession. Emphasis is now being directed to color furniture arrangement and overall planning for commercial institutions: yes, businessmen (even though they may not be top executives) want well-designed and -appointed offices to satisfy and to fulfill their business and business entertaining requirements, as well as to delight their preferences in color and style of furniture; the board of directors of a large corporation or of a bank realize that a well-designed building provides not only a more functional work area for the employees but also a more pleasant atmosphere for the customers' business; even religious organizations are using the services of a commercial designer to create appropriate surroundings for classrooms, libraries, and social areas. If you like variety, the opportunity to meet and to work with people in business, and the challenge of creating functional yet aesthetic interiors and are willing to face strict competition, deadlines, and extra hours of work, then commercial designing is perhaps the field for you.

Besides the university and school requirements, the following suggestions, which could be picked up in electives or in an additional term or two, would be most beneficial and worthwhile to the commercial designer. A thorough knowledge of business practices and methods is an extremely vital asset. It is not hard to realize that if you are to work with business people, you must be business oriented. Secondly, because most of your

* Written for this volume. Mrs. Jill Siwicki Smith is an Interior Designer, George Stuart, Inc., Orlando, Florida. She is a graduate of Southern Illinois University, Carbondale, and is a member of the National Society of Interior Designers and the Institute of Business Designers.

work originally begins with a set of blueprints, you are expected to be able to read the prints and to understand them. To accomplish this, it is advisable to enroll in some architectural technology and drafting courses outside of the school of home economics. Although you are not expected to become an architect, you are expected to be able to make suggestions on interior partitions and exterior façades. Your training in this field is invaluable. Finally, any experience you can obtain in relation to any aspect of interior designing—apprentice work, selling, measuring (drapery and carpet), color coordinating—would prove advantageous to the "fresh-out-of-school designer." Not only would you have an idea of what the profession is like, but you would also have the pretraining experience that most employers are now demanding.

The Home Economist in Social Welfare and Public Health

"Home economists in health and welfare positions provide aid to the handicapped homemaker, help to troubled families, nutrition facts for clinic or community, planned care for the aging, advice to new citizens, and other services to families or to community agencies, concerned with welfare and health."[39] The home economist in social welfare or public health may work for a state, county, or city public welfare or public health department, the Peace Corps, or rehabilitation centers; or, the work may be with voluntary health or social welfare agencies such as the Red Cross, visiting nurse associations, tuberculosis and other health associations, family service agencies, and community aid organizations. He is often one of a team of professional people working through the public or private agency.

A home economist in public health often (1) helps people to learn what good nutrition is and why it is important; (2) works with co-workers helping to train new ones in the field; (3) teaches in a clinic, helping with problems in nutrition; (4) prepares and evaluates educational materials and audiovisual aids; (5) presents radio and television programs; (6) speaks at club or community meetings; (7) gives service to related institutions and agencies; and (8) works with many groups for community health.[40]

A home economist who is a specialist in a social welfare agency

[39] American Home Economics Association, *Unfold Your Future in Home Economics* (Washington, D.C.: The Association, 1959), p. 8.

[40] American Home Economics Association, *For You a Double Future in Home Economics* (Washington, D.C.: The Association, 1957), pp. 19–20.

generally (1) helps provide the administrators of the agency with information as to what families need in food, clothing, and other necessities; (2) confers with the staff and the families on "management, family financial plans, work simplification methods, and buying practices"; (3) suggests special programs for homemakers with particular problems, such as a handicap or disability, debts, or the double role of homemaker and wage earner; (4) joins other home economists in improving family living; and (5) cooperates with other groups in planning and carrying out community welfare programs.[41]

Because nutritionists are in demand in social welfare and public health positions, the student interested in such positions should refer to the earlier section, "The Nutritionist," in this chapter, where more detail is given about the duties and requirements.

SPECIAL REQUIREMENTS

A bachelor's degree is required, but a master's degree is desirable for this position. A degree in home economics with a specialization in home and family is most helpful preparation. Courses in family economics, food and nutrition, home management, child care and development, housing and equipment, textiles and clothing, and family relations are most important. It is also desirable to elect courses in sociology, journalism, anthropology, public speaking, and script writing. Experience, too, in community centers, camps, and settlement houses will profit the prospective social and welfare worker, giving a better understanding of relationships among people and social conditions and problems.

Graduate work in family economics, family life, and home management is valuable or required for many positions. The graduate program should also include human behavior and personality development, public health and welfare, community organization, case work, and social administration.

ADVANTAGES

Social welfare and public health can offer a very challenging and satisfying opportunity for serving others and contributing to the health, well-being, and security of all people. There is opportunity for using initiative, imagination, and ingenuity and for professional advancement and specialization. The professional organizations of this profes-

41 Ibid., p. 20.

sion are the American Home Economics Association and the Health and Welfare Section of the AHEA.

POSSIBLE DISADVANTAGES

Training may be long and salaries are often low, yet pay has been improving. There also may be considerable emotional and physical strain involved. Another disadvantage may be that mobility by the person so trained may be important for employment opportunities; some areas of the country offer more opportunities for employment than do others.

The Home Economist in Rehabilitation

Although rehabilitation has been mentioned in the previous section on social welfare and public health, it seems that the employment of the home economist sometimes borders on the casual or is nonexistent. For example, we find that a comparatively few states and territorial public welfare agencies employ one or more home economists on their staffs. It seems certain that if we look at individuals and families in this twentieth century and predict for the year 2000 or beyond, the apparent need is for a home economist with specialized training who can function as a member of a team in helping the physically, emotionally, and mentally handicapped as well as the culturally and financially handicapped to reach their maximum potentials.

A task force organized by the Rehabilitation Committee of the American Home Economics Association prepared a pilot publication in February, 1970, entitled *Home Economist in Rehabilitation.* The following statements are from that publication:

The home economist in rehabilitation is found . . .
  . . . in the community, in schools, with extension, in hospitals, on television, in rehabilitation centers, with health agencies
  . . . in cities, towns, rural areas, and foreign countries
The home economist in rehabilitation . . .
  . . . holds a degree in home economics from an accredited college of home economics
  . . . has had specialized training in working with the socially, physically, emotionally, and mentally disabled
The home economist in rehabilitation . . .

... provides direct service to the socially, emotionally, physically, and mentally disabled

... works closely with families, doctors, nurses, social workers and other team members in helping an individual become independent

... plans and coordinates workshops and training programs for the disabled and other professionals

... assists the individual to develop home management skills as related to:

> family money management
> child care and family relations
> use of time and energy
> selection and arrangement of equipment
> meal planning and preparation

... teaches and coordinates field experiences for students and interns in the multiple fields of rehabilitation

A home economist in rehabilitation is first of all a . . .

Home Economist . . .

who has a broad basic education with courses in social sciences, physical sciences, and the humanities

plus

courses in the subject matter areas of home economics which include: art, family economics, home management, family relations, child development, food and nutrition, housing, home furnishings, equipment and clothing and textiles

plus

additional study and internship in rehabilitation

The AHEA Rehabilitation Committee's task force in its statement of "Philosophy, Educational Objectives, and Core Content for Home Economics Programs in Rehabilitation," prepared for and accepted by the AHEA Board, carried these statements, noting that they had been designed to promote individualized programming within any academic institution, whether presented on the baccalaureate, master's, or doctoral level.

Broadly defined objectives of programs designed to prepare the home economist to assume her role as a member of the rehabilitation team are:

... to acquire background information on rehabilitation theory and processes

... to acquire background information on the series of adaptive processes: physiologic, sociologic, psychologic, cultural, intellectual, educational, and economic

... to gain competency in identification of problems for the handicapped individual and his family and in isolating alternative solutions to these problems

... to gain competency in identifying availability and function of community resources necessary for the alleviation of problems

... to gain competency in home economics subject matter as well as adaptive application to rehabilitation

... to gain competency in interpreting research.

ADVANTAGES

Rehabilitation can be a challenging opportunity for serving others and in seeing results. There is an opportunity for using the skills, knowledge, ingenuity, and initiative that one has or has attained. There are many opportunities for positions for persons with this specialized training as well as opportunity for advancement. The professional organizations of this profession are the American Home Economics Association, the Health and Welfare Section of the AHEA, and, with the specialized training, the National Rehabilitation Association.

DISADVANTAGES

The specialized training may be long. It is not always easy to gain acceptance as a member of the team. There may be considerable emotional and physical strain.

*The Home Economist in International Programs**

by Helen LeBaron Hilton

Improving living conditions for people is a major goal of every society. Countries that are struggling to develop industry and agriculture find they also must forge new programs to make sure that progress made in the economy is reflected in a better life for their citizens. It follows that educational programs to help people with daily living problems of sanitation, nutrition, housing, clothing, family planning, and management of resources are in order.

When a country does not have a program for preparing professional home economists or does not prepare enough of them to cope with its

* Written for this volume. Dr. Helen LeBaron Hilton is Dean of the College of Home Economics at Iowa State University. Her degrees are from Vermont, Cornell, and the University of Chicago. Her experiences represent a wide range: teaching homemaking in high school in Vermont; state supervisor in the State Department of Education in Vermont; Assistant Director of Home Economics at Pennsylvania State University. She has held numerous state and national offices in home economics associations and has served on countless committees and boards, such as the Sloan Foundation and the American Home Economics Association Foundation Board. Under her direction Iowa State University has made outstanding contributions to home economics programs in other countries.

problems, it may request assistance from abroad. Home economists from the United States have served in other countries under the aegis of several different organizations and agencies of the United Nations, the United States government, foundations, universities, and churches. If the need is for assistance with university programs or for the administration of extension, community development, or public health nutrition, experienced home economists with advanced degrees are needed.

Often there are opportunities for inexperienced home economics graduates for direct work with women and girls in the villages. The Peace Corps has used more young home economists than any other agency. Although many young home economists have served in it, there have been more requests for home economists than volunteers available.

Preparation for work in another country can be accomplished through careful planning of college courses and of personal experiences. Courses in all areas of home economics are appropriate, with special emphasis (perhaps additional work) in nutrition, management, and child development. Subject matter to help one understand people of a different culture is important: cultural anthropology, philosophy, land economics, world geography, comparative political systems, history of the Far East, Africa, or South America, language.

Summer experience in this country working with people of other cultures and with those of a different socioeconomic status can serve as preinduction training, for it introduces one to the kind of problems that may be encountered in working abroad. Some government programs, e.g., VISTA, offer such opportunities. Others can be found with church or university extension programs that are designed for families of the inner city or for those living in the disadvantaged rural regions.

It is difficult to enumerate the personal traits important for those working in other countries without appearing too inclusive and describing a paragon who does not exist. A minimum list of essential characteristics would include a natural empathy for people, appreciation and understanding of the values of others, a mind open to new ideas, flexibility, humility, imagination, a practical approach to problems, and sensitivity to the feelings of others.

Home Economists in the Peace Corps

A home economics volunteer in the Peace Corps enters a challenging field—a challenge to himself as well as a challenge to his home economics training. The efforts he puts forth may not show in immediate improvements, but advancements in the standards of the people in developing countries will show in time. Occasionally improvements can be seen by the volunteer himself, but he does not give up when goals appear far away.

Home economics has for many years been making a contribution to . . . intellectual understanding around the world by providing a reservoir

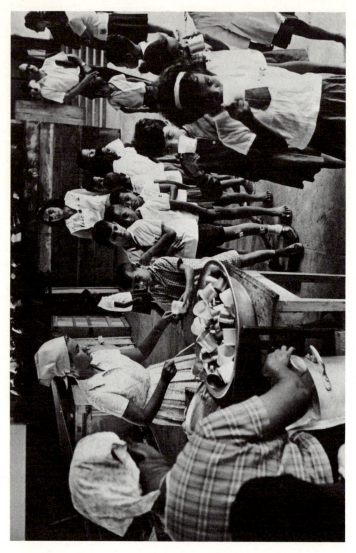

FIGURE 3-44. *Volunteer Carol Ann Vest of Jackson, Mississippi, works on the school lunch program in Vitoria, Brazil. The school feeding program is primarily for children who would otherwise go to school on an empty stomach.* (Courtesy of the Peace Corps Office of Public Information, Office of Economic Opportunity.)

FIGURE 3-45. *Volunteers Celeste Turcotte and Gaye Longyear work with a women's group in the barrio in Colombia. They are promoting a high-protein vitamin supplement. Here they give a demonstration in their back yard, showing the women how they can add "incaparina," a high-protein vitamin supplement, to their basic dishes. (Courtesy of the Peace Corps Office of Public Information, Office of Economic Opportunity.)*

of practical knowledge, versatility, and dedication to public service. The concern of home economics with the home and family is a common meeting ground for peoples of all cultures. Today home economists in colleges and universities are ready to make a real contribution internationally by cooperating with the Peace Corps. Furthermore, they are well suited to participate in the Corps itself.[42]

Home economists are currently helping in Brazil, Pakistan, Chile, Honduras, Ethiopia, Nepal, Turkey, India, and Ecuador—to name a few countries. Volunteers with degrees or experience in home economics have been requested by Bolivia, Colombia, the Dominican Republic, the Ivory Coast, Peru, and Sierra Leone. Volunteers teach adult courses in child care, sewing, nutrition, hygiene, and home improvement. They help develop curriculum, assist in community development work, help with rural youth clubs, work as home demonstrators, and help plan and prepare nutritious diets in schools and hospitals.

In most of the developing countries home economics is not an art and a science as we know it. Homes are likely to be managed in the traditional way. As in many of our own homes, food preparation is carried on in the same way as in past generations, in spite of evidences of malnutrition and of disease. The manner of dress may be decided by religious dogma rather than practicality or desire. Again as in our own country, ignorance may affect child training, although superstition is also a factor that may cause the neglect of children in the developing countries. The washing may be done on the rocks at the river. Thus, the home economist in any Peace Corps assignment will find that he must be understanding, adaptable, and resourceful. Emotional stability and physical stamina are also vital.[43]

Although Peace Corps work differs from country to country, the following quotations from the Peace Corps pamphlet *Home Economists Needed This Summer for Peace Corps Programs* do provide some insight into the type of work in which some Peace Corps Volunteers will find themselves.

The Ivory Coast Program: This program, under the Ministry of Education, will assist young Ivoirienne girls in broadening their vocational skills and in qualifying them for further education or employment opportunities. The Centre des Métiers Féminins in Abidjan and Bouake offers a three-year course in nutrition, child care, sewing and hygiene, in addition to

[42] Phillips, op. cit., p. 229.
[43] *Home Economists Needed This Summer for Peace Corps Programs,* Peace Corps Publication (Washington, D.C.: Peace Corps Office of Public Information, 1965), p. 2.

FIGURE 3-46. *Volunteer Mary Lou Callahan is a teacher in the Brush Town of Dabola, Guinea. (Courtesy of the Peace Corps Office of Public Information, Office of Economic Opportunity.)*

studies in French, mathematics, science, physical education, music and art. Students are admitted to the schools if they have completed primary school and have passed an entrance examination. First-year students are between fourteen and seventeen years old. Upon completion of the three-year course, the girls are awarded vocational proficiency certificates that enable them to work as assistants in social work centers, kindergartens or women's adult education centers. If students return for two additional years of training, they may qualify as teachers of domestic science and housecraft. In 1965 the two Centres had a total enrollment of 425 students, and a considerable increase is planned for 1966. The Centres are equipped with pedal sewing machines and gas stoves. Volunteers will instruct students in all areas of housecraft, using both lecture and laboratory sessions. Because the Centres are equivalent to Ivoirien secondary schools, teachers will have to expect high proficiency from their students.

The Centre de Formation Ménagère, established in 1962, is designed to give vocational training to girls who do not complete primary school or are unable to enter secondary schools. This Centre offers a two-year course that prepares its students to become seamstresses, cooks and clerks in commercial enterprises. The girls study homemaking skills, hygiene, child care and basic academic subjects.

The Centre de Formation Ménagère is not as well equipped as the other Centres. Instruction will be simple and practical with the goal of adequately preparing students for a job related to the domestic arts. These students must be taught with imagination and patience, and they must be challenged to perform at their maximum capacity. Teachers for all the Centres will have enough time to become involved in activities outside the classroom. They will do special projects during the summer school vacation, July to September.

The Ministry of Education has drawn up an excellent program for the year's work: reading, writing, arithmetic, hygiene, child care, household management, cooking, sewing and related domestic studies. It is a completely realistic program based on local concepts and needs and does not set out to "burn bridges" but to mend them, underpin them and add to them. The hoped-for by-product is that the home will become a place where some level of intellectual give-and-take can occur, where ideas can be created and carried out and where, on some scale, the amenities of life can be practiced.[44]

Becoming a Peace Corps volunteer is not difficult. One must be a United States citizen, at least eighteen years old, in good health, and, if single, have no dependents under eighteen. A prospective volunteer must fill out a Peace Corps volunteer application and take a Peace Corps Placement Test. An application form may be secured from: Peace Corps, A Part of Action, 806 Connecticut Avenue N.W., Washington, D.C. Knowledge of a foreign language is not necessary. One

[44] Ibid., pp. 4–5.

need not be a college graduate, but completion of college before Peace Corps volunteer work is strongly encouraged. College training in home economics is good preparation for work with homes and families in other lands.

The Peace Corps volunteer spends a twelve- to fourteen-week training period in one of the six training centers operated by the Peace Corps. Approximately three hundred hours of this period is spent on concentrated study of the language of the country. Working ability will be developed in one language, ranging from Amharic to Swahili. The normal tour of service will last twenty-four to twenty-seven months, including the training period. The volunteer may request extensions up to one year or reenroll for another two-year period for service in the same or in a different country. He receives an allowance to cover food, clothing, housing, and incidentals. Medical care and transportation are also provided. In addition, an allowance of $75 per month accumulates as a readjustment allowance; this is subject to U.S. taxes.[45]

ADVANTAGES

Peace Corps work is a rich experience. A volunteer will become familiar with another culture, its language and people. College credit is sometimes given for Peace Corps work. Sometimes scholarships are offered to returning volunteers. The majority of the benefits, though, are personal and these are the ones that mean the most.

POSSIBLE DISADVANTAGES

Accomplishments are not always apparent and progress is slow. In some areas there are increasing health hazards, but health rules and instructions are given during training that, if followed, will take the danger from the work. And, too, "volunteers are not placed in work sites where health hazards pose a real danger."[46] There may be a culture shock when the Peace Corps volunteer enters the host country and again when he reenters the United States. Volunteers are prepared for their own initial reactions. Living conditions and pay are kept at the same level as those of the co-workers in the community, and this is

[45] *Peace Corps: One Part of ACTION,* Action Publication (Washington, D.C., 1972), pp. 2–22.
[46] *A Special Message to Parents of Peace Corps Volunteers,* Peace Corps Publication (Washington, D.C.: Peace Corps Office of Public Information, 1965), p. 3.

what the volunteers themselves want in order to help those around them better. Although postal service in some areas is reliable, there remain some places in which delivery of mail is not reliable. The final disadvantage is the possibility of internal political or civil power struggles. Inasmuch as volunteers work on a person-to-person level, they are generally unaffected by governmental changes and effectively continue work in time of political unrest.

The Home Economist in Research

Of the many definitions of research, the common core is that it is an effort to provide new knowledge whether it may be in testing accepted views or finding new facts. There are also many classifications of types of research, and here we get an even greater variance. Natural scientists are likely to consider as research only the basic, fundamental, pure research in which the concern is for the establishment of facts or broad generalizations and in which there is no, or little, concern for the practical use of the findings. Behavioral scientists may be more interested in applied, practical, or action research in which the concern is to use the new knowledge for the improvement of practice. Any problem that needs an answer, any idea that needs testing can be scientifically adapted to research.

Nature of the Work

The common purpose of all home economics research is to provide new knowledge that can be used for the improvement of home and family life. Such research may be aimed toward the well-being of individuals and family members, toward the improvement of human relationships, toward the improvement of homes, or simply toward the determination of family needs and/or desires.

The student interested in a career in home economics research has many broad areas from which to select: foods, nutrition, textiles, clothing, housing, home furnishings, equipment, home management, family economics, child development, family relations, home economics education, institution management, and related art. Home economists have the responsibility of contributing through research to the knowledge needed for the improvement of family life throughout the world, particularly in such complex areas as food, nutrition, shelter, mobility, divorce, delinquency, education, leisure-time activities, consumer problems, and problems of the aging.

The methods used by the researcher are largely dependent upon the particular problem, and the area of reserach may indicate the method most likely to be used. For example, experimental research is more likely to be used, though not exclusively, in the areas of textiles, food, and nutrition; these involve the use of laboratories and equipment, a knowledge of chemistry, and skilled laboratory techniques.

The descriptive method is more likely to be employed in home economics education, family economics, and home management, for example. Survey studies are often used in the descriptive method, in which the aim is to seek facts and to develop guiding principles. The findings often serve as bases for predictions or may serve as information for experimental research.

The historical method is more likely to be used by the home economics researcher who is interested in the past as it relates to the present or the future. This method may be employed by those in the areas of clothing, family relations, housing, and home furnishings, for example. The historical researcher is more likely, too, to have literary objectives.

The day of the individual researcher has not passed, but the team approach to research is increasingly used. Teams of specialists cooperate on the more ambitious projects, with each individual making a contribution. The beginning researcher and the student researcher may have segments of studies that have been designed by those with more experience. Home economics researchers of the future may often find themselves involved in longitudinal, interdisciplinary studies in which specialists from several disciplines may work as a team on a research project. Research on the family might thus involve home economists, art researchers, psychologists, engineers, sociologists, or researchers from other areas depending upon the problem and its magnitude.

The researcher may find employment in government, business, industry, colleges and universities, international agencies, and public and private foundations.

The home economics student with a keen intellectual curiosity—who is interested in the why, how, why not, and so what—may wish to consider research as a career. Other qualities needed are superior intellectual ability, initiative, patience, persistence, preciseness, ability to maintain an open mind, responsibility, imagination, good judgment, analytical ability, dependability, ability to organize, ability to cooperate, and a deep interest in some aspect of home economics as well as a belief in its values. The student should also consider the area of his future employment for other personal qualities that may be needed. For example, one interested in research in an international agency needs respect for the values of others and the respect of their rights to hold those values, flexibility, and the ability to recognize the difference between literacy and intelligence.[47] These characteristics are, of course, assets in any research position.

SPECIAL REQUIREMENTS

The student interested in a career in research should carefully consider the educational requirements. There are beginning positions in research open to those holding a bachelor's degree with basic training in the subject matter involved in the research. The student should realize, however, that for advancement one must have a master's degree and that for the top positions and maximum contributions, a doctoral degree is necessary. A broad background in home economics at the undergraduate level is considered by many a necessary part of the education for all home economics research in that it affords an insight into the interrelatedness of the many facets of home and family life and thus makes research results more meaningful. At some level of study, all home economics researchers must acquire competency in the tools of research; these include mathematics, statistics, computer programming, and methods of research. English courses that enable the researcher to write reports easily, accurately, and clearly should be included as a part of the educational training. The student should realize, too, that at some level of study he must gain depth as well as breadth in his field of special interest. A core of courses in the field or fields fundamental or allied to the area of special interest is necessary; these courses vary according to the specialization or even according to the particular facet of the specialization in which one is interested.

Related fields to the various areas of specialization may include, but are not necessarily limited to, the following:

Food and Nutrition—chemistry, biology, physiology, and bacteriology, as basic; histology, anatomy, psychology, and sociology, as supplemental.

[47] American Home Economics Association, *New Dimensions in International Programs in Home Economics* (Washington, D.C.: The Association, 1954), p. 71.

Textiles—chemistry and physics, as basic; art, biology, psychology, economics, and sociology, as supplemental.

Clothing—chemistry, art, psychology, economics, and sociology, as basic; physics, biology, and history, as supplemental.

Child Development—psychology, sociology, and physiology, as basic; economics and anthropology, as supplemental.

Family Relations—sociology, psychology, and anthropology, as basic; economics and physiology, as supplemental.

Housing, Home Furnishings, and Interior Design—art, architecture, psychology, and physics, as basic; economics and sociology, as supplemental.

Equipment—chemistry, physics, and economics, as basic; art, psychology, and engineering, as supplemental.

Family Economics—economics, marketing, psychology, and sociology, as basic.

Home Economics Education—education courses in tests and measurements, philosophy of education, learning processes and motivation, psychology, and sociology, as basic; anthropology and guidance, as supplemental.

Home Management—sociology, psychology, economics, and management, as basic; art, philosophy, chemistry, physics, and anthropology, as supplemental.

ADVANTAGES

Opportunities are unlimited and salaries for the competent are unusually good. Recognition and prestige come to those who are successful. The work is challenging and interesting. Perhaps the greatest advantage for the home economics researcher comes through the satisfactions realized in discovering new facts, new methods, and new materials that will contribute toward improved home and family life and the betterment of human welfare and thus make a contribution toward a better world. Many university professors, particularly those teaching at the graduate level, combine teaching and research and find this combination advantageous.

POSSIBLE DISADVANTAGES

Research work involves a great deal of routine and detailed work, which may become monotonous. Long hours may be necessary at some stages and in some kinds of research. Results may be frustrating or disappointing. The meticulous care necessary for record keeping, analysis, and writing has brought nervous stress to some.

AS THE RESEARCHER SEES HIS RESEARCH

A few outstanding research people were asked to write a brief statement on "As the Researcher Sees His Work in the Future." No effort was made to cover every field of research in home economics. With these examples, it is thought that the student can investigate the possibilities in his area of major interest. These illustrations are given to stimulate and challenge the student who has or might develop an interest in research.

RESEARCH IN MANAGEMENT AND THE ECONOMIC PROBLEMS OF THE CONSUMER*

by Sarah L. Manning

The need and opportunities for research in management and the economic problems of the consumer are, perhaps, greater than they have ever been. This is a result of the increasing interest in the welfare of consumers, both individuals and families. It results also from the growth of home economics itself. Early concern for this welfare tended to be centered upon food and the human requirements for it. Now the welfare of consumers is emphasized in broader aspects with an increasing awareness of the contributions of the social sciences to overall welfare.

One current research project that involves several of the social science disciplines is NC 90, funded by the U.S. Department of Agriculture. In this project family economists are investigating the effect of dependability of income and income fluctuations on the financial problems of the family, including the use of fixed commitments to spend. Two of the states involved are cooperating on a smaller portion of the study concerning perceptual and conceptual foresight with regard to the managerial ability of the respondents. All of this is done cooperatively with researchers in other disciplines from other state Agricultural Experiment Stations.

Households consume services as well as goods. One such area of services is house cleaning. Although it is possible to go out and buy this service

---

* Written for this volume. Dr. Sarah L. Manning has been head of the Department of Home Management and Family Economics at Purdue University since 1967, joining the staff there in 1959. She received her B.S. degree in home economics education from Buffalo State Teachers College and her M.S. and Ph.D. in household management and economics from Cornell University. Her experience includes teaching in high school and college plus four years as an extension specialist in home management and family economics. In addition she has been a supervising house mother in a resident school for dependent Indian children. She is currently on leave from Purdue, working with the Cooperative State Research Service, U.S. Department of Agriculture in Washington, D.C.

FIGURE 3-47. *A meeting of the Regional Committee for Agricultural Experiment Stations Project NC 90: Factors Affecting Levels of Living in Disadvantaged Families. This is an interdisciplinary project with researchers from schools of home economics and agriculture in approximately fifteen states cooperating through their Agricultural Experiment Stations to examine resource procurement and use; values, goals and orientation; and social structure and social process as they affect disadvantaged rural and urban families. Shown above in a picture taken at the annual meeting at the University of Nebraska are some of the committee members and advisers— back row: Dr. Hazel Reinhardt, Rural Sociology, Wisconsin; Dr. John Woodward, Human Development, Nebraska; Dr. Edward Metzen, Family Economics, Missouri. Front row: Dr. Mary Beth Minden, Cooperative State Research Service, USDA; Dr. Francille Maloch, Home Management, Ohio State University; Miss Jean Pennock, Consumer and Food Economics, Research Division, USDA; Director Herbert Kramer, Agriculture Experiment Station, Purdue University; Dr. Ronald T. Daly, Family Life, University of Nevada. (Courtesy of the University of Nebraska.)*

in some instances and it is possible for certain people to sell their own services in cleaning houses to those wishing to buy, there exist many actual problems in this labor market situation. With the ultimate aim of improving the satisfactions of both the buyer (or consumer) of this service, and the seller (or producer) of the service, a research project is underway at Purdue University, funded by the U.S. Department of Health, Education, and Welfare. A team of workers is exploring criteria for estimating the time necessary for cleaning parts of a home, regardless of how homes differ one from another.

Research undertaken in schools and colleges of home economics provides and will continue to provide the basis for expanding studies of the use of resources by households. An examination of some recent titles of theses completed by graduate students in the Department of Home Management and Family Economics at Purdue University in Indiana suggests areas to which home economists are directing their attention. An annual listing of all such research done in this country may be found in the American Home Economics Association publication, "Home Economics Research Abstracts, Family Economics–Home Management." Recent titles:

"Consumer Preferences for Selected Expenditures Related to Levels of Consumption," Janet Armstrong, Ph.D., June 1970.

"Characteristics of Money Income and Employability in Some Disadvantaged Families," Priscilla S. Gautier, M.S., August 1969.

"Work Time Estimation for Cleaning Tasks in Household Employment," Dorothy L. Schauer, Ph.D., January 1971.

"High School Youth and Their Money Management," Lenora G. Smith, M.S., January 1971.

"Factors Related to Net Worth Change of Selected Indiana Families," Flora L. Williams, Ph.D., June 1969.

As the Clothing Researcher Sees His Work[°]

by Marilyn J. Horn

Clothing is generally accepted as one of the fundamental needs of individuals and families the world over. In its most functional and utilitarian aspects, we are concerned with the design and construction of garments that will provide the optimum in physical comfort and durability. Yet as we examine clothing in its relationship to custom, values, fashion, and other social and psychological forces, we find that there are amazingly few people who would be adventurous enough to wear a body covering that was purely functional in design.

Clothing becomes an inseparable part of the total perceptual field within which an individual is observed and evaluated. As such, it is a symbol of crucial importance that communicates to others impressions of one's social status, role, personality attributes, and many other characteristics. Clothing behavior, i.e., the way in which people select and use clothing, is rarely random and purposeless. In any field of inquiry, a sci-

[°] Written for this volume. Dr. Marilyn J. Horn is Director of Graduate Study and Research, School of Home Economics, University of Nevada. Most of her research has been done on the sociopsychological aspects of clothing. She has made outstanding contributions to the work of the American Home Economics Association, including service on the Accreditation Committee and the Cooperative Relations Committee.

FIGURE 3-48. *A research team analyzes details of clothing taken from a sample of college men in a study of conformity to normative patterns of dress. Data collected through observation and interview are coded onto cards and fed to the computer for detailed statistical analyses. (Courtesy of the University of Nevada.)*

entific approach depends upon the organization of observations and experiences. In the ordering of our observations of clothing behavior, we seek to identify the common, regular, and repetitive elements in the action patterns of individuals and groups. Secondly, we attempt to account for such patterning by noting the relationships that exist with other phenomena in the environment. Obviously, those patterns that are followed by the greatest number of individuals, and that are repeated in many successive situations, offer a relatively high degree of predictability.

The ultimate purpose of such analysis is not just to find out what may happen tomorrow in the way of fashion change but to understand the consequences of such behavior in the lives of individuals and to society as a whole. Thus, clothing research can help the individual to make clothing decisions that will satisfy his personal needs, communicate to others the image that he seeks to convey, and at the same time contribute to the best interests of others in society.

Clothing behavior may be interpreted from many points of view.

Psychologically, clothing expresses our inner needs and desires; historically, it provides a record of past events; physiologically, it affords protection and comfort. To the anthropologist, clothing is a pattern of culture; to the sociologist, it is a manifestation of collective life, whereas the economist sees it in terms of consumer demand and business cycles. It becomes obvious that many disciplines contribute to our understanding of why people choose to wear the clothes that they do.

Graduates who wish to enter the field of clothing research should have a fairly broad background in the behavioral disciplines that contribute to an understanding of clothing. In addition to the research qualifications previously outlined, a person must be unusually perceptive in regard to the details of dress and have a respect for precision in observing and recording data.

RESEARCH IN CHILD DEVELOPMENT*

by James Walters

Research in child development in home economics has had for its primary focus an analysis of the factors affecting normal growth. Beginning with observational studies of infants and young children, research in the area has been expanded to include school age youth and adolescents and has stressed the importance of the family in understanding behavior. Utilizing the findings and procedures developed in the social and behavioral sciences, research in child development in home economics is designed to discover answers to problems facing the family and to facilitate the development of knowledge that will enable parents and others who are responsible for youth to guide children more effectively. Because of their focus on the applications to be made of information from the sciences and the arts, home economists in child development are concerned with the integration of knowledge, the effective use of the family's resources, and the discovery of new constructs that will enable families to achieve greater satisfaction in everyday living.

Research work in child development in home economics requires graduate education. The opportunities for the imaginative, well-educated,

* Written for this volume. Dr. James Walters is Professor of Family Relations and Child Development at Oklahoma State University, Stillwater. His B.A. degree in sociology is from Washburn University, his M.A. degree in child welfare is from the University of Iowa, and his Ph.D. in child development is from Florida State University. His professional affiliations include the American Home Economics Association, the American Psychological Association, the National Council on Family Relations, Sigma Xi, and Omicron Nu. He has served as chairman of the family relations and child development section of the American Home Economics Association, as chairman of the National Commission on Family Life Education, and as chairman of the Special Emphases Section of the National Council on Family Relations. He has served on the boards of directors of the American Home Economics Association and the National Council on Family Relations. He is the recipient of the Osborne Award, an award given annually by the National Council on Family Relations for the outstanding teacher of the year in family life education.

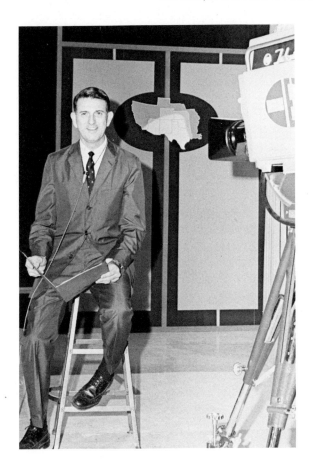

FIGURE 3-49. *Dr. James Walters, Professor of Family Relations and Child Development at Oklahoma State University, teaching by television.*

and motivated student are excellent. It should be emphasized, however, that the doctorate is normally required for positions in this area and that students need considerable work in such allied areas as psychology, sociology, education, and statistics.

Researchers in child development are learning that the traditional boundaries of disciplines must be replaced by the understanding that can come only when the discoveries of researchers in a variety of areas are examined in relation to each other. Thus, to obtain an understanding of the many factors that influence a child's behavior, the researcher needs to be aware of investigations in many disciplines if he is to design studies that will enable man to predict and control his environment with greater efficiency. Researchers in child development in home economics are making valuable contributions to knowledge that can assist families to function more competently, to achieve greater fulfillment, and to make more significant contributions to communities.

171

The listing of publications by Dr. Walters should be of interest to the potential researcher inasmuch as they indicate some of the concerns of the researcher in child development. They also indicate the contributions that a researcher in this field can make.

Publications

James Walters and Ralph H. Ojemann, "A Study of the Components of Adolescent Attitudes Concerning the Role of Women," *Journal of Social Psychology*, 52 (1952), 101–110.

Harold Hawkins and James Walters, "Family Recreation Activities," *Journal of Home Economics*, 44 (1952), 623–626.

James Walters, "The Measurement of Attitude Components in Family Life Education Research," *Journal of Home Economics*, 45 (1953), 729–732.

Thelma Bennett and James Walters, "Personal and Social Adjustment of College Home Economics Freshmen," *Journal of Home Economics*, 45 (1953), 29–31.

Ruth Connor, Theodore Johannis and James Walters, "Parent-Adolescent Relationships: II. Intrafamilial Concepts of the Good Father, Good Mother, and Good Child," *Journal of Home Economics*, 46 (1954), 187–191.

Ruth Connor, Theordore Johannis and James Walters, "Parent-Adolescent Relationships: I. Parent-Adolescent Conflicts: Current and in Retrospect," *Journal of Home Economics*, 46 (1954), 183–186.

Ruth Connor, Theordore Johannis and James Walters, "Family Recreation in Relation to Role Conceptions of Family Members," *Marriage and Family Living*, 17 (1955), 306–309.

James Walters and Barbara Bridges, "Attitudes of Single Men Toward Child Guidance," *Journal of Home Economics*, 48 (1956), 109–113.

James Walters, Doris Pearce and Lucille Dahms, "Affectional and Aggressive Behavior of Preschool Children," *Child Development*, 28 (1957), 15–26.

James Walters, Frances Stromberg and Geraldine Lonian, "Perceptions Concerning Development of Responsibility in Young Children," *The Elementary School Journal*, 57 (1957), 209–216.

Ruth Connor, Helen Greene and James Walters, "Agreement of Family Member Conceptions of 'Good' Parent and Child Roles," *Social Forces*, 36 (1958), 353–358.

Victor Christopherson and James Walters, "Responses of Protestants,

Catholics, and Jews Concerning Marriage and Family Life," *Sociology and Social Research*, 43 (1958), 16–22.

James Walters and Clara Fisher, "Changes in the Attitudes of Young Women Toward Child Guidance over a Two-Year Period," *Journal of Educational Research*, 52 (1958), 115–118.

James Walters, "The Effects of an Introductory Course in Child Development on the Attitudes of College Women Toward Child Guidance," *Journal of Experimental Education*, 27 (1959), 311–321.

James Walters, "Relationship Between Reliability of Responses in Family Life Research and Method of Data Collection," *Marriage and Family Living*, 22 (1960), 232–237.

Patricia H. Henderson, Ruth Connor and James Walters, "Family Member Perceptions of Parent Role Performance," *Merrill-Palmer Quarterly of Behavior and Development* (1961), 31–37.

James Walters, "A Review of Family Research in 1959, 1960, and 1961," *Marriage and Family Living*, 24 (1962), 158–178.

James Walters, "A Review of Family Research in 1962," *Marriage and Family Living*, 25 (1963), 336–348.

James Walters, Ruth Connor and Michael Zunich, "Interaction of Mothers and Children from Lower-Class Families," in Medinnus, G. R. (Ed.) *Readings in the Psychology of Parent-Child Relations*, New York: John Wiley & Sons (1965).

James E. Montgomery and James Walters, "The Impact of Social Mobility in the Family," in Bonniwell, B. L. and Witherspoon, R. L. (Eds.) *Studies in Social Mobility*, Villanova University Press, (1966).

Hortense Glenn and James Walters, "Feminine Stress in the Twentieth Century," *Journal of Home Economics*, 58 (1966), 703–707.

Nick Stinnett and James Walters, "Parent-Peer Orientation of Adolescents from Low-Income Families," *Journal of Home Economics*, 59 (1967), 37–50.

James Walters and Nick Stinnett, "Should Family Life Education Be Required?" *Journal of Home Economics*, 60 (1968), 641–644.

Chung Kim Chungsoon, R. J. Dales, R. Connor, J. Walters and R. Witherspoon, "Social Interaction of Like-Sex Twins and Singletons in Relation to Intelligence, Language, and Physical Development," *Journal of Genetic Psychology*, 114 (1969), 203–214.

Ruth J. Dales and James Walters, *Factors Related to Educational and Occupational Aspirations of Adolescent Males from Culturally Deprived Families* (Washington, D.C.: Office of Education, Bureau of Research, U.S. Department of Health, Education and Welfare.)

James Walters and Nick Stinnett, "Parent-Child Relationships: A Decade Review of Research," *Journal of Marriage and the Family,* 33 (1971), 70–111.

James Walters, Karol K. Parker and Nick Stinnett, "College Students' Perceptions Concerning Marriage," *Family Perspective,* 7 (1972), 43–49.

Mary Jo Weale and James Walters, "From Bauhaus to Baroque: Designers Predict Furniture Trends," *Journal of Home Economics,* 65 (1973), 7–11.

FAMILY RELATIONS—AS THE RESEARCHER SEES IT[*]

by J. Joel Moss

How much do you really know about family relations? Many people feel they are experts in the matter. After all, they grew up in families and

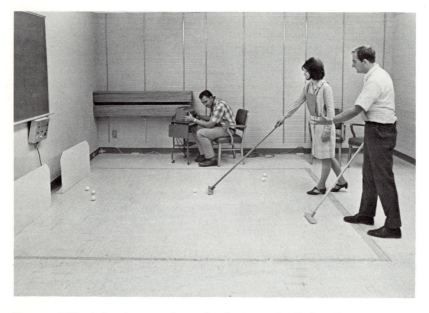

FIGURE 3-50. (a) *A married couple playing a shuffle-board type of game called SIMFAM (Simulated Family Activity Measurement) while an experimenter operates a switchboard to give colored light signals to indicate correct and incorrect moves. (Courtesy of Brigham Young University.)*

[*] Written for this volume. Dr. J. Joel Moss is Chairman and Professor of Child Development and Family Relationships at Brigham Young University. His degrees are from Brigham Young University and from the University of North

there are many common-sense prescriptions for family living floating about.

The family relations researcher is a frontiersman and a watchman. He explores a fascinating jungle of information about which we really know very little. He is a watchman who reminds students that much of what we think is correct has never been proved so. He feels that only as we explore and test ideas can we label what is really contributive and noncontributive to family life. Much of what we believe may be only bias, and love is by no means a cure-all in the sense that most people conceive of love.

There are several research areas in which home economists may find opportunity for research in family relations in the future. One area of concern is the development of children's personalities with the focus upon family relations as they contribute to such development. Another area of research interest is concerned with family patterns as they affect the family as a unit. Issues such as family unity, family conflict, family crises, and family processes are of major concern. In these two research areas, the poten-

FIGURE 3-50. (b)   *A videotape recording of husband-wife interaction and behavior during SIMFAM is played back as many times as necessary for the classification and scoring of social interaction and behavior. (Courtesy of Brigham Young University.)*

Carolina, Chapel Hill. He has served as Head, Division of Family Relations and Child Development at the University of Nebraska, and as Research Professor at Southern Illinois University, Carbondale. He has done extensive research in marriage and family relations.

175

tial home economist who would participate must like abstract reasoning and the experimental method; he should also have a sound background in personality and learning theory, child development, family relations, group dynamics, and small group sociology.

Another area of interest to many home economists is the patterns by which individuals move from the single into the married state and their consequences. Helping people become more ready for marriage becomes a major task of the home economist teaching in a high school or college setting. Because patterns of dating and courtship are innovations developed by youth, knowledge is needed about how the youth perceive the world and the consequences of the various innovative patterns they are developing. The teacher who operates in this area must almost be a researcher with his class, exploring with them the issues rather than merely passing on information gathered from other research studies.

In a world where family patterns are changing and becoming more specific to the personalities who make up the family, the family begins to chart its own developmental course throughout its life cycle. Some home economists may find that they must be concerned with the developmental happenings occurring within families as they grow older. Concern for middle- and older-aged individuals and their family patterns gives us the clues to help people know what to do to progress throughout the family life cycle. Those who would do research of a developmental nature need background in fields that give them a developmental perspective along with the basic family relations and social gerontology knowledge that is available.

The area of family decision-making has usually been seen as a focus of those in home management. In the modern world, where consumer behavior is a serious concern, the linking of the interactional approach of the family relations researcher with the resources and decision-making, problem-solving approach of the home management specialist offers better answers than either can individually. Consumer behavior is role behavior. The more secure one is in the roles he plays the more readily he can operate in the marketplace and provide the strength to help a family do so. Role behavior in interactional settings has its roots in family interaction. Those desiring to do research in this area would do well to be well grounded in both management and the understanding of interactional human behavior.

Finally, some family relations researchers are teaming up with counselors and educators who have research interest to explore better ways by which families can be helped to move from one systematic behavior pattern to a more productive one. These researchers capitalize on the educational and counseling ideas of behavioral objectives, negotiation of interested parties, evaluation, and experimental activity.

As the Foods Researcher Sees His Work[*]

by Andrea Mackey

Career opportunities fall into three broad groups: business, universities, and government laboratories and services. In business, foods graduates are

[*] Written for this volume. Dr. Mackey is Professor of Foods and Nutrition in the School of Home Economics at Oregon State University, Corvallis. She is in

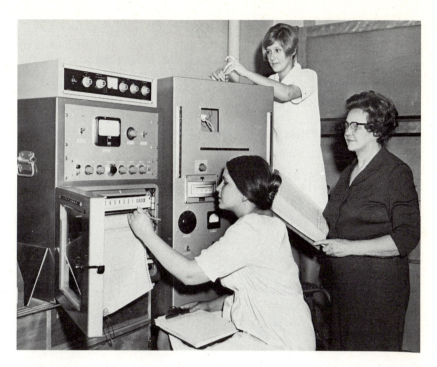

FIGURE 3-51. *Chromatography helps isolate volatile food components. Nancy Kline and Janet Wozenski, graduate students in Food and Nutrition, are analyzing the flavor of rye flour with several techniques. Dr. Andrea Mackey studies the chromatograms. (Courtesy of Oregon State University.)*

employed by public service companies, where they may work with foods and equipment. They work in test kitchens and in analytical laboratories and for research institutes supported by industry. In work of this type the home economist may test recipes, develop new food products, and write articles and reports of work in scientific laboratories. He may be in charge of the food-testing laboratory and the taste panel. In the development of new foods, such as soy protein products, the home economist often works on a team with food technologists and chemists.

A university career usually consists of teaching foods, working on research projects, or being a foods specialist in home economics extension. A home economist may work for the government as a food specialist in the U.S. Department of Agriculture research laboratories, or he may work as a food marketing specialist. The USDA research laboratories are located in several different regions of the country, including Washington, D.C.

charge of food research in the Department of Home Economics Research. Dr. Mackey has published many scientific papers in national journals and has written bulletins and leaflets of information. She received her Ph.D. degree from Iowa State University in 1945.

Food research can be strengthened by a background in any of the sciences, including chemistry, physics, mathematics, the social sciences, and psychology. The picture illustrating this article shows the application of modern chemical methods to food analysis. The volatile flavor constituents are evaluated by a panel of expert flavor judges for their contribution to the total flavor. The fields of chemistry, foods, and psychology are brought together to solve the riddle of food flavor.

AS THE NUTRITION RESEARCHER SEES HIS FUTURE WORK°

by Ruth M. Leverton

World leaders are becoming increasingly aware of the promise of nutrition for improving the lot of mankind. Therefore, nutrition research in the

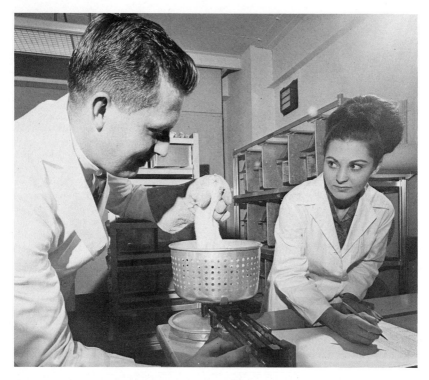

FIGURE 3-52. *Nutrition research, U.S. Department of Agriculture, Agricultural Research Center, Beltsville, Maryland. (Courtesy of the U.S. Department of Agriculture.)*

° Written for this volume. Dr. Ruth M. Leverton is Science Adviser, U.S. Department of Agriculture, Washington, D.C. She has earned national and international recognition for her research in human nutrition. She was twice recognized

future, beginning as soon as tomorrow, must find answers to their urgent questions about what and how much food.

In the developing countries, often referred to as the food deficit countries, leaders are asking, "How little food can people get along on and still be adequately nourished? What is the least amount or the floor of a food or a specific nutrient that will prevent retarded growth of children, symptoms of dietary deficiency, susceptibility to infection, low levels of health, and shortened lifespan?"

The economically developed countries are asking, "What are the nutritional goals toward which we should aim in order to ensure the kinds and amounts of food that will maintain a high level of nutritional well-being?" As a logical sequence, they are also asking, "What are the maximum amounts for energy and the different nutrients, a ceiling of intakes, above which we would not expect any added nutritional benefit, and indeed in some instances, above which it may be unsafe to go?"

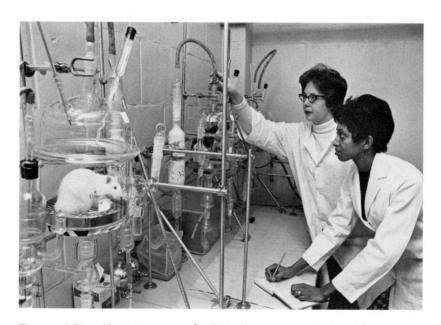

Figure 3-53. *Nutrition research, U.S. Department of Agriculture, Agricultural Research Center, Beltsville, Maryland. (Courtesy of the U.S. Department of Agriculture.)*

through the Borden Award, in 1942 and in 1953, for fundamental research in nutrition. Her numerous publications on nutrition and the types of positions she has held indicate that she is extremely well qualified to write on the future of such research. Her experiences include positions as research assistant and director of nutrition research in an Agricultural Experiment Station, professor of nutrition, a Fulbright professor, and a member of the United States delegations to international nutrition conferences.

Nutritionists are vital members of the teams of research scientists that must find the answers. Home economics students who are interested in such a future need to concentrate on phases of the sciences that are related to health and nutrition—physiology, biology, and chemistry. These are the sciences that equip the specialist to study human nutritional needs, interrelationships and metabolism of nutrients, and nutritive values of foods and to appraise the adequacy of diets, evaluate food habits, and interpret research findings for use in nutrition programs.

In this chapter the major careers in the home economics profession were discussed. Actually the career opportunities are nearly unlimited. New positions are opening as the need develops. Home economists must remain aware of the possibilities through which home economics can ever broaden its scope and be applied to new family, community, national, and international situations.

Part II

Utilizing Your College Years
for Maximum Impact
and Satisfactions

Introduction

The author wishes to emphasize that Chapters 4, 5, and 6 are basic reviews. However, they discuss abilities and practices that the university professor expects the student to have and be able to put into practice from high school studies. The university professor using this text may wish to give a pretest to see if the student does, in fact, have these abilities and practices. After years of teaching from coast to coast and in the Midwest, the author has found that a pretest will show that the majority of students do not, in actuality, have these abilities and practices even though they may maintain that they do.

To you, the student, the author would emphasize that if you are to utilize your college years for maximum impact and success in college and after graduation in the professional world, these abilities, habits, and practices are fundamental.

Chapter 7, "The Ethical Dimension of a Career," was added because of student requests and statements, such as, "Every-one talks about ethics but where do we learn anything about ethics?" It is hoped that Chapter 7, then, will give you some insight into this philosophical subject, stimulate your interest for additional study and reading on this subject, and ultimately earn for you such praise as "his professional ethics are excellent." Good professional ethics *are* needed in today's and tomorrow's worlds.

Utilizing Your College Years for Maximum Impact and Satisfactions

4

Developing Good
Study Habits

The Importance of Good Study Habits

High school was fun. There were club activities and basketball and football games; there were plenty of dates and some studying, too. Have you heard that college is a lot of fun, too? It can be. But then there must be a difference between college and high school, and there is.

When you first arrived on campus, you were probably awed, not so much by the buildings and new students but by a weight of *responsibility* that suddenly fell upon you. The decisions you make in college will affect a major portion of your life. What courses will you take? How much time will you spend on this activity and that? Where will you study? Your parents, friends, or advisers may have asked you some of these questions. You may already have made numerous decisions or you may still be fumbling. This is to be expected: almost everyone is shaky at first. This book was written for you, the college freshman in home economics, to help you make plans for your college career.

High school reading assignments were not as long or as technical as those in college. In some courses the outside reading will be heavier than in others, and the load will increase somewhat in more advanced courses. For example, in a 100-level mathematics class two fifteen-page chapters may be covered weekly, whereas a 200-level history course may require one hundred pages of the text per week, plus one outside book for the term. It is expected that you will increase your *reading efficiency* to meet the demands of college.

We will discuss the improving of your reading skills later in this chapter.

A third difference between high school and college is the heavy reliance upon *class notes*. In high school, teachers may not require any notes: they may tell you what is important enough to note, they may write on the chalkboard things they wish you to remember, or they may hand out study sheets of the major points of the class. When you arrived in college, this situation changed considerably. Here much emphasis is placed on class notes and it is your responsibility to decide on the important aspects of a lecture. Class notes usually are the major source of examination questions. (The textbook usually ranks second, and sometimes other reference books are important, too.) You will want to make notes for a second reason also: they may be valuable in related courses and in your future profession. Class notes will play a significant role in your college career and are discussed in more detail in a later section of this chapter.

Term paper assignments may reach you during your first term at the college level. In high school the writing of a term paper may have been studied in an English class. A few high schools expect two or three, whereas some high school students graduate without having written a term paper or even a theme or an essay. The emphasis again shifts at the college level. These papers may be a primary source of a term grade: they are to be expected in many courses. They are considered in detail in this chapter.

Finally, at the secondary level your grade may have been determined by class participation, daily assignments, laboratory work, short quizzes, and a few longer examinations. The increasing enrollments on college campuses and the ever-increasing class size have necessitated the strong emphasis on one, two, or three written *examinations*. You will want to learn how to study for them as well as how to take written examinations. These topics are also treated in this chapter.

The greater responsibilities, longer, more intensive reading assignments, heavier reliance on class notes, frequent term papers, and heavier emphasis on written examinations may appear frightening at first. Yet two things seem important to adjustment at this crossroad: one is the studying of a text such as the one appearing before you and the second is the setting up of obtainable goals for your college years.

Goals and objectives were discussed in Chapter 1. As indicated there, making good grades may be one of your intermediate goals or objectives. In order to achieve high grades, you will want to plan your work, make usable class notes, improve your reading skills, write worthwhile term papers and reports, study effectively, and write successful examinations. In order to reach self-satisfaction and greater learning, too, you will want to achieve these objectives. Part II of this book is intended to help you achieve your goals, but first you must have a good set of mind and body.

Proper emotional and physical set are essentials for college success. Nearly every source on study habits and college success names these factors as basic requirements for college study. They are also very important to one who sets up a well-rounded personality as one of his goals.

Physical
Mental   Maturity = Well-rounded Personality + College Success
Emotional

Physical maturity is sought by regular health habits of eating, sleeping, exercising, and personal grooming, which will be reviewed in Chapter 5. Mental maturity is sought through learning and keeping one's mind questioning and seeking. Sound mental health, or emotional maturity, is sought through meeting problems calmly and squarely, facing reality, and avoiding the dodging of facts.[1]

Self-confidence is a part of emotional maturity. Lack of it may bring defeat in any undertaking, be it sport, conquest, or study; it hinders the use of the knowledge one possesses, making him overcautious and thus afraid to put down possible worthy ideas. In order to gain confidence, the student may try preparing extensively for the job, studying past mistakes, and looking at others and himself objectively.[2] Self-confidence is an important part of emotional maturity, as emotional security, coupled with physical and mental maturity, is vital to a well-rounded personality and success in college.

Planning Your Work

One of the responsibilities of college work is the need for planning time effectively. Ability alone is insufficient for achieving scholarship.

[1] Phi Eta Sigma, "Hints on How to Study" (Phi Eta Sigma, 1961), p. 2.
[2] Joseph C. Heston, *How to Take a Test* (Chicago: Science Research Associates, Inc., 1953), pp. 11–12.

Ability coupled with its effective use is necessary. The first step toward efficiency or the effective use of ability is the planning of time to meet goals best. Because scholarship is generally an important intermediate goal (self-imposed responsibility) of college, planning for efficient use of time becomes a prime responsibility.

Many authors believe that the only way for students to plan time is to make time schedules and stick to them. The objectives of this technique[3] are to afford time and freedom to do all the things that a student wants to do and to avoid spending too much time on one type of activity. Most students will accept these objectives as their own and will probably want to try out a time schedule.

Two sample schedules are illustrated to suggest ways of planning time. One schedule includes considerable laboratory work and thus less need for study time. The other student has mostly lecture classes with an average amount of studying needed, but he works part time.

In the first schedule, the young woman majoring in home economics took sixteen hours of credit, but because she had two laboratory courses, she was in class twenty-one hours a week. Considering two hours of study for every hour of lecture class, the student planned on twenty-two hours of study per week. This, then, is only a forty-two-hour week. With eight hours of sleep nightly, seventy hours a week remained for personal hygiene, letter writing, conversation with roommates, church, clubwork, and other recreation.

The second schedule is slightly more "tight." This young man in interior design carried a fourteen-hour course load, which kept him in class sixteen hours weekly. After receiving his schedule he planned a working schedule with his employer that involved another sixteen hours. Planning his study on the two-to-one basis gave him twenty-two hours of study. Having planned his work well, this student still had fifty-eight hours of free time after sleep.

For the average full-time student a forty- to forty-five-hour week of classes and studying is sufficient. Gerken[4] suggests that no less than ten hours be spent in studying per week and no more than thirty. Notice that generally the study periods in the illustrated time schedules were in two- to three-hour blocks. This was done purposely, because time spent each period should be "long enough so that you can get thoroughly 'warmed up' to your work, but short

[3] Luella Cole, *Students' Guide to Efficient Study*, 4th ed. (New York: Holt, Rinehart and Winston, 1961), p. 1.
[4] C. d'A. Gerken, *Study Your Way Through School* (Chicago: Science Research Associates, Inc., 1953), p. 11.

enough to avoid excessive fatigue."[5] Three main suggestions of the time schedule are: a class and study week should total forty to forty-five hours; no less than ten nor more than thirty hours should be spent on study; and study blocks should be sufficiently long to warm one up for studying but not excessively long, causing fatigue.

Some students attempt setting up a schedule that includes time for studying specific subjects, break time, and so on. These have been found to be very difficult to follow. If a schedule is not flexible, it will be useless. At the first minor interruption a student will give it up. It is to be expected that changes will be made, but without a specific goal set down (the hours to be spent studying), one may wander around without finding what he wants. If one realizes that the schedule is for his *use*, he can use it to guide him without allowing it to be his master. It must be flexible to his needs.

Rigid time schedules in which you allow certain definite amounts of time for classes, for studying, for eating—even for brushing your teeth—are cumbersome, too machine-like, and rather useless for most students. Students who follow them don't need them; students who might benefit can find more excuses for not following them than for using them.[6]

There are always students who cannot work on a weekly time schedule, but they can plan day by day those items that need to be accomplished in the time that is available. (Some planning by the week and term is absolutely necessary.) The following hints in planning a day's work come from Gerken's[7] study. They may especially help the student who cannot make weekly plans.

1. Studying by the job or the assignment rather than by the hour results in more efficient work. A job finished is the reward to oneself.
2. Between classes free time can be well spent in summarizing the preceding class notes or reviewing.
3. Flash cards can be used to learn foreign words, technical terms, formulas, history dates, new vocabulary, and other material to be memorized. Frequent short periods of memorizing can provide better results than less often longer periods.
4. Two- or three-minute breaks at a convenient time will refresh one and allow him to return to studying with renewed energy.
5. Rest also includes closing the eyes for a moment, stretching the

[5] Phi Eta Sigma, op. cit., p. 1.
[6] Gerken, op. cit., p. 7.
[7] Ibid., pp. 8–9.

	Monday	Tuesday	Wednesday	Thursday	Friday	Saturday	Sunday
8:00	Clothing Lecture	Clothing	X	Clothing Lecture	Clothing		
9:00	X	Laboratory	X		Laboratory		
10:00	X		X				
11:00	English		English		English		
12:00				EAT			
1:00	Chemistry	Chemistry Lecture	Chemistry		Chemistry Lecture		
2:00	Lab.	X	Lab.		X		
3:00	X	X			X		
4:00	Government	Government		Government	Government		
5:00				EAT			
6:00							
7:00	X	X		X			X
8:00	X	X		X			X
9:00	X	X		X			X
10:00							

X indicates study periods.

190

STUDENT'S TIME SCHEDULE

	Monday	Tuesday	Wednesday	Thursday	Friday	Saturday	Sunday
8:00	English	English		English			
9:00	Interior Design	Physical Ed.	Interior Design	Physical Ed.	Interior Design	Physical Ed.	
10:00	X	X	X	X	X	O	
11:00	X	X	X	X	X	O	
12:00				EAT			
1:00	Home and Family		Home and Family		Home and Family	O	
2:00		Speech Lecture		Speech Lecture			
3:00	O	O	O	O	O	O	
4:00	O	O	O	O	O	O	
5:00							
6:00				EAT			
7:00	X	Speech Lab.	X	Speech Lab.			X
8:00	X	X	X	X			X
9:00	X		X				X
10:00							X

X indicates study periods; O indicates work blocks.

191

shoulder muscles, and so on. Rest those muscles that were being used and exercise those that were not.

Planning work includes more than the weekly time schedule itself. It includes making plans for the term. Here the most appropriate word for such a quality is *foresight*. This kind of planning includes mapping out the dates when various papers and reports or reading assignments should be completed and recording periods of days that will be used for review for examinations. The last significant aspect of planning is done each time the instructor speaks or gestures. A student with foresight will note the instructor's methods, peculiarities, and attitudes about attendance and class participation.[8] These play a decided role in the grading in a course. If he is a "fact" man and gives essay examinations, if he places strong emphasis on the very practical side of home economics, if he has a decided belief about the original cause of World War II—these things should be carefully noted for future use.

Improving Your Reading Skills

The instructors' lectures, to a great extent, come from numerous books. The instructors help the student by showing him the essential messages of the books, relating illustrations of principles from their own experience, and stimulating further insight or creative thoughts about the subject matter. They try to effect in the student an interest that will compel him to search further and deeper into the subject by reading textbooks, reserve reference books, or an assortment of related volumes in the library. Often a specific number of pages or chapters or a specific topic is assigned. The depth is generally greater than that encountered in high school; the reading assignments will be longer and more frequent. It is to be expected that the student will have to improve his reading skills. Even the best readers can improve and would probably like to learn how.

It is difficult to define a good reader, because this is not a static position. One who works to increase his speed and understanding but stops trying to improve when he believes that he is a good reader is no longer a good reader. Thus, when Lass and Wilson attempt to de-

[8] Abraham Lass and Eugene Wilson, *The College Student's Handbook* (New York: David White Company, 1965), pp. 27–28.

scribe the characteristics of a good reader, the student should bear in mind that here is a working situation in which the good reader is trying to better his ability.

What Is the Good Reader Like?

He reads easily and rapidly. He understands what he reads—readily and fully. He remembers what he reads.

He reads with a purpose. Before he starts to read, he knows what he wants to get out of his reading: facts, ideas, answers to questions, pleasure, etc.

He reads groups of words—"thought units."

He reads rapidly or slowly, adapting his reading speed to his reading purpose and the kind of material he is reading.

He has a wide, varied, accurate vocabulary. He keeps adding to his vocabulary.

He reads critically. He does not accept anything he reads without first questioning its accuracy, validity, motives.

He reads many kinds of materials in many fields.

He enjoys reading.[9]

The "good reader" principles will give the student a foundation to begin reading. Like the confidence that a system of writing notes gives a student, the organization of having a method of reading is of great personal benefit, too. Various methods will be discussed, including the four-step method of Dr. Charles Bird, the five-step method by Robert M. Bear, and the PQRST method suggested by Southern Illinois University. The basic principles of all three are the same, yet each has its individual suggestions that may help the student.

Regardless of the method followed, the preliminary step in beginning to read a new book will generally be the same. This involves reading the preface, the introduction, and the table of contents. There are three significant advantages to this procedure. First, the student gets an immediate suggestion as to the author's point of view. Second, the entire book may be condensed in the table of contents, affording the student a preview and base for continuing study. And last but not least, tying in new material with past knowledge by reading the table of contents thoroughly makes learning "faster, easier, and more permanent."[10]

The method suggested by Dr. Charles Bird[11] of the University of Minnesota is simple and easy to remember. In condensed form, the method follows these steps:

[9] Lass and Wilson, op. cit., pp. 61–62.
[10] Gerken, op. cit., pp. 17–18.
[11] Ibid., pp. 19–20.

1. First, read the assignment rapidly; concentrate on major divisions, new terms, and summaries.
2. Reread, section by section, for content. Plan possible examination questions and note these on the left half of the left-hand note page. Close the textbook and answer the questions.
3. Section by section, open the book and correct the answers if they need clarification or change.
4. Cover all of the answers, expose one at a time and answer each *rapidly*. If the answers come haltingly, this is the time to clarify them.

The four-step method summarized is a read, reread, test, retest system, which is very similar to the five-step method of Robert M. Bear. The principles in each of the methods are the same; only some small suggestions vary. Bear's steps follow this order:

1. Make a preliminary survey.
2. Read for understanding.
3. Test yourself.
4. Take notes.
5. Review.[12]

During the preliminary survey the student will relate the title of the chapter to the preceding parts and check for any further hints of organization. He then reads the summarizing paragraphs carefully, picking out the generalizations. The end of the chapter should be skimmed for summarizing and reviews. Thus, in the preliminary survey the student should make a practical individual adaptation of trying to tie materials together and looking for organization, summaries, and generalizations.[13]

In the second step reading for understanding will involve asking questions as the material is read. It is helpful for the student to change the bold-type phrases at the beginning of sections into questions to ask himself. He continues to look for relating parts and the transition. Reading for understanding involves continually asking oneself why, how, who, when.[14]

Testing oneself incorporates the answering of the questions that were posed in the preceding step. This is the time to check back for

[12] Robert M. Bear, "How To Get the Most Out of Your Textbooks" (New York: The American Textbook Publishers Institute, 1959), p. 3.
[13] Ibid., p. 3.
[14] Ibid., pp. 6–7.

uncertainties. Following this method of testing oneself helps the student to concentrate during the reading.[15]

The next step is a longer one. This is the time in which notes can be made. Bear suggests employing a system of taking notes in the text itself. (This is an advantage of buying rather than renting textbooks.) Bear suggests bearing in mind these points of outlining.[16]

1. Distinguish the main points from the subordinate ones.
2. Include enough detail.
3. Use markings that make the relationships between points clear.
4. Suit your system to the subject matter.

Further points to consider include avoiding underlining too much and obscuring the main points. Any system can be overdone. Using brackets around key phrases of important ideas and parentheses around less important ideas is a helpful technique. Also, using an outlining method of I, II; A, B; 1, 2 will show relation, organization, and importance of concepts. This step of making notes should be done after the reading of each entire section.[17]

The final step of the five-step method is the review. One should try to recall the key points or generalizations. Here the notes that have been taken will be of extreme importance. Questions at the chapter end, too, can be beneficial. Then, in order to clarify hazy points and once again set the principles in one's mind, the student should reread the section of the chapter that is involved.[18] The reader will want to individualize any system that he chooses so that it will be his very own.

The method suggested by Southern Illinois University may differ slightly from the others. It is called the *PQRST method.*

P Preview
Q Question
R Read
S Study
T Test

Again the preliminary step is a preview of the material, catching the main ideas and summaries. Then the topic headings are made into

[15] Ibid., p. 7.
[16] Ibid., p. 8.
[17] Ibid., p. 9.
[18] Ibid., p. 10.

question form, whereas in the first two methods this was done during the thorough reading. R then stands for "read," the third step, which is simply that—reading in detail. Fourth, the material is studied; this involves the making of an outline. (This was not included in the four-step method but fell after testing one's understanding and before the final review in the five-step method.) Last in PQRST is the testing. This involves both self-testing and reviewing the sections of which one is uncertain.[19]

Hence, the main ideas are the same in all three techniques. More than one was illustrated to stress to the student the idea that no one method is the best method, and that whichever one is chosen should be personalized in its use. Once a method is adapted, the confidence and organization that it brings will hasten greater learning and reading efficiency. All three methods involved a concentrated effort; in some courses that involve heavy reading assignments the preceding methods will not be possible. In such a case an exception may be made by the student. Thus, five steps[20] are suggested as an alternative:

1. Read the main points of the chapter, which are often outlined in the table of contents.
2. Skim the chapter, reading the main points.
3. Rapidly read the chapter, going a bit deeper into the material. Jot down the important words and phrases.
4. Close the book and write a brief summary.
5. Open the book and rapidly check the summary against the chapter itself.

In certain courses in which particulars rather than generalizations and principles receive great emphasis, memory or memorizing becomes extremely important. A home economics student may find such a need in a foreign language, a science, or a history course, for example. Before one considers a technique, one precaution is memorizing only when it is necessary; as much as possible, think and reason and learn by association.[21]

Memorizing has been found to be most effective when it is done in scattered, short practice periods. Three-by-five note cards have been suggested as flash cards. These can easily be pulled out and reviewed

[19] Student Counseling and Testing Center, Office of Student Affairs, "Study Hints" (Carbondale, Ill.: Southern Illinois University, n.d.), p. 3.

[20] Gerken, op. cit., p. 21.

[21] Cole, op. cit., p. 31.

before a class begins or while one is waiting for a date or standing in a line. There are pros and cons to the use of memory devices. For some students these devices have failed. In the end it is up to the individual student, but flash cards are suggested as a method proven by its use.

"Is there merit in speed reading?" "When should it be used?" "How can one increase his reading speed?" These are questions that students ask or about which they vaguely wonder. There are many reading assignments in college and little time in which to cover them—there *is* a need for speed reading. Yet courses differ in their assigned amount of reading and the depth of the context. In one course speed reading may be important; in another intensive depth reading is a necessity. According to Lass and Wilson[22] the rate should be determined by what is being read, why it is being read, and the individual goals for the material. Speed reading is important when the material assigned is long and not very deep and the purpose is to understand the major principles of the work.

The answer to the third question requires more extensive consideration. Inasmuch as understanding must always come first, efficient reading aids must coincide with effectiveness. Phi Eta Sigma, a men's scholastic honorary, suggests the following aids:[23]

1. Have something definite to look for when you read.
2. Extend your work knowledge.
3. Read silently.

A definite purpose helps one to concentrate. Learning the new vocabulary of a discipline will help the student to read the material faster and more effectively. Avoiding excessive lip movement allows faster reading. Mouthing the words takes far more time than seeing words in thought units. Further speed reading suggestions come from the Counseling and Testing Center of Southern Illinois University:[24]

1. Eliminate word pronunciation and lip movements.
2. Read for *ideas*, not words.
3. Try to get the main thought of each paragraph.
4. Have in mind something definite for which you are reading.
5. Focus your attention only upon the meaning.
6. Reduce re-reading to a minimum.

[22] Lass and Wilson, op. cit., p. 71.
[23] Phi Eta Sigma, op. cit., pp. 3–5.
[24] Student Counseling and Testing Center, Office of Student Affairs, op. cit., p. 2.

197

7. Try to read more rapidly.
8. Spend a regular time each day reading easy material at an ever-increasing speed.

These rules summarize and add to those previously made concerning reading speed and efficiency. Therefore, the question. "How can one increase his reading speed?" can be answered first by understanding, then by practice.

One of the suggestions for more rapid reading is the broadening of one's vocabulary. This is also a requirement for thorough understanding of the subject matter of a discipline. Another advantage of building a vocabulary is that:

Every new word adds something to your understanding of yourself, of the people and the things in the world around you. Every new word gives you another avenue of entry into the world of books and ideas. Every new word you master enables you to communicate with others with greater clarity and vividness.[25]

Building a vocabulary is not a two-week process as some books may attempt to make one believe. It is a lifetime process, just as increasing reading effectiveness is. Therefore, any statements of vocabulary building that are included in this chapter are not shortcuts or hard-and-fast rules; they are only suggestions for building a more effective vocabulary.[26]

1. The number of books read is vital to increasing a vocabulary. The more one reads of the better books, the more likely it is that his vocabulary will be increased.
2. The habit of using a dictionary will increase word knowledge. It means that the new term will be learned as soon as it is read; time is spent on thinking about the word—valuable for memory, and the habit will aid in developing an inquiring mind.
3. A notebook especially for vocabulary may be valuable. The student can more easily find all his new vocabulary words when he has a few moments to spend on them.
4. Greek and Latin roots, prefixes, and suffixes play a vital part in the words of a language—both common and technical. Learning some of these will help the student when he encounters new words.
5. Interest developed in the origins of words will reinforce one's attempts to increase his vocabulary.

[25] Lass and Wilson, op. cit., p. 65.
[26] Ibid., pp. 66–69.

6. The more experiences the student encounters, the greater depth and breadth of vocabulary he will establish.
7. The habit of collecting words is important in making this a lifetime process. One becomes a "word collector."
8. A thesaurus is a further aid to vocabulary building. This is an extraordinary book of synonyms, antonyms, and related words.
9. Each time the student learns the meaning of a word, the learning of its synonyms and antonyms will make it more firm in his mind.
10. Basic vocabulary lists for the various subjects may help in the organization of thinking for each.
11. The addition of a few words to one's vocabulary every day, too, will help increase his vocabulary to become a habit and a lifetime interest.

Many students will tend to skip over graphs, charts, or diagrams, believing that time will be saved. Yet these representations are included for the student's reading. They summarize in a small space a

COLLEGE EXPECTANCIES*

Reasons for Going to College	Per Cent of Students Checking Each Reason
1. In order to prepare for a certain vocation	71.8
2. For general self-improvement in culture and ideals	64.5
3. Because a person with a college degree can obtain a better position and earn more money	47.6
4. Because of my interest in specific studies and my desire to pursue them further	31.9
5. Because a person with a college degree has more prestige and a higher social standing	31.8
6. Because my parents wished it	20.8
7. Reasons unknown	9.9
8. Because of the social attractions or athletic opportunities of college life	8.2
9. Because so many of my friends and relatives had gone to college that it seemed the thing to do	5.4
10. In order to show people that I have as good a mind as anyone	2.3

* Mildred Thurow Tate, *Home Economics As a Profession* (New York: McGraw-Hill Book Company, Inc., 1961), p. 13.

number of facts and relationships that would take many words to express.[27] Two examples are included here to illustrate to the student the interest as well as the concise organization of ideas that can be gained from representations.

In the chart "College Expectancies," the relation of each reason to the others can be plainly seen. The percentages of students checking each reason can be compared at a glance. The first reason, that of preparing for a vocation, was checked 71.8 per cent of the time, whereas the tenth reason, showing others that one has a good mind, was checked only 2.3 per cent of the time. The information is concise in the chart, whereas it would have taken considerable space and possibly less interesting reading to present the material in paragraph form.

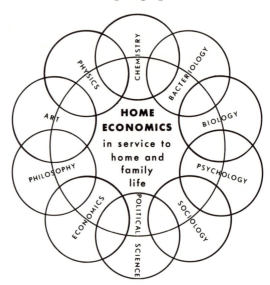

FIGURE 4-1. *The relation of home economics to other fields.*

The diagram shown is not complete by itself, but it illustrates from the context of *Home Economics Careers for You* the unique responsibility that the profession has in integrating contributions from biology, sociology, art, political science, and so on into "one functional whole for service to families."[28] The illustration shows at a glance the relation of home economics to these other fields.

In the student's reading of college assignments, reports, term papers,

[27] Cole, op. cit., p. 23.
[28] Velma Phillips, *Home Economics Careers for You* (New York: Harper & Row, 1962), pp. 88–89.

and research, he will often need to refer to professional journals and related periodicals. It is believed that a list of home economics professional sources will be valuable to the freshman home economics student. The student is not expected to memorize this list or to use all of these sources during the first year. Instead, this list may help him to begin to become familiar with the names of the professional volumes in his area of interest for future use.

Clothing and Textiles:

The Ambassador
The American Fabrics Magazine
The Department Store Economist
Harper's Magazine
House and Home
Interiors
Textile Organon
Vogue
Women's Wear Daily

Food and Nutrition:

Composition of Foods (bulletin by USDA)
Handbook of Food Preparation (by AHEA)
Journal of Home Economics
Nutritive Value of Foods (a USDA bulletin in common household measurements)
Other U.S. Department of Agriculture bulletins and books
Articles in newspapers, current magazines, and advertising—evaluate carefully
Information from UNICEF and FAO

Home and Family:

Changing Times
Consumer Education
Consumer Reports
Journal of Childhood Education
Journal of Educational Research
Journal of Experimental Education
Journal of Home Economics

Journal of Home Management and Family Economics
Journal of Marriage and Family Living
Journal of Nursery Education

Home Economics Education:

American Vocational Journal
Changing Times
Illinois Teacher of Home Economics
Illinois Vocational Progress
Journal of Home Economics
NEA Journal
Practical Forecast
What's New in Home Economics

Evaluate the attitudes and values reflected and the points being stressed
in lay magazines, such as:

Good Housekeeping
Ladies' Home Journal
Better Homes and Gardens

Studying Effectively

Webster defines study as the "application of the mind to books, arts,
or any subject, for acquiring knowledge." This is where studying goes
beyond reading effectively, because it involves more than books. It
involves concentration on ideas and concepts, on class notes, and on
many other materials, whether they be magazines, newspapers, reference books, pamphlets, paintings, sculpture, or musical works. Studying
is a questioning, analyzing, creative, reflective concentration, which will
become a habit for the student—a habit that will provide motivation.
The student will find that studying benefits him in gaining:[29]

1. More from the work.
2. Better grades.
3. Better chances for admission to graduate or professional schools.

[29] Lass and Wilson, op. cit., pp. 90–91.

FIGURE 4-2. An *environment conducive to study.*

4. Greater chances at getting a desired job.
5. Prestige.
6. A feeling of relaxation.
7. Enjoyment of college.

Learning to concentrate is not a simple task. One suggestion for facilitating concentration is to arrange a study environment that is conducive to concentration. Luella Cole gives five rules[30] to follow: using the same place for studying most of the time, keeping distractions off the desk, keeping one's back to one's roommate, developing a routine of work, and beginning to study immediately upon sitting at the desk. People concentrate differently, of course. Some are able to concentrate with others present, with a radio playing softly, while singing or whistling, or even being in a noisy setting. This, too, is an individual problem. There is an advantage to using a radio for some people—the noise may give a secure feeling of companionship. For these people, silence could be oppressive and isolation could be distracting.[31] Thus concentration is an individual problem—the background for studying should depend upon the student's efficiency.

Yet a student just beginning in college generally would like to have

[30] Cole, op. cit., pp. 12–14.
[31] Ibid., p. 16.

some suggestions about a study environment before he adapts it to his own needs. Gerken[32] has presented some ideas to consider in choosing this environment:

1. Almost all studying should be done at one table or desk far from distractions.
2. The chair should not allow one to sink down. A straight-backed chair will help one maintain an erect, concentrating position.
3. The light should have no glare, shadows, or light-and-dark spots. If possible, it should be indirect or semidirect.
4. Only study materials should be on the desk.
5. "Giving it all one has" musters a set of mind that brings continued concentration.
6. Accuracy comes first, then speed.
7. Study should be done in relation to coming examinations, in reference to speed, problems, analyses.
8. A study routine will afford more time for nonroutine activities.
9. When interest and ability are applied, one does not need to wait for inspiration.
10. The question of a radio and soft music to study by is left to the individual's good judgment. Television takes more concentration— it involves seeing and hearing; it cannot be a background to worthwhile studying, as a radio may be in some cases.
11. Worry may cause inability to concentrate. If a student cannot face his problems openly, a counselor can be of help.

How much time should be spent in studying? This question was reviewed earlier, but we repeat that not so much time should be spent that one overworks or so little time that one underworks.

The student should begin studying as a course commences. Because one forgets rapidly after the first encounter, it is best to review soon after each lecture. Immediate reinforcement will cause longer remembering. In order to reinforce learning, repeat or review from the onset of a course.

"How should I review?" students ask. A few suggestions at this point may give a better understanding of the relation of studying throughout the term and a review for an examination. For some people, small-group study can be effective. This will depend on keeping to a small group (two or three persons) and making a list of topics and

[32] Gerken, op. cit., pp. 12–15.

sticking to them. A fourth suggestion is that all those involved in the group be about the same in knowledge of the subject to avoid wasting time tutoring. Small-group study has its value when used well throughout the term.

One should review the questions that he predicts will be on the examination during reading for class and note taking. The student should recognize the points stressed by both the teacher and the text and review them. Always, while studying, one should keep alert to the ways of transferring his knowledge to other subjects, from one chapter to another, and from a class to a television program, a game, or an outside activity. Prediction, emphasis, and transfer throughout the term may be three key approaches to studying.

Heston[33] suggests that one study vocabulary; formulas, laws, and rules; famous people and important dates; and relationships. We add principles and applications to that list.

Writing Class Notes

One of the significant differences between high school and college is the stronger emphasis upon class notes in the college classroom. In high school sometimes an entire class hour is spent on making one point. The point may have been said in many different ways, it may have been illustrated, and the class may have discussed it. In contrast, a college instructor generally makes numerous points and often never repeats them. Yet a student may expect to have them appear on an examination. What can the student do? The most strategic advice we can give the student is that he learn how to write class notes.

It has been suggested that there is a difference between "taking" class notes and "making" notes. Gerken[34] suggests that taking notes involves only the ears and the hand holding the pen. The thoughts of the instructor enter through the ears and flow directly out in writing. Making notes, he suggests, involves the important in-between stop—the brain. Here one digests facts, analyzes opinions, and questions the thoughts and the ideas left unsaid. When the notes then flow from the pencil, they are in the writer's own words and include the questions he wishes to ask or check upon. The terms *taking* or *making* notes may not be so significant as the idea behind the terms—one should be less

---

[33] Heston, op. cit., p. 8.
[34] Gerken, op. cit., pp. 33–34.

concerned with writing than with thinking; both are necessary for the effective making of notes.

There are significant advantages to digesting and analyzing the lecture while writing notes. From Gerken's[35] *Study Your Way Through School* come these suggested benefits:

1. Interest is built.
2. More attention is paid—an activity contributing to learning.
3. Learning from day to day may be interconnected. Tying up the ideas of a lecture brings learning as a unit.
4. Good schoolwork brings success, which in turn breeds more successes in other work—a fine habit.
5. A final review for the examination by a reading of one's notes is the most efficient type of preparation for the evaluation.

Six simple rules[36] may aid the student in writing notes. Practice them for at least a month and they will become a habit of which you will seldom need to be conscious.

Figure 4-3. *Correct posture in class.*

[35] Ibid., p. 34.
[36] Ibid., pp. 35–36.

1. Leaning forward and avoiding relaxing too much will help focus attention.
2. Keeping a large notebook results in more effective notes.
3. Dating each page will keep one from getting lost.
4. Making notes legibly and rapidly and using abbreviations will be invaluable.

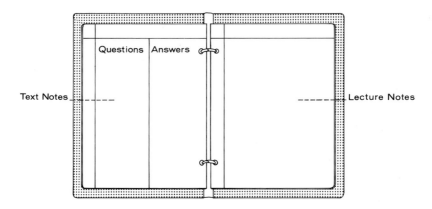

FIGURE 4-4. *Take notes effectively.*

5. Taking notes on the right-hand page and outlining the chapter on the left will keep similar material together.
6. Keeping course notes together by either using a spiral notebook for each course or using separate sections of a loose-leaf notebook will provide the organization that is necessary to effective study.

You may be asking, "How will I know what the more important points of a lecture are?" Of course it takes practice to catch readily the emphases of the instructor, but some suggestions may help. (Even though hints throughout this book may tend to be associated in your mind with common sense, it is wise to think about them. A reminder of common-sense ideas has helped many a person.) The lecturer underlines the important points by:[37]

1. The time he spends on a particular point.
2. The number of times he makes the point.
3. His gestures and the tone of his voice. His gestures will be more

[37] Lass and Wilson, op. cit., pp. 111–112.

forceful and animated and his voice will become rapid, deliberate, dramatic, urgent, or insistent, as he makes a significant point.

In large college classes you may be surprised to see students reading a newspaper, writing a letter, or sleeping. These people are not there to gain an insight into the ideas of the course or the thought of the instructor; they are in class to be marked present. You too may be tempted in some classes that seem boring or are not taught well to follow suit. A college instructor lectures for the people who are there to learn and he may disregard the others, so go ahead and sleep if you want to. No one will tap you on the shoulder and ask you if they can help you in the class. It is your responsibility to *yourself* to succeed, and failure will hurt no one but you. But we believe that the student who was just described is not you, for otherwise you would not be studying this text. Instead, maybe you would like to know what can be done to gain an interest in what appears boring. Making a subject that is boring at first interesting is not simple, but it is quite possible with some effort on your part.

Concentrating is a process that psychologically is a good deal like sleep. Neither will come in response to a conscious effort, but both will occur naturally when the circumstances are favorable.[38]

It is easy for others to say, "Be interested in your subjects, so that you can concentrate in classes." But it can be very difficult when one does not know how to go about it. First must come the understanding that interests are made, not born, and thus, it is possible to develop interests. It follows that there is lack of information when concentration is lacking. The best suggestion that can be made at this time is that one muster the determination to study the subject enough to find a practical use for the information. Then concentration should be easy, with an ever-increasing interest.

A second reason for lack of interest is a block or prejudice against courses that are not in a student's major field. Gerken[39] reflects that living in a vacuum is not a characteristic of a well-educated person. One must understand the relationship between his field and others, as well as being familiar with many different areas of knowledge. With this attitude of usefulness and need for knowledge in other fields, an interest will develop.

[38] Cole, op. cit., p. 14.
[39] Gerken, op. cit., pp. 4–5.

Once a system has been adopted, most tasks are found to be considerably easier. You have probably found this to be true in washing dishes, frying a chicken, or even typing a letter. A system, according to Webster, is "regular method or order." Thus, it follows that when a method of writing notes has been individualized and adopted, it too will be easier.

Two note-writing methods have proved workable. One is a three-column and the other a two-column form. Neither is purported to be superior to the other, and it is not to be assumed that these two are the only note-writing devices. The student must decide for himself which method will best fulfill his needs and adapt it for greatest efficiency.

The three-column system uses two vertical lines drawn on each note page from the top to the bottom. One should be approximately two inches from the left edge and the other is one inch from the right edge. Notes are written in the middle large section. This includes charts, tables, graphs, illustrations, definitions, equations, formulas, new terms, and other aids to learning. This section should be in the student's own words. After the class the notes should be summarized or a skeleton outline should be made in the left column of the page. Tie-up lines or arrows in colored pencil from main points in the outline to the center may be a further aid. The third step, done during the review for the examination, is condensing the page into a few lines written on the right side of the page. Then the student can make a quick final review by turning the notebook on its side, flipping each page, and studying the condensed sections.[40]

The two-column method involves dividing each sheet into two parts by drawing a line down the center. The left-hand column is used for recording the important points of the lecture. The right-hand column is used for comments, questions, recommended readings, or personal reminders suggested by the lecture.[41]

Writing a Term Paper or Report

Do the words *term paper* send shudders down your spine? Does *report* spell confusion and disorganization? They need not, if the student learns a systematic approach to the writing of term papers and

[40] Ibid., pp. 36–38.
[41] Lass and Wilson, op. cit., p. 110.

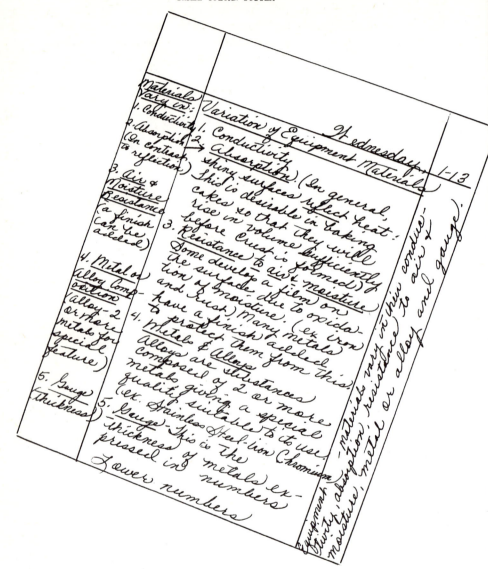

* The notes come from an equipment lecture by Dr. Betty Jane Johnston, when she was Chairman of the Department of Home and Family, School of Home Economics, Southern Illinois University. Dr. Johnston is currently Chairman, Department of Home Economics, Northern Illinois University.

* The notes come from an equipment lecture by Dr. Betty Jane Johnston, when she was Chairman of the Department of Home and Family, School of Home Economics, Southern Illinois University.

reports. Once a student learns to organize his approach to writing, he can tackle any size assignment.

An instructor generally will not define *term paper* unless it is assigned in an English class. Thus, it is explained here for the student's benefit. A term paper has a point of view—a specific attitude or vantage point of the writer; it is limited in scope—the topic is neither too broad nor too narrow to cover adequately in a paper; it is logically planned and developed; it contains appropriate quotations and references; it uses a variety of sources; it supports statements with authoritative evidence—opinions are given weight when an authority has reflected on the subject or researched it; it is clearly written; and it lacks grammatical errors in punctuation and usage.[42]

College instructors assign or suggest term papers, because they believe that planning, preparing, and writing a paper are valuable in:[43]

1. Choosing and limiting a subject.
2. Using resources.
3. Reading purposefully.
4. Selecting meaningful data or ideas.
5. Taking notes on selected material.
6. Organizing material into a paper.
7. Outlining.
8. Developing writing skills and vocabulary.

Throughout life people write for the purpose of expressing their thoughts and opinions and describing the world accurately and effectively. One develops good writing by writing. "We learn by doing and by overcoming our errors. We learn by practicing the activity we want to learn."[44]

If the subject choice is left to the student, he should select one that is of individual interest, is specific enough for adequate covering, is broad enough to write about, and is of enough importance to be worth the time spent.

When a topic is assigned by the instructor or after it has been chosen, it is helpful to carry cards and jot down ideas as one goes about his day. Then these ideas will be used for an outline. The student can formulate many ideas in a library by browsing or seeking specific advice from a librarian.

[42] Ibid., p. 115.
[43] Ibid., pp. 114–115.
[44] Gerken, op. cit., p. 25.

An outline becomes a "framework about which you may build a coherent and meaningful theme."[45] It includes all the main topics that will be brought out in the paper along with support of the main topics.

After choosing the topic, considering possible areas to cover, and writing a tentative outline, the student will visit a library. Here one of the first steps generally is using the card catalogue. Books throughout the library are listed on small cards by author, title, and subject. For a term paper or report, when one has done little previous reading on the subject, he will first consider the subject cards. Later, if he wants to see what other books one author has written or if one reference leads him to another, the student can then use the author or title cards.

On a catalogue card will be found the call number enabling the student to find the book, the author's name—last name first—the author's date of birth, the title of the book, the publisher, the date of publication, and the number of pages in the book.

362.14
B612e
1965

> Brooks, Josephine (1920–   )
> Economic Research Affecting the Consumer,
> Joseph Brady & Company, 1965, pp. 372.

Cross-reference: consumer, economics, title, and author.

Explanations of the data that appear:

362.14	The classification of the subject by the Dewey Decimal System gives each book such a call number. This is one method in which volumes are organized on the shelves.
B612e	*B* stands for the first letter of the author's last name and 612 is the author's number; *e* is the first letter of the first important word in the title of the book.

[45] Ibid., p. 26.

1965	This is the publication date of the book. It is placed prominently, because in many cases the date is vital to the research. If the student is searching for the latest consumer economics research, he would not want to bother searching for a book dated 1965.
Brooks, Josephine	The *B* in the call number stood for *Brooks.* The first name of the author follows the surname.
(1920–)	The author was born in 1920 and is still living.
Economic Research Affecting the Consumer	Often on a catalogue card the title of the book is not underlined.
Joseph Brady & Company	The publisher.
1965	Publication date.
pp. 372	Number of pages in the book.
Cross-reference	This tells where else the same card is listed in the catalogue. Sometimes the cross-reference will suggest to the student related topics to check.

For the latest information on a subject, periodicals should be consulted. Various indexes group all the periodicals of a given period of time under their subjects. Thus, one can turn quickly first to the volume of the year he would like to consult and then to the subject listed alphabetically. Some of these indexes[46] are

Reader's Guide to Periodical Literature (probably the most-used index)
International Index to Periodicals (includes foreign periodicals)
The New York Times Index (articles are listed by the subject from *The New York Times* newspaper)
Special indexes in art, agriculture, education, engineering, and psychology
Indexes for abstracts (summaries of books and articles in special fields)

[46] Lass and Wilson, op. cit., p. 57.

Encyclopedias are sometimes useful in listing new sources for reference. Inasmuch as an article in an encyclopedia is condensed to the major topics, it may give the student a preview of the subject matter. Hence, he may seek further information in the resources cited. Examples of encyclopedias are

Encyclopedia Britannica
Encyclopedia Americana
New International Encyclopedia
Columbia Encyclopedia
Collier's Encyclopedia
Catholic Encyclopedia
Jewish Encyclopedia

Generally a good desk dictionary is sufficient, but occasionally an unabridged dictionary would be helpful. For the most part one of the following desk dictionaries[47] will suffice

American College Dictionary
Webster's New Collegiate Dictionary
Thorndike-Barnhardt Comprehensive Desk Dictionary
New College Standard Dictionary

Other occasionally helpful sources are[48]

Bartlett, John. *Familiar Quotations*
Stevenson, Burton E. *Home Book of Quotations*
Fowler, H. W. *A Dictionary of Modern English Usage*
Roget, P. M. *Thesaurus of English Words and Phrases*
Webster's *Dictionary of Synonyms and Antonyms*
Webster's *Biographical Dictionary*
Webster's *Geographical Dictionary*

When using these sources, a student copies down all the references (title, author, and call number, or title of article, periodical, author, and volume) that appear to relate to his topic. This list is the forerunner of his bibliography. From here he finds the sources and begins to read. Notes are taken in various ways and in various forms. The

---

[47] Ibid., p. 59.
[48] Ibid.

suggestion by most authors, though, is to take notes on large cards, keeping just one subject per card.

These cards later can easily be separated and arranged according to the outline. As notes are taken a student will generally find the need to alter his tentative outline. Finding new information not expected and failing to find expected information will make this alteration necessary. Thus the library steps involve finding all the available sources on a subject, reading them, taking notes (preferably on note cards), and rearranging the outline, if necessary.

Rhythm, life, and vividness are some of the requirements for an interesting theme or paper. It is suggested that one write the paper rapidly at first for freshness and smoothness. Condensing, correcting, and making transitions can come later.

What are footnotes and when are they used? A footnote is a reference to the source of the information used in a paper or a reference to a source to which the reader can go for further information. A third purpose for using such a reference is to protect oneself from a charge of plagiarism. When an author publishes a work, he is given a right of ownership; no one may use his ideas without giving credit to him. Therefore, footnotes are given for the benefit of the reader, the author cited, and the writer himself.

The form of footnotes varies occasionally and often instructors will give their preference. If no mention is made of this, it may be wise to use the basic form as given by Turabian.[49] (Kate L. Turabian is recognized as one of the authorities on term paper, thesis, and dissertation format.) Her suggested form for a reference to a book is

No. Author, *Title* (Publishing City: Publisher, Publishing Date), page.

Ex. [1] Kate L. Turabian, *A Manual for Writers of Term Papers, Theses and Dissertations* (Chicago: The University of Chicago Press, 1967), p. 19.

For a periodical the basic form is somewhat different.

No. Author, "Title of Article," *Title of Periodical,* Volume Number in Arabic Numerals (Date), page number(s).

Ex. [1] Eva Medved, "Television in Nutrition Education," *Journal of Home Economics,* 58 (March, 1966), 167–170.[50]

[49] Kate L. Turabian, *A Manual for Writers of Term Papers, Theses and Dissertations* (Chicago: The University of Chicago Press, 1967), p. 19.
[50] Ibid., p. 34.

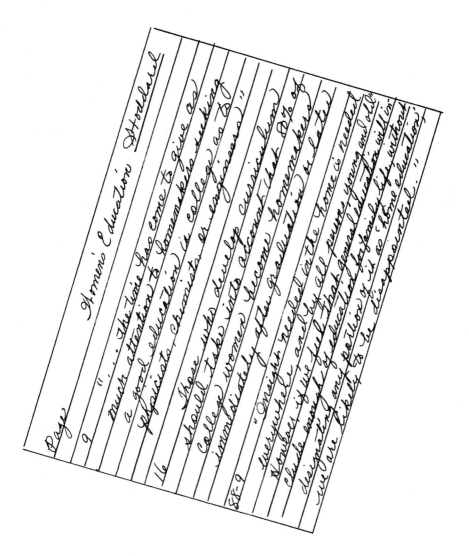

Women's Education Stoddard

Page 9

"...The have has come to give as much attention to homemakers as to a good education' (is college) as to physicists, chemists, or engineers."

16 Those who develop curriculum should take into account that 80% of college women become homemakers immediately after graduation or later.

88-9 "Everywhere and by all means, if we feel that the home is neglected, the numbers if we feel that all parents young and old should be warned that domestic education will in no parior of an education to family life without designating any portion of it as 'home education'. We are likely to be disappointed."

* George D. Stoddard, *On the Education of Women* (New York: Macmillan Publishing Co., Inc., 1950).

217

When a reference is cited a second time or more, the writer need not repeat the entire footnote. The term *Ibid.* is used when no citation of another work has intervened between the first citation of the work and this second one. *Ibid.* comes from Latin and stands for "in the same place." Sometimes it is underlined because it is a foreign term. The basic form[51] is

No. Ibid., page.

Ex. [12] C. d'A. Gerken, "Study Your Way Through School" (Chicago: Science Research Associates, Inc., 1953), p. 6.

[13] Ibid.

[14] Ibid., p. 13.

When one or more citations have intervened, rather than *ibid.*, *op. cit.* is used meaning "in the work cited." When only one work by the author has been used, only the author's surname, *op. cit.*, and the page are needed after the original citation. When there is a second book by the same author, the complete title should be included. If more than one author has the same surname, the first name should be included. The basic form[52] follows:

No. Surname, op. cit., page.

Ex. [16] Luella Cole, *Student's Guide to Efficient Study*, 4th ed. (New York: Holt, Rinehart and Winston, 1961), p. 1.

[17] Abraham Lass and Eugene Wilson, *The College Student's Handbook* (New York: David White Company, 1965), pp. 27–28.

[18] Cole, op. cit., p. 14.

Loc. cit. is the third abbreviated term used from Latin, meaning "in the place cited." This means not only that it is in the same work cited previously with intervening reference(s), but it is *from the same page*. Thus, if Lass and Wilson, pp. 27–28, were again documented as footnote 19, it would appear as:

[19] Lass and Wilson, loc. cit.

[51] Ibid., p. 43.
[52] Ibid., p. 47.

The basic form[53] is

^{No.} Surname, loc. cit.

At the very end of the paper all the relevant sources are listed in a bibliography. Some writers prefer to include only those most complete and useful sources in a "selected bibliography." Commonly, references are grouped first by classification, such as books, articles, and periodicals; public documents; reports; unpublished material; and other sources. Within each group the sources are alphabetized by the surname of the author. If no author is included, the first major word of the title is alphabetized along with the authors. If more than one work by the same author is used in those works after the first, the author's name is substituted for by a line about eight spaces long, ending with a period. The features of the format contrasting with that of a footnote are that the first line is even with the left margin and a second or third line is indented; the surname comes first followed by a comma, the first name or initials, and a period; and no parentheses are placed around the publication information.[54] (For more information on rule exceptions and specific differences on the format of footnotes, bibliographies, and other details of a paper, the reader is asked to consult Kate L. Turabian's *A Manual for Writers of Term Papers, Theses and Dissertations* or a similar reference.)

At this point the paper has been written in its rough-draft stage. It is time for proofreading and revision. Here words become more important in their usage, rhythm, and effectiveness. It is well to avoid slang and too formal, stiff, or pompous words. The only use of these would appear in a quotation. Words connoting action are effective. Adverbs and verb-adverb combinations are suggested for frequent use. Adjectives should be avoided, because they may become trite. When they are needed, they should be carefully chosen. Sentences should be kept short for clarity. A final suggestion is the use of attention devices between straight explanatory writing to stress points and keep the readers interested and entertained.[55]

Revising is done in order to replace dull or hackneyed words and check the transition of words or ideas. Having a friend read the paper aloud helps one to see the rough spots.[56]

[53] Ibid., p. 47.
[54] Ibid., pp. 75–77.
[55] Gerken, op. cit., p. 28.
[56] Ibid., pp. 28–29.

Writing an Examination

At the onset of a college career the importance of long-term goals is stressed. The student will understand that getting good grades is a legitimate short-term goal that helps in achieving the more important later ones. Through the student's careful planning, conscientious note-taking, thoughtful reading, and efficient studying, he can be well versed in a particular subject. Yet for grades consistent with one's knowledge, the student must be able to let the instructor know the content of his learning. Telling the content of one's knowledge and using one's own abilities more effectively in an examination are the essence of this section.

There are personal advantages to taking examinations, which the student will recognize. First, the content of the test as well as the results will show strengths and weaknesses. These may help a student to judge his own potential and make decisions accordingly. In both the review for an examination and the test itself, a student can gain new ideas about relationships and principles. And third, the test results can show others one's achievements for scholarships, job acceptances, and other similar needs for results.[57]

The instructor or examiner also has purposes in mind. He seeks to measure progress, find out what has been achieved in class, and decide what areas still need concentration.[58] Examinations help him to evaluate his own teaching as well as the increase in student understanding.

Examinations may be classified as to their purpose or their form. Purpose classifications involve the evaluating of interests, appreciation, understanding, ability, knowledge, and so on. The general forms are the objective and the subjective, or essay, examination. An objective test is one with answers that are clear-cut, brief, and factual. It measures the *"accuracy* of your knowledge and reasoning" and the *"breadth* of your knowledge."[59] In contrast to the breadth that an objective test can cover, the essay tests give a "chance to discuss thoroughly a few questions—each of which covers a wide area."[60] An examination is usually objective, essay, or somewhere between the two. Usually an

[57] Heston, op. cit., pp. 3–4.
[58] Ibid., pp. 2–3.
[59] Ibid., p. 20.
[60] Ibid., p. 31.

objective test covers breadth of knowledge, whereas an essay test emphasizes depth.

Objective ———→ True and False ———→ Short ———→ Subjective
                        Qualified   Essay   Essay

There are many types of objective tests, and often a test includes more than one kind of objective question. These objective tests can be true and false, yes and no, completion, matching, multiple choice, or variations of any of the preceding. One variation is the classification[61] question, a reverse of the multiple choice, asking the student to mark the one wrong answer. College instructors assume that the freshman has taken tests of the majority of these types. If the student has not, he should seek an explanation of the test now, before entering the examination room.

"How will I know what kind of test will be given?" a student asks. The kind of course usually determines the kind of examination that will be given, but if the student is in doubt, the majority of instructors will gladly tell their classes. Understanding the difference between an objective and a subjective test will mean that the student may want to study differently, depending on the test form.

An essay examination deserves individual attention, because some simple suggestions can mean the difference between an "A" paper and a "C" paper. It is very important to read the directions and all the questions carefully first. The second step is to divide one's time. If there are four questions and fifty minutes in which to write the answers, a logical time schedule might involve ten minutes per question with five minutes at the beginning for planning and five minutes at the end for rechecking. When the student is ready to tackle the first question, he makes an outline of the question on scratch paper or on the reverse side of the test. The student makes a list of the facts to be included, sorts them into major and minor points, and arranges them in a logical order. Finally, he can begin to write, remembering that a somewhat longer answer that lacks "padding" and is well organized tends to receive a better grade. (The instructor's time is as valuable as the student's, so when the instructor sees obvious padding or a poorly organized paper, he may unconsciously be prejudiced against it, regardless of the content.) Some further hints coming from Gerken[62] are

[61] Ibid., p. 29.
[62] Gerken, op. cit., p. 42.

1. Remembering the later questions while organizing an earlier one will keep one from presenting in one answer information that really should be included in another.
2. Attention should be paid to whether the student is asked to "describe, list, evaluate, sketch, outline, criticize, or discuss."
3. If the answer to one question is related to another, one should note this on the test, showing the instructor his ability to relate.

Heston suggests some additional pointers:[63]

1. Avoid padding.
2. Include pertinent information to show you have mastered the subject.
3. Use illustrative material whenever possible.
4. Turn some of your major points into headings.
5. Tailor your information to match the course. (This approach is determined by course emphasis. It is not apple polishing; instead it is demonstrating that the point of view important for the class has been grasped.)

Grammar and handwriting are influential in this type of examination also. It is important to check for "appropriate vocabulary, capitalization, grammar forms, sentence structure, spelling, variety of vocabulary and punctuation."[64] Sometimes an instructor plans in grading that a specific number of points will be forfeited for poor grammar and handwriting. At other times, a student is just naturally handicapped, because the teacher cannot understand the handwriting or the organization of thoughts.

An essay examination requires skill in organizing and presenting information, but often students prefer this kind. The reason is that here they may be given a chance to explain in depth the facets of the course with which they are most familiar and which are very important, whereas in an objective examination, a student must be familiar with the main principles and important facts of every area of the subject.

Specific suggestions regarding each of the types of objective tests, as well as objective tests in general, can help the student considerably. A true-false test can be particularly tricky. Sometimes an instructor will plan to subtract the wrong answers from those correct to discourage guessing on the part of students. This fact will generally be

[63] Heston, op. cit., pp. 38–39.
[64] Ibid., p. 40.

explained in the directions of the test or the instructor will make such an announcement. If the matter is not mentioned, then the student should ask. If the wrong answers are subtracted, then he should not guess on very puzzling questions. A "scientific" or "intelligent" guess may be profitable though. If the chances are 50-50 that he will get it wrong, he should not guess. A second rule to follow is that if any part of a true-false question is false, the entire sentence is false. Also, statements that include the words *always* or *never* are generally false, because any feasible exception would keep the answer from being true.[65]

In a completion test it is wise to look for clues, such as a broken line calling for two or more words. In this case remember to guess rather than leaving a blank, because teachers are often flexible in marking completion tests.[66] In a multiple-choice test a rule[67] to follow in three words is

1. "Analyze"—look for what the question asks.
2. "Eliminate"—reject those answers obviously incorrect.
3. "Discriminate"—choose the best answer of those remaining.

A matching-test question combines multiple-choice questions with multiple-choice answers. Often the questions are on the left and the answers are on the right. Extra answers are sometimes used to force the student to choose carefully. A second device used is the inclusion of an answer that must be used for more than one question.[68] For the last type of objective test, the rearrangement question, if one is uncertain, he should start with the known facts and then work toward the unknown.[69]

A few further general suggestions for objective tests are (1) if you guessed on the first time through the test, do not change the answer—generally a student's first hunch is his best—and (2) do not overemphasize one word in a question; this may change its intended meaning. Also, consider suspiciously such terms as *always, usually,* and *seldom.*[70]

There are a considerable number of suggestions[71] on general examination-taking that may be found to be helpful:

[65] Ibid., p. 27.
[66] Ibid., p. 28.
[67] Ibid., p. 29.
[68] Ibid., p. 30.
[69] Ibid., p. 30.
[70] Gerken, op. cit., p. 41.
[71] Ibid., pp. 42–43.

1. Review throughout the term.
2. Plan the final review period so that you can relax the night before the examination.
3. If study must be included the night before the examination, sleep afterwards, do not perform other activities.
4. Work on developing speed continually, so as to be ready for the pressure during a test. Accuracy, though, comes first.
5. If unsure of the kind of test, study as though it will be an essay test.
6. Have some recreation during the week prior to the examination.
7. Get enough sleep and stay in good physical and mental condition.
8. Be punctual for the test. Bring the necessary equipment, but not extras.
9. "Remember it's not what you know that earns your grades; it's what you let the instructor know that you know."

When surveying the examination, it is wise to look for such information[72] as:

Length of test.
Scoring plan.
Weight of questions.
Types of questions.
Directions applying to the phases of the test.
Order of answering questions.
Prerogative of choosing questions to answer.
Related items or "leads."
Form of answers.
Use of aids, such as rulers.
Use of scratch paper.

There are advantages to saving the difficult questions until last. This ensures that a student gets credit for those questions of which he is confident. Also, by postponing the hard items the student places them in his mind for incubation.[73] The fear that was aroused when he first looked at the difficult question may leave, and with a clear mind he may more easily think of the answer. The points earned in delaying the difficult questions will often have a significant effect upon a student's grade.

During the examination the student will profit from a few well-

[72] Heston, op. cit., pp. 14–15.
[73] Ibid., p. 17.

timed relaxation periods. He may want to look up from his paper to rest his eyes, shift his position to relieve muscle fatigue, stretch, and take a few deep breaths.[74]

In the material previously given on surveying the examination, it was suggested that a student examine the test length, scoring plan, and weight of questions. If there are any "weighted" sections, it is especially worthwhile to plan one's time. One should be certain to cover the less important questions, but he should spend less time on them.

Some students try to figure out a scoring pattern that an instructor may have made, such as "F T F F T T F T." A test maker is more likely to shuffle the questions in an accidental order. Working out a pattern will only waste a student's time.[75]

Taking the necessary equipment to an examination is especially important in a mathematics or drafting class. Other examinations require thought on the question. One may need paper, pencils, erasers, pen and ink, ruler, compass, protractor, slide rule, math tables, or a foreign-language dictionary.[76]

One final suggestion pertains to the time of arrival. A student will want to be at the examination room soon enough to get comfortable before the examination, but arriving too early is unwise. Students who enter the room ten to twenty minutes in advance tend to cram nervously and may forget all that they had learned, besides putting themselves into a nervous state that handicaps them in taking the examination.

Evaluating Progress

One of the advantages of taking examinations was cited as giving the student the chance to look at his strengths and weaknesses realistically in order to make decisions related to his potential. Some self-evaluation takes place as one takes a test and some is done throughout life as one examines his achievements, but primarily students look at themselves more objectively when they see the results of their study in tests returned to them.

Tests that help the student to look at himself realistically are not all related to ability. Many are known as personality tests. The difference between them lies in the answers—ability tests have right or

[74] Ibid., p. 18.
[75] Ibid., p. 22.
[76] Ibid., p. 14.

wrong answers, whereas in a personality test "the only right answers are those which correctly describe the person tested."[77] These other tests measure interests, appreciation, values, attitudes, and so on, and are sometimes called inventories, questionnaires, or checklists, to distinguish them from ability tests. Personality tests, as well as ability tests, are used to help the student measure and place a value judgment upon his personality characteristics—a realistic approach.

Tests scorers—instructors, guidance counselors, or testing organizations—place the results of tests in terminology that they believe the student can best understand. Three familiar forms of ability test results are educational age, percentile, and intelligence quotient. All three attempt to show the relation of the individual student's score to the scores of the others taking the examination. This relation is what makes the test results more easily understood by the student.

The educational age compares an individual score with the ability of the average child in a particular grade.[78] Thus, a score such as 11.3 places the child's rank in the eleventh grade, third month. A college freshman can interpret an educational age score that is lower than his placement to mean that he should take a lighter than average course load, that he may desire special help by a counselor, or that he cannot attempt to do part-time work while he is in school. The student may interpret a high score somewhat conversely.

A percentile also compares individual performance with that of the group. A student's rank is the per cent of people who fell below him on the test results. If an individual ranks in the fifty-second percentile, 52 per cent of those taking the test rank below him. A further interpretation of the score is that it was slightly above the median mark, which would have been at the fiftieth percentile.

The test result that may be most feared by students and most avoided by faculty is the IQ or intelligence quotient. It is a score derived by multiplying the ratio of mental age to chronological age by 100. The mean score by national norms is 100. The students often fear it because they do not understand its relation to success; many instructors often avoid it because they are concerned that it may prejudice their thinking about a particular student. The college freshman may have been told his score but may never have been helped to understand it. Each intelligence test gives only an estimate of an intelligence quotient in comparison to the ability of others. This

[77] Herschel T. Manuel, *Taking a Test* (New York: World Book Company, 1956), p. 12.
[78] Ibid., p. 14.

quotient may vary from test to test as it will fluctuate over a period of time. The most successful person is not necessarily the brightest. Instead, success depends upon special abilities, the amount of effort one puts forth, personality, and character. One succeeds by realistically looking at what he is and what he is not. Building upon one's abilities will lead to success.[79]

College course grades are the results of tests and are often stated in relation to the grades of others taking the test or course. They are often inaccurate measures, overstressed and insignificant in terms of the individual's total life. Yet while the student is in college, they control awards, dropping out, graduating, and being admitted to graduate schools.

Marks are only symbols of learning, not learning itself. Marks are by-products of learning, not its goal. Concentrate your thoughts and energies exclusively on learning and on the excitement of new discoveries. Even though you must work for marks, remember that ten or twenty years after college your marks will be hidden away in your scrapbook, but your learning will contribute constantly to the richness and meaning of your daily life.[80]

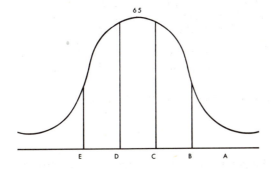

FIGURE 4-5. *The bell-shaped curve.*

Lass and Wilson believe that although learning is the lasting goal, grades are an important in-between step valuable for success. They feel that some "instructors give each student what he deserves even if this means giving all A's and B's. Some instructors don't believe in failing students, and others seem to believe that their professional integrity demands failing from 10 to 30 per cent each term."[81] Many instructors, though, grade "on the curve," which means that they

[79] Ibid., p. 10.
[80] Lass and Wilson, op. cit., p. 41.
[81] Ibid., p. 29.

plan a distribution of grades. Usually it is assumed that there will be a majority of marks at a central point and that there will be approximately the same number of scores above average as below.[82] It is assumed, when grades are curved, that there will be a normal distribution falling on what is known as the bell-shaped curve.

If the student who self-evaluates finds that a course or an area of study such as his major field is too difficult, it may be wise for him to make a change, whether it be the course of study or the type of school. "There is, of course, a difference between giving up trying to do something and trying to find something you can do effectively."[83] Choosing the area that one can be successful in may be "good" adjustment.

In the course of self-evaluation a need for self-confidence may become apparent. This may become evident only during the time of examinations, or a student may consistently show lack of confidence in himself. Three suggestions may aid the student in this plight: practice, forget yourself, and think about satisfying things. A profitable suggestion for when examinations are the major problem comes from "Study Hints."

> Look upon a test as a competitive game with yourself. Regard a test as an opportunity to show your mettle. Develop the attitude of the sportsman —win if you can, lose if you must, but do the best you can.[84]

All college work can be viewed as such competition. Adapting such a challenging outlook may bring the self-confidence that is so vital to success.

The problem of adjustment often hits the high school honor students worst of all because:

1. Competition is stronger.
2. Assignments are over a longer period of time, requiring an adjustment in planning and thinking.
3. Often memory is most important in high school. At the college level understanding and the use of knowledge is most important.
4. Honor students seeking the top schools, which admit only the highest students scholastically, may find themselves at the bottom half of their class. These students must learn to see themselves realistically.

[82] Manuel, op. cit., p. 13.
[83] Gerken, op. cit., p. 45.
[84] Student Counseling and Testing Center, Office of Student Affairs, Southern Illinois University, op. cit., p. 5.

5. College standards vary from school to school. An example is that some give A's to the top 25 per cent and some give A's to the top 10 per cent.

STUDY HINTS*

	Term Beginning		Term Ending	
	Yes	*No*	*Yes*	*No*
1. Do you work rapidly, planning your work efficiently, and with a purpose?				
2. Have you planned a definite time and place to study each subject?				
3. Do you avoid "frittering" away time unnecessarily?				
4. Do you study each assignment just as soon after the class as you can and review just before going to class? Do you rest completely from study for a day on the weekend?				
5. Have you agreed with your roommate about study hours? Do you refrain from talking to each other unless both are idle?				
6. Do you clear your desk and get out necessary materials before beginning to study so that you need not break into your concentrated thought?				
7. Have you reserved a suitable amount of time for conversation with others?				
8. Have you made plans to avoid too much time consumed in self-support?				
9. Do you assume a positive attitude toward required courses, looking for the pleasure and profit that they hold for you?				
10. If you have pressing worries, do you plan ways of removing or overcoming them? Are you doing your best at living with those conditions about which you can do nothing?				
11. Can you concentrate and rise above petty annoyances?				

* Adapted from *Study Hints,* Office of the Personnel Deans, Southern Illinois University, Carbondale, Illinois.

Reading	*Term Beginning*		*Term Ending*	
	Yes	*No*	*Yes*	*No*

1. Do you first pay attention to the subject of the large divisions of the book and then to the chapter headings?

2. Do you look for the topics of the main divisions of the chapter and then at the paragraph headings?

3. Do you read the chapter summary, if there is one, both before and after reading the chapter?

4. Do you first give the entire chapter a quick reading for the main ideas and then go back a second time, reading more slowly for the details related to the main ideas?

5. Do you underline or write out important sentences?

6. Do you know the meaning of the technical terms? Other words? Do you use the dictionary?

7. Do you jot down questions or problems that occur so that you can go back to them?

8. Do you take time to study the charts, graphs, maps?

9. Do you try to speed up your reading, taking in at one glance several phrases at a time or even whole sentences?

10. Do you recite to yourself in your own words the gist of the whole chapter, then of each section and paragraph?

11. Do you think as you read? Do you get clear-cut, active impressions of what you read, reacting to the ideas expressed?

12. Do you approach your assignments with confidence in your ability to remember?

Writing Lecture Notes

1. Do you give the instructor your complete attention? Do you react to each idea that he sets forth?

	Term Beginning		Term Ending	
	Yes	*No*	*Yes*	*No*

2. Do you know what the general topic or problem is that is being considered? Usually the instructor summarizes at the close of each main topic and states clearly what main topic is going to be discussed next.

3. Do you comprehend the main thought units presented under each main topic? Often a statement is followed by illustrations, examples, and explanations. Do you lose sight of the main idea while the explanations are being given?

4. Do you listen effectively, then take notes? Do you write down enough and avoid too many abbreviations, so that after class you know what the notes mean?

5. Do you put a definite heading over each group of notes so that you can keep track of the notes later on and see at a glance what they are about? Do you follow main heads with subheadings for each new unit of thought? Do you indent to show main topics and subtopics?

6. Are your notes neat, legible, *accurate?* Do you restate and summarize in your own words the main ideas? Do you write complete statements? Are you careful to put down facts and figures correctly? Do you put your notes in such a form that they need not be recopied?

7. Do you, as soon after class as possible, fill in, revise, and review your notes while the lecture is well in mind?

8. Do you discuss the lecture with fellow students?

9. Do you ask the instructor questions about what you do not understand clearly?

10. When you study for an examination, do you underline, use colored ink, or some other method for emphasizing the important points? Do you recite to yourself the main gist of each lecture with its subthought units?

Review your notes often. If you find yourself swamped, ask for a conference with your instructor. See your adviser or the deans for help also.

5

Developing Good
Health Practices

A Concern for Personal Health

Part I began with an awareness of the new responsibilities of the college freshman regarding decisions that affect a major portion of life. The essentials of health also become a vital concern for the individual who, with increasing maturity, takes on the responsibility of his own well-being.

In Chapter 5 some aspects of mental and physical health will be considered. Rather than a deep consideration of mental health as taught in most colleges during a health education course, "Understanding Emotional Health" concerns some of the practical aspects that may help the freshman toward a better understanding of his own feelings and reactions to experiences. "Employing Dietary Essentials" pertains to a portion of physical health that is of immediate concern to the beginning college student. Because of the increased use and misuse of medication and drugs a section on these has been added. A consideration of various health rules is included because of the total effect on physical well-being.

Good health, both mental and physical, is necessary to the well-being of the individual. With entrance into college, the student should be concerned about health because it affects study habits, personality, and adjustment to and success in and after college.

Understanding Emotional Health

Good emotional health may be nearly synonymous with emotional stability or security and the meeting of problems with courage and strength. Emotional security can be marked by:[1]

1. Letting life happen and increasingly observing it more fully.
2. Getting the most out of what there is.
3. Coordinating what is and what might be. (We are neither so hopeless nor so perfect as we sometimes think.)
4. Realizing that one is "becoming" more mature—a continuing process.
5. Realizing the difference between physical and emotional maturity.

Personal or emotional adjustment appears to be one of the major problems of college students. In a study of 576 college freshmen at Ohio State University, the following ranking of problems was compiled.

1. Education.
2. Personal temperament.
3. Social and recreational activities.
4. Citizenship.
5. Health and physical well-being.[2]

A study of one hundred men and one hundred women college students by Hunter and Morgan[3] included "being self-conscious," "lacking self-confidence" and "wanting a more pleasing personality" in the top eleven problems of students.

One of the major adjustments in college seems to be finding one's place in a new group. New acquaintances at first will not know one's assets and liabilities. Other students will have equal and sometimes greater ability in college. It may take some time for the student to find placement in a congenial group; until one finds his place, adjustment may be a problem. Conflicts arise when one's motives, impulses, or instincts contradict each other. Similar conflicts of college

[1] Esther W. Stearn and Allen E. Stearn, *College Hygiene* (Philadelphia: J. B. Lippincott Company, 1961), p. 31.
[2] Mildred Thurow Tate, *Home Economics as a Profession* (New York: McGraw-Hill Book Company, 1961), p. 6.
[3] Ibid., p. 7.

students in general are those related to social life, scholastic life, the selection of a vocation, daily communication, friendship with the opposite sex, social behavior, and religious convictions.[4]

During college the student faces many personal and social adjustment problems, which reflect upon college success. All age levels have their problems and the college age is no exception. Yet problems are added by the school environment and college life. These can be "distracting, confusing, and fatiguing."[5] These emotions will affect both success in academic work and enjoyment of college life.

Besides the problems of adjustment to college, individuals have problems stemming from their needs and desires. All people have emotional cravings, regardless of their age. Human desires common to stages of maturity that give rise to problems and conflicts requiring personal adjustment are getting married, having a home and children, having friends, and establishing the religious or philosophical beliefs by which one lives.

Everyone needs a working philosophy. This is one's attitude toward life—what he plans to contribute to life and what he expects to receive from it. The student who has definite objectives, attainable major and immediate goals, will have stepping stones that, upon being reached, will build confidence and success. As one reaches his goals, he will want to project them further. Although high goals will give motivation, goals set too high may cause feelings of failure and regression when they cannot be reached. We will consider personality goals in relation to maturity, the family, personal relationships, and oneself.

Students entering college are at various stages of development, not only intellectually and physically but also socially and emotionally. Understanding this will help one to set his goals in relation to his own present stage.

It is advisable to be aware of one's own progress in the various phases of development when entering college. In other words, if students are eighteen years of age chronologically at this time, they should strive to become eighteen years of age intellectually, emotionally, socially, physically, and spiritually.[6]

In youth, emotions rather than reason govern. The child is subject to self-pity and fits of anger. As he matures he learns to govern him-

---

[4] Stearn and Stearn, op. cit., pp. 20–21.
[5] Lita Bane and Mildred R. Chapin, *Introduction to Home Economics* (Boston: Houghton Mifflin Company, 1945), p. 13.
[6] Tate, op. cit., p. 14.

self through reason. This is the time of meeting life's problems. Thus, the goal for maturity may be to govern one's emotions and behavior through reason to the extent that he is able to do so at his developmental stage.

Home economics places major emphasis upon the home and family. Problems related to the adjustment of the individual in relation to the family will be dealt with in numerous courses during the college career. Etheredge[7] speaks of the family as a great influence upon adjustment in society. Although such adjustment begins within oneself, it stretches to the family and then to others in society.

Carl R. Rogers, the noted psychologist and researcher of client-centered therapy, has done considerable study on the relationships of people. From him come suggestions of goals for personal relationships.[8] A personal relationship should be genuine; second, one should be aware of his own feelings and be willing to express them. The relationship should be based on reality—what really is. The fourth goal for the strong relationship is that one should be accepting of others and desire to understand others. Fifth, the relationship should afford a freedom for exploration of concepts and ideas. And finally, there should be freedom from the feeling of being judged or evaluated.

Emotional stability is the conscious and unconscious goal of every cultured human being, of every life-loving person. It leads the boy to sound manhood; the girl to glorious womanhood; nations to the greatest efforts for the attainment of lasting world peace.[9]

From Rogers, again, come likely goals of personality in respect to oneself. He suggests that one become more open to his experiences, more trusting of himself, more aware that the place of evaluation lies within himself, and more content to view his personality as a process rather than a product.[10] A goal of life that is becoming a pattern is to show the person that one truly is. This means moving away from what one "ought" to do, from what the culture seems to expect, and from trying to please others, and moving toward directing one's own life, toward being a process rather than fearing any change

[7] Maude Lee Etheredge, *Health Facts for College Students* (Philadelphia: W. B. Saunders Company, 1959), p. 29.

[8] Carl R. Rogers, *On Becoming a Person, a Therapist's View of Psychotherapy* (Boston: Houghton Mifflin Company, 1961), pp. 33–34.

[9] Samuel Shulman, *How to Attain Emotional Maturity* (New York: Exposition Press, 1952), p. 5.

[10] Rogers, op. cit., pp. 16–21.

in emotion, toward being a complexity—often a conflict of emotions—and toward openness to experience.[11]

To be mentally healthy one must understand himself. He should be honest with himself and willing to endure pain and disillusionment. He must be able to endure criticism from both himself and others. Only by believing that he can improve will he so do. It takes both desire and determination to reach one's goals. Having broadly outlined some possible goals in relation to maturity, the family, personal relationships, and oneself, we ask that you think about your own problems, needs, and desires and then set down your goals.

In order to gain a better understanding of your emotions, you may want to complete the following two questionnaires.

The two questionnaires may help you to evaluate your assets and liabilities. Understanding your liabilities may help you work to eliminate them. Some emotional liabilities commonly spoken of are fear and anxiety, frustration and conflict, and pressure and tension.

Emotion is brought about by a feeling that something is beneficial or harmful—strongly moving one either pleasantly or unpleasantly. Anxiety, fear, anger, love, joy, hope, and courage are among the basic emotions. Pleasant emotions, although they may be accompanied by unpleasant emotions, are not problems in themselves. Therefore, we

AT HOME, ON THE JOB, OR IN YOUR PERSONAL
RELATIONS ARE YOU:

	Occasionally	Frequently
Getting more irritable over petty things?	———	———
Becoming hypercritical of people?	———	———
Feeling more neglected, left out?	———	———
Growing more distrustful of people?	———	———
Beginning to believe you are indispensable?	———	———
Becoming more impatient to get things done?	———	———
Feeling increasingly sorry for yourself?	———	———
Worrying more about future decisions?	———	———
Growing bored with everything about you?	———	———
Finding it difficult to praise others?	———	———
Feeling you must be first in everything?	———	———

Wherever you have checked the "Frequently" column, consider objectively the pressures being put on you—including those you put on yourself.

[11] Ibid., pp. 166–170.

At School, at Home, in Your Personal Relations:

	Yes	No
1. Do you enjoy life? Have fun?	_____	_____
2. Are you interested in other people? In their ideas?	_____	_____
3. Do you have confidence in yourself?	_____	_____
4. Do you have confidence in others?	_____	_____
5. Have you analyzed the kinds of friends you have?	_____	_____
6. Do you read for pleasure in addition to reading done for course work?	_____	_____
7. Have you analyzed the *kind* of reading you do in your leisure time?	_____	_____
8. Have you analyzed your leisure time activities? Have you developed special interests?	_____	_____
9. Are you able to control your temper? Are your feelings easily hurt?	_____	_____
10. Do you rationalize?	_____	_____

Source: From the book, *The Life Extension Foundation Guide to Better Health* by Henry J. Johnson, M.D. © 1959 by Life Extension Foundation. Published by Prentice-Hall, Inc., Englewood Cliffs, N.J., and used with their permission.

turn toward some of the unpleasant emotions in order to consider adjustment.

One reacts to a specific danger with fear; anxiety is a reaction to vague and uncertain stimuli. Many people, including some beginning college students, have their fears and anxieties; if you are one of them, perhaps you should consider taking a course in psychology early in your college years. Briefly, the person striving for good mental health will meet anxiety and/or fear with the belief that there is more to be gained from moving ahead than by escaping. As one faces, moves through, and conquers fear and/or anxiety cresting experiences, he will be developing the positive aspects of himself.[12]

Many confuse the meanings of frustration and conflict. Some believe that they are synonymous terms, some believe the former leads to the latter, and others believe that the latter causes the former. Learning to view himself and his world realistically and building self-

[12] Rollo May, *The Meaning of Anxiety* (New York: The Ronald Press Company, 1950), p. 234.

238

confidence may be of significant value to the person weighted down by frustrations and conflict.

Dr. Harry J. Johnson emphasizes the fact that it is not abnormal to feel pressure.[13] This is a very natural feeling in one's home, but more often in one's job. The college student finds many pressures with part-time work, reading assignments, term papers, and examinations. When one loses the ability to meet daily pressures, tension may result. Everyone has a breaking point at which he can handle no more pressures. It is important to know where one's breaking point lies in order to balance one's life. Tenseness is a personal reaction to problems. Because it is personal, it is believed that the individual can handle the situation himself in most cases without professional help. Tension or approaching one's "breaking point" can be recognized in both physical and emotional signs. Functional ailments may include sleeplessness, constant fatigue, dizziness, constipation, frequent headaches, stomach pains, back aches, or indigestion. Probably more common tension signs are despair feelings, persecuted loneliness, extensive irritability, and impatience. There is a need for concern when these emotions occur often over a long period of time.[14]

Johnson has suggested these methods of handling pressure when symptoms of tension arise:

1. Do not neglect your physical health.
2. Change your perspective. (The necessary attitude for good mental health is that you can do so much and no more.)
3. Build up your self-confidence.
4. Be moderate in your habits and attitudes. (Avoid excessive ambition.)
5. Seek release in a change of routine.[15]

Adjustment is a continuous process throughout life. Just as one never arrives at the point of being completely educated but always strives for more education, he can never become fully adjusted but continually strives toward healthy adjustment. We speak of an evaluating process rather than evaluation, the educating process rather than education, and finally the adjusting process rather than adjustment.

Emotional health is defined by Stearn and Stearn as a "state in which our emotional responses enrich ourselves as well as others."[16] Some people deny expression of their emotions because of an un-

[13] Johnson, op. cit., p. 41.
[14] Ibid., pp. 37–40.
[15] Ibid., pp. 42–44.
[16] Stearn and Stearn, op. cit., p. 24.

happy experience. Instead, the well-adjusted person will learn to change the situation that brought about the unhappiness. The mentally healthy and emotionally mature person will allow involvement of his emotions in order to seek happiness.[17]

The young child is told that he must express his emotions in acceptable ways. Recalling the advice of Rogers, that becoming a person means that we move away from what we "ought" to do, it seems that the expressing of emotions by college students should be in a manner that will give the most ultimate happiness. It has been suggested that personality elements such as a highly explosive temperament can be channeled into more productive ends such as competition. Others stress vigorous exercise and creative work as harmless ways of expressing emotions. The point to be kept in mind is that the avenue of emotional expression should be one that will bring further contentment.

Another method of adjustment involves talking one's problems over with someone else. Often when a personal problem is kept within oneself, it appears to be insoluble. Finding a person with whom one can talk out a problem brings clarification and a second point of view. A third advantage of talking out a problem is that another can help one to see his progress—an aid to further adjustment. Some have suggested that talking a problem over with a college counselor, a faculty adviser, or a house mother may help. This will depend on the individual student and his problem but always there will be someone who wants to help.

A third method of adjustment is diversion. In regard to homesickness, Phillips makes these suggestions:

Get acquainted with the college and make new friends. . . . Keenly observing all things around you, orienting yourself to new situations and constantly questioning with an alert attitude should make it possible for you to become adjusted to your new home after the first week or two. Forget about yourself. Watch others. Help those that need help. Take outdoor exercises and walks on the campus.[18]

There seem to be many discussions in health education and mental hygiene courses about the final adjustment method considered here—adjustment mechanisms. This is a technical term for the methods con-

[17] Ibid., p. 31.
[18] Velma Phillips, *Home Economics Careers for You* (New York: Harper & Row, 1962), pp. 22–23.

ventionally used, such as some of the preceding suggestions. The person seeking sound adjustment will seek relief by acceptable mechanisms. Basic drives and impulses can be converted into acceptable responses as the individual substitutes one goal for another with the result remaining satisfying; new goals can be interchanged; one can attempt to reduce conflicts; and one can reason using those ideas that justify his feelings and actions to himself and others. Finding the means of adjustment that will help one toward emotional health is a responsibility left to the individual and his specific problem.

College presents a fine opportunity for adjusting to society, if one has not already done so. This process involves class participation, sharing ideas between classes, speaking at the dinner table, and many more opportunities. It involves listening as well as talking. Fine friendships and an understanding of life may be the result of wholesome play and recreation. A person who is well integrated into society will have the ability to meet the problems of social adjustment; will have the ability to integrate his thinking on the political, economic, religious, and ethical problems that confront his community and mankind; and, will have the ability to solve some of these problems.[19]

Employing Dietary Essentials

Emotional health is only one facet of well-being that affects the student's life in college. A great many collegians neglect their physical health, and especially an adequate diet, in order to give time, money, or thought to other activities they believe to be more valuable at this time. One might assume that students are to some degree interested in nutrition and that they may even value it to some extent. However, in reality one may find that even though students have adequate knowledge, their diets are inadequate compared to the established minimum daily requirements. In order to be in optimum health, with the ability to succeed in mental and physical activity, a student must feel strongly enough about his own well-being to prefer the value of proper nutrition over lesser values. He will eat three balanced meals, maintain his desirable weight, and achieve health, happiness, and a full vigorous life.

[19] Etheredge, op. cit., p. 31.

A person can be well nourished and still not be totally fit, but he can never be totally fit without being well nourished.[20]

The following attitude questionnaire should aid your thinking about some food habits. It is not to be graded.

ATTITUDE QUESTIONNAIRE

Place a checkmark after "yes" or "no," according to your attitude:
1. Do you think that it doesn't matter if you skip breakfast?　　　　　　　　　　　　　　　　　　YES＿＿＿　NO＿＿＿
2. Do you think that people should choose carefully the foods they eat?　　　　　　　　　　　　YES＿＿＿　NO＿＿＿
3. Do you believe in a balanced diet?　　　　　　YES＿＿＿　NO＿＿＿
4. Can snacks contribute to a balanced diet?　　YES＿＿＿　NO＿＿＿
5. Do you think that you are overweight or underweight?　　　　　　　　　　　　　　　　　　　　YES＿＿＿　NO＿＿＿
6. Are there some foods that you do not like?　YES＿＿＿　NO＿＿＿
7. Do you like to try new foods?　　　　　　　YES＿＿＿　NO＿＿＿
8. Is it essential that we eat foods that contain vitamins and minerals?　　　　　　　　　　　　YES＿＿＿　NO＿＿＿
9. Do you think that middle-income and rich people ever suffer from malnutrition?　　　　　　YES＿＿＿　NO＿＿＿
10. Do you often like to eat sweets?　　　　　　YES＿＿＿　NO＿＿＿
11. Should we drink milk after we are adults?　　YES＿＿＿　NO＿＿＿
12. Is it possible for your food patterns to affect your scholastic standing?　　　　　　　　　　YES＿＿＿　NO＿＿＿
13. May careful selection of food help one to live longer?　　　　　　　　　　　　　　　　　　YES＿＿＿　NO＿＿＿
14. Should we eat what we need before eating what we want?　　　　　　　　　　　　　　　　YES＿＿＿　NO＿＿＿
15. Does it matter what we eat as long as our hunger is satisfied?　　　　　　　　　　　　　　YES＿＿＿　NO＿＿＿
16. Calories are the most important thing to consider in food selection?　　　　　　　　　　　YES＿＿＿　NO＿＿＿

Elements of an Adequate Diet

Adequate nutrition is believed to be necessary for emotional and physical well-being. The three major functions of food in the body are providing materials for building and repairing body tissues, sup-

[20] Philip L. White, "Fitness of Youth for the Challenge of Today," *School Lunch Journal*, 20:1 (January, 1966), p. 19.

plying fuel for energy, and furnishing regulating substances for body processes. In order to receive the full benefit of food, one must have an adequate diet.

The term "balanced diet" is simply the practical expression of the inter-relationships among the various nutrients in an adequate diet. In the very early days of the science of nutrition and with the relatively few foods available 75 years ago, much emphasis was placed just on the balancing of carbohydrate, fat and protein in the diet. Research has since shown that the functions of all the nutrients—vitamins, minerals, amino acids, fats, carbohydrates and water—are closely related. This concept is important. . . .[21]

The elements of an adequate diet could be classified into two groups:[22]

1. The carbohydrates, proteins, and fats which supply energy.
2. The vitamins which act as body regulators, promote growth, and help protect against disease. In this same group are the minerals which are essential to the formation of hard and soft tissue and the fluids of the body and also assist in regulating body processes. Water, too, is important in regulating body processes.

Most students receive enough foods of the first group, but few eat enough of those that are necessary for the utilization of the nutrients in the former group. The body cells are dependent on these dietary essentials for growth, repair, and regulation.

The dietary need that is often considered the most important is protein, the main growth material. Protein is composed of an assortment of amino acids, out of a possible twenty-five presently known kinds. Food must supply eight specific amino acids of plant or animal origin that must be present at the same time for effective tissue building. Some other amino acids can be synthesized in the body from the amino acids consumed. The essential foods, then, provide what cannot be made by the body or cannot be made fast enough and must therefore be supplied by food. Protein is used for the growth and repair of cells as well as for food energy, when there is an absence of fat and carbohydrates in the body.

Fats are another cell requirement; they are used by the cells for producing energy. More than twice as much energy is gained from fat as from an equal amount of protein or carbohydrate. Fats go through the process of combustion in the body, producing both heat and work

[21] Philip L. White, *Let's Talk About Food* (American Medical Association, 1967), p. 3.
[22] Johnson, op. cit., p. 57.

energy. When fat is not needed or oxidized by the cells, it is converted into fat tissue and deposited throughout the body. Because vitamins A and D are fat soluble, they are found only in the fat of foods such as milk fat, meat fat, or vegetable fat. The presence of fat-soluble vitamins and the production of work energy make fats necessary in the diet.

The third essential food element is the vitamin group—the complex chemical compounds manufactured by plant and animal cells that are necessary to normal growth and nutrition. Broadly, they function in affecting growth, reproduction, and defense activities.

Extremely rich vitamin-source foods are egg yolk, heart, kidney, liver, whole milk, cream and butter, fruits and vegetables, whole-grain cereals, muscle meat, and cheese. More specifically, citrus fruits, cabbage, and tomatoes are rich in vitamin C; whole-grain breads, cereals, milk, and meats in the B complex; milk, butter, and cheese in A; and milk and sunlight in D. K and E are found in most meat and whole-grain or enriched cereal products. The specific vitamins and their functions are shown in the following chart.

FUNCTIONS OF VITAMINS*

Vitamin	Important Function	Important Sources
A (retinol)	Prevention of xerophthalmia	Liver
Provitamin A (carotene)	Helps prevent night blindness	Green and yellow vegetables
	Helps keep mucous membranes firm and resistant to infection	Egg yolk
	Helps control bone growth and faulty tooth formation	Whole milk, cream, butter, fortified margarine
	Helps keep skin clear and smooth	Yellow fruits
D (calciferol)	Helps absorb calcium from the digestive tract and promotes calcification of bones	Vitamin D milk Fish liver oils
E (tocopherol)	Helps in prevention of anemia	Vegetable oils Leafy vegetables
K (menadione)	Necessary for synthesis of prothrombin, blood clotting	Green leafy vegetables Liver Egg yolk Cheese

* Frank Konishi, Chairman of the Department of Food and Nutrition, Southern Illinois University, Carbondale; Gladys E. Vail et al., *Foods* (Boston: Houghton Mifflin Company, 1967), pp. 14–15; Sue Rodwell Williams, *Nutrition and Diet Therapy* (St. Louis, Mo.: C. V. Mosby Company, 1969), pp. 85–113.

C (ascorbic acid)	Helps make cementing materials that hold body cells together Helps make walls of blood vessels firm Helps in healing wounds and broken bones	Citrus fruits—orange, grapefruit, lemon, lime Strawberries and cantaloupe Tomatoes Green peppers, broccoli Raw greens, cabbage Potatoes Chili peppers
B_1 (thiamine)	Helps promote normal appetite and digestion Helps keep nervous system healthy and prevents irritability Helps body release energy from food	Meat, fish, poultry—pork supplies about 3 times as much as other meats Eggs Enriched or whole-grain bread and cereal Dried beans and peas Potatoes, broccoli, collards
B_2 (riboflavin)	Helps cells use oxygen Helps keep skin, tongue, and lips normal Helps prevent scaly, greasy skin around mouth and nose	Milk All kinds of cheese Ice cream Meat, especially liver Fish, poultry, and eggs Enriched cereals
Niacin (nicotonic acid)	Helps keep nervous system healthy Helps keep skin, mouth, tongue, digestive tract in healthy condition Helps cells use other nutrients	Peanut butter Meat, fish, poultry Milk (high in tryptophan) Enriched or whole-grain bread and cereal
B_6 (pyridoxine)	Helps in prevention of anemia, neuritis, hyperirritability, and convulsions	Liver Meat Wheat Corn
Folic Acid	Necessary for blood cell regeneration in pernicious anemia Helpful in curing and/or preventing chronic diarrhea and other digestive disturbances	Liver Green leafy vegetables, asparagus

Vitamin	Important Function	Important Sources
B$_{12}$ (cobalamin)	Coenzyme in protein synthesis Forms red blood cells (with folic acid) Helpful in prevention and/or cure of chronic diarrhea and other digestive disturbances (with folic acid)	Liver Meats Milk Eggs Cheese

Vitamin deficiencies occur among the poor as well as among the ignorant and those who have a limited food choice, such as pregnant women, infants, children, people with digestive disturbances and thus little absorption of vitamins, and those dieting unwisely.[23] Vitamin deficiencies have been diagnosed only in the last forty to fifty years.[24] Diseases caused by vitamin deficiencies such as rickets, scurvy, pellagra, beriberi, and other vitamin deficiencies are still common in some of the developing countries of the world and also are encountered in the United States.

The student should remember that the vitamins are important to optimum health. The symptoms of vitamin deficiency are lack of energy, nervousness, irritability, poor eyesight, blemished skin, swollen gums, cracked lips, sore tongue, poor posture, and so on. It must be recognized, however, that other things may also cause these symptoms. When any of these symptoms is noted, a member of the medical profession should be consulted.

One need not ever suffer a vitamin deficiency if he follows the essential guide to balanced meals. Even when the rich food sources are incorporated in one's diet, precious vitamins can be lost unless extra care is taken to preserve them. Certain vitamins may be lost by heat, oxidation during storage and cooking, the presence of an acid or alkali, or being dissolved in water and thrown away. Vitamin C especially is destroyed when cooked at a high temperature, in the presence of air or light, or with soda. The amount of the loss depends upon the length of time the food is cooked, the intensity of heat, and the amount of oxidation. Vitamin C is also lost when fresh vegetables are exposed to air and become wilted or bleached. Twenty-one to eighty per cent of

[23] Stearn and Stearn, op. cit., p. 119.
[24] Cleveland P. Hickman, *Health for College Students,* Second edition © 1963. Reprinted by permission of Prentice-Hall, Inc., Englewood Cliffs, New Jersey.

the vitamins may be lost in canning, when the foods are cooked for too long a period of time; freeze-drying is less detrimental.

In order to avoid the loss of these natural vitamins, one must follow certain rules of cooking. In brief, these can be stated:

1. Use covered cooking equipment.
2. Avoid extra stirring.
3. Avoid unnecessary cutting of food.
4. Use a minimum amount of water.
5. Use the leftover juice of fruits and vegetables in soups, gravies, and so on.
6. Use as little soda as possible, if it is necessary at all, and decrease the cooking time.
7. Cook food for the shortest possible period of time for tenderness.

The seventh rule explains why deep-fat frying is less destructive of vitamins than prolonged boiling.[25]

Fourth in the list of cell requirements are minerals—more elements believed to be essential to the body. Man has some twenty-five minerals present in his body. They need replenishing as they are used. The importance of some of the necessary amounts and specific kinds that are essential are yet to be established. Those functions that are believed to be due to some minerals are still vague. They appear to be necessary for enzymatic action and for the growth and repair of bones and teeth; they are found in hormones and are a part of vitamins; they are necessary for the production of hemoglobin and in the forming of body fluids and secretions.[26]

Needed body minerals include calcium, phosphorus, iodine, fluorine, iron, copper, magnesium, manganese, chlorine, cobalt, and others. Grouped as to function or source, certain minerals appear similar to each other. Calcium and phosphorus are both important to the body and both are provided in a sufficient quantity of milk. Iodine and fluorine are similar in that both can be provided in drinking water if it contains iodine or iodized salt and if it contains fluorine naturally or as an additive. Iodine functions in the body in forming the important hormone thyroxine in the thyroid gland. Fluorine appears to be necessary for normal tooth development, although an excess may cause yellow teeth in children. Iron is essential in formulating the hemoglobin needed for transporting oxygen to the tissues. Iron is found in

[25] Stearn and Stearn, op. cit., p. 121.
[26] Hickman, op. cit., p. 191.

eggs, meat, green leafy vegetables, and molasses. Very little copper is needed and what is needed can be supplied by that "dissolved from copper-lined cooking vessels or from the copper pipes of pasteurizing milk machines."[27] Other necessary minerals are magnesium, manganese, cobalt, zinc, and others in minute traces.

Real tired blood is fatigue caused by anemia, a condition in which the hemoglobin content of the blood is below normal because the body does lack iron. Although your body requires no more than about one-quarter of an ounce of iron, a deficiency of this mineral can lead to an anemic condition. But treatment for anemia should be prescribed by a doctor, who will most likely have no trouble solving the problem by prescribing iron in the form of pills or by adding certain foods to your diet.

But very few people are really anemic. Three out of four who complain of fatigue are simply bored. Yet fatigue is such a widespread complaint in modern times that it apparently has become relatively easy to sell millions on buying "tired blood" medications.[28]

The last food group necessary for body cells is the carbohydrate group, which includes sugars, starches, and cellulose. Digestion breaks down complex sugars and starches into simple sugars, which can be absorbed and used by the body as energy. Carbohydrates can be stored, when in excess of body needs, in the liver, in the muscles, or in fat deposits in various forms. The chief carbohydrate sources are potatoes, sugars, cereals, legumes, and bread. Carbohydrates appear as starch foods in bread, potatoes, rice, cereals, and many vegetables; as sugar foods in fruit, sugar cane, sugar beet, milk; and also in forms of the sugar contained in foods like candy and soft beverages.

The body cells require two last elements that are not food in themselves. These are water and fiber. Water is a carrier of materials; it travels through the stomach and intestines to the blood stream and is excreted through the lungs, the skin, and the kidneys. Approximately two thirds of the water requirement is furnished by one's diet; the remainder must be supplied by what one drinks. Some of the many functions of water in human nutrition are the following:[29]

1. Water serves as a medium in which many body chemical changes take place.
2. Food is digested in a water solution.
3. Water eliminates waste in solution.

27 Ibid., p. 192.
28 Johnson, op. cit., p. 66.
29 Etheredge, op. cit., pp. 69–70.

4. Water is vital to body secretions. It is a major component of saliva, gastric juices, tears, and so on.
5. Water is an important part of the blood.
6. Water is an important part of the spaces between cells.
7. Water is an important part of tissue cells.

Fruit and vegetable fiber, too, enters into a discussion of nutritive requirements. Although fiber, which is cellulose, is not a food material, it does have a regulatory function in the diet.

Cellulose is only softened by cooking processes and is practically indigestible in man, so that it is not a true food substance. Cellulose and the closely related hemicelluloses make up the structural or fibrous part of plants (leaves, stems, roots, and seed and fruit coverings) and also the cell walls. Since most of this material taken in plant foods remains undigested, it serves to give bulk to the food residues in the intestine and promote their evacuation. Individuals vary in how much bulk they need to prevent constipation and whether they tolerate cellulose in rougher or only in softer forms.[30]

TYPICAL LOW- AND HIGH-RESIDUE FOODS*†

Low-Residue Foods	High-Residue Foods
Sugar	Fruits (esp. if eaten with skins)
White Bread	Vegetables (except potato), legumes, and nuts
Highly milled breakfast cereals— e.g., Cream of Wheat and white farina	Whole-wheat bread
Meat	Breakfast cereals from whole grains —e.g., oatmeal, shredded wheat, and dark farina
Potato	
Fats	

* Although milk contains no fiber, its lactose content tends to promote the formation of rather bulky stools.
† Lotta Jean Bogert et al., *Nutrition and Physical Fitness* (Philadelphia: W. B. Saunders Co., 1966), p. 145.

When there is insufficient bulk in the upper intestine, the muscles are not stimulated to push the waste through the body. The result is the stopping of the food materials, which collect, stagnate, and putrefy, waiting a day or two for bulk food to push the waste.

It is thought to be better to receive the cellulose in the form of

[30] Lotta Jean Bogert, George M. Briggs, and Noris Howes Calloway, *Nutrition and Physical Fitness* (Philadelphia: W. B. Saunders Co., 1966), p. 24.

fruits, vegetables, and whole grain foods rather than as bran. Too many high-residue foods, particularly accompanied by bran, may cause an irritation of the intestines. Those foods with little bulk or those with a high amount are shown in the table.

Foods may be grouped into four basic groups: (1) Milk and milk products; (2) meat, fish, and poultry, with nuts and legumes as alternates; (3) fruits and vegetables; and (4) breads and cereals. A good selection of foods from each group will provide an adequate diet.[31]

An adequate diet will maintain the body in a moderately satisfactory state of health and provide for the growth and repair of the body tissues and bones. The student should remember that these are basic needs and that for optimum health, maximum growth, resistance to disease, highest body vigor, and vitality, additional foods should be selected from the fruits and vegetables, milk, eggs, or whole grains.

Nutritional requirements vary for the individual according to age, body weight, rate of absorption, activity, and sex. For example, a woman who is pregnant or in lactation will have special requirements. Regardless of small variances, most people can follow a daily food guide that will provide the necessary protein, minerals, vitamins, fats, carbohydrates, water, and fiber. The "Basic 7" was introduced to make it easy for the consumer to choose all of the necessary foods to meet the requirements. The "Basic 4," an adaptation of the "Basic 7," has now become popular with professionals and consumers. The guide most commonly used is outlined in the U.S. Department of Agriculture leaflet "Food for Fitness—A Daily Food Guide."

BASIC 4*

Milk Group
  Some milk for everyone
    Children under 9   2 to 3 cups
    Children 9 to 12   3 or more cups
    Teen-agers   4 or more cups
    Adults   2 or more cups
Vegetable-Fruit Group
  4 or more servings
    Include
      A citrus fruit or other fruit or vegetable important for vitamin C

---

[31] "Food for Fitness—A Daily Food Guide," Leaflet No. 424 (Washington, D.C.: U.S. Department of Agriculture, 1964).
  * "Food for Fitness—A Daily Food Guide," Leaflet No. 424 (Washington, D.C.: U.S. Department of Agriculture, 1964).

A dark-green or deep-yellow vegetable for vitamin A—at least every
    other day
Other vegetables and fruits, including potatoes
Bread-Cereal Group
  4 or more servings
    Whole grain, enriched or restored
Meat Group
  2 or more servings
    Beef, veal, pork, lamb, poultry, fish, eggs
    As alternates—dry beans, dry peas, nuts
Plus other foods as needed to complete meals and to provide additional food
energy and other food values.

The milk and cheese group, as just described, will furnish proteins,
calcium, phosphorus, riboflavin, and vitamins A and D; the fruits and
vegetables will provide vitamins A and C; cereals and breads will
supply iron, several of the B vitamins, carbohydrates, and some protein; meat and the alternates will furnish protein, thiamine, riboflavin,
niacin, and iron.

FIGURE 5-1.
The milk group.
(Courtesy of the
National Dairy
Council.)

251

FIGURE 5-2.
The vegetable-fruit group.
(*Courtesy of the National Dairy Council.*)

FIGURE 5-3.
The bread-cereal group.
(*Courtesy of the National Dairy Council.*)

BASIC SCORE CARD FOR ADULTS*

Basic 4 Food Group	Foods	Daily Requirements	Daily Check S M T W Th F S	Possible Score	Your Score
Milk & Butter Group	Milk First cup of milk Second cup of milk Third cup of milk or more	1 pint of milk or more 2 tablespoons of butter or fortified margarine		10 10 5 $\overline{25}$	
Fruits & Vegetables	1 serving of green or yellow vegetables 1 serving of citrus fruits, tomato, or cabbage 2 or more servings of other fruits and vegetables, including potato	1 serving leafy green or deep yellow vegetable 1 serving citrus fruit, tomatoes, or raw cabbage 2 or more servings additional fruits or vegetables		10 10 5 $\overline{25}$	
Breads & Cereals	4 servings of whole-grain or enriched cereal or breads	2–4 servings		20 $\overline{20}$	
Meat Group	1 serving of egg, meat, fish, poultry, or cheese (or dried beans or peas) 1 or more additional servings of egg, meat, fish, poultry, or cheese	1 serving meat, fish, poultry 4 eggs per week 2 or more servings per week of cheese, dried beans or peas, peanut butter, or an additional meat serving		15 10 $\overline{25}$	
	Water (total liquid)	6–8 glasses		5 $\overline{5}$	
Total Score				100	

* This chart was adapted from Bogert, Briggs, and Calloway, *Nutrition and Physical Fitness*. Water was added by the author and points were subtracted from the cereal group; the word *cheese* was changed to *butter*.

Figure 5-4.
*The meat group.
(Courtesy of the
National Dairy
Council.)*

For one week test your own selection of food by completing the following score card. At the end of the week total your score. Does it total 100? If it does not, what should you add?

NUTRIENT SUPPLEMENTS

In the late 1920's and early 1930's medical literature was filled with reports of deficiency diseases such as pellagra (the niacin deficiency disease), beriberi, mild anemia, and ariboflavinosis in the United States. Dr. Thomas Parran, then Surgeon General of the U.S. Public Health Service, pushed adequate nutrition for improved health through the enrichment of bread and cereal products as World War II neared.[32] The refining of breads during the milling process had been removing the B complex vitamins. Enrichment restores the thiamine, riboflavin,

[32] Ellen H. Semrow and Mary K. Moore as told to them by Thomas Parran, M.D., "The Bread and Flour Enrichment Program," *Journal of Home Economics,* 53 (October, 1961), 660–662.

254

niacin, and iron in the proportions recommended by the Federal Drug and Cosmetic Act.

> . . . since the inauguration of the enrichment program, the death rate decline from pellagra alone has been dramatic. Within two years of the appearance of niacin-enriched foods on the market, the pellagra death rate had dropped to the rate of one per 100,000 and by 1950 to a rate of 0.2, which represented an unprecedented low of two hundred sixty total deaths as compared with the seven thousand deaths in 1928.[33]

Bread and cereal have not been the only foods enriched for improved nutrient consumption. Margarine is now fortified with vitamin A. Milk that has been irradiated has had its 7-dehydro-cholesterol changed to active vitamin D and is sometimes fortified with vitamin D concentrates.

Since the education of the public to the importance of vitamins, supplements in the form of tablets have been developed and sold widely to many people, regardless of their adequacy of food intake. Dr. Johnson[34] considered the argument of the vitamin salesman. The usual sales approach is that vitamins are being lost through food processing, that the soil is being depleted by farmers, and that harmful chemicals are being injected into the crops. In reality, the food-processing industries are refortifying food often to a greater vitamin content than before, modern farming techniques call for enriching the soil with depleted minerals, and the effect of crop chemicals upon vitamins is questioned.

Dr. Johnson stresses that "Between the ages of eighteen and sixty-five, there is rarely a medical need for vitamin supplements to be taken habitually."[35] According to Stearn and Stearn,[36] "It is the consensus of medical authorities that self-prescribed doses of vitamin pills are a waste of money, because an individual thrives best on a balanced diet which should provide all necessary vitamins."

An excess of vitamins has no value and can even be harmful. As was discussed previously, an excess of fat-soluble vitamins is stored in the liver and the fat of the body and an excess of water-soluble vitamins leaves the body in waste materials. Storing up too many fat-soluble vitamins will cause what is known as hypervitaminosis, a disease probably as dangerous as a deficiency. An excess of water-soluble vitamins

[33] Ibid., p. 662.
[34] Johnson, op. cit., p. 89.
[35] Ibid., p. 90.
[36] Stearn and Stearn, op. cit., p. 121.

is just an unnecessary additional cost, because these vitamins will be lost from the body.

OTHER NUTRITIONAL NEEDS

Many college students have some poor eating habits. Surveys made of college freshmen have shown that even as few as 19 per cent maintain "good" diets. Men generally consume better diets than women; approximately one out of four eat no breakfast; only 64 per cent have "fair" diets; and 17 per cent have decidedly "poor" ones.[37] Eating no breakfast and lacking variety in food may be two of the more prominent reasons for the poor nutritional level of some college students.

According to studies, the day's protein intake is best used by the body when it is divided among the three meals rather than concentrated in one or two.[38]

Generally breakfast should provide from one third to one fourth of the day's needs in protein, vitamins, minerals, and calories. Included in the reasons given by college students for not eating breakfast are lack of time, not liking breakfast, and/or being on a diet. Yet, "after a long overnight fast, breakfast food is digested and used during the active morning hours so that it is least likely to be stored as fat. Protein foods last through a busy morning while carbohydrates may result in a mid-morning slump."[39] There is almost general agreement, in numerous studies, that the omission of breakfast causes

1. Less physical effort.
2. Quicker onset of fatigue.
3. Less strength and endurance.[40]

The second habit of many young adults is to limit the variety of their food. One study showed that those foods most disliked were green and yellow vegetables, fish, and organ meats.[41]

[37] Hickman, op. cit., p. 199.
[38] Janina M. Czajkowski, "Better Breakfasts," *Instructor*, 75 (September, 1965), 43.
[39] Ibid., p. 48.
[40] Hickman, op. cit., p. 200.
[41] Deeda Sessoms, "Learning to Like a New Food," *Instructor*, 75 (September, 1965), 140.

Here are a few suggestions for increasing food likes:

1. When a new food (especially a vegetable) is offered, try it.
2. Take only a small helping of a new or disliked food.
3. Do not finish the serving if you do not feel you can, but try it again sometime soon.
4. Variety in color, texture, size, and temperature of foods on the plate will make each food more appealing. It is wise for a college student to learn to like different foods. As he enters his chosen field and during preparation for it, he will often be in a situation, in which he is eating with someone in a position of influence. Impressions are often made in regard to one's "choosiness" or broadness with regard to food. If the student or young professional is hard to please in food selection, an employer or a possible employer or an associate may generalize and conclude that the individual may be narrow-minded and not accepting of new ideas. This is just one possible unfavorable reaction, but it is not as unlikely as it may first appear to be.

Energy Needs

CALORIES AND BASAL METABOLISM

The calorie is a unit of energy. The definition of a calorie is the amount of heat that is required to raise one kilogram of water one degree centigrade. In terms of food, a calorie is measured by the amount of heat produced by an energy food. When more calories are provided than are needed, the excess finds its way to fat deposits. Inasmuch as food energy can be measured by calories, it has been found that an average number of calories is required daily for the maintenance of body weight. Everyone first needs a specific amount of energy for the body at complete rest, or basal metabolism. The basal metabolism rate shows the amount of energy used by the heart in pumping blood, the intestines in digesting food, the lungs in breathing, and so on. Basal metabolism is only part of the energy requirement. Work output and forms of exercise constitute the major need for energy. Generally men have a somewhat higher metabolic rate than women per unit of body surface; children have a higher rate than adults, adults than older people, and people who are physically active than those less so.

NORMAL WEIGHT

"Your best weight is one at which you feel well, look well, are alert, and resist fatigue and infections."[42] This will depend upon one's age, height, and bone structure. The table of weights given here was taken from the Metropolitan Life Insurance Company publication *Four Steps to Weight Control* to help the student find his "best weight." The first weight listed in each age-height group is that for a small frame; the middle figure is for medium frame; and the last is for a large frame. The student should remember that these ranges of weight will give him only a general idea of his correct weight. Only a physician, using tests, can give each individual his accurate weight range.

Numerous reasons can be given for maintaining the proper weight. A long list of the hazards of abnormal weight are shown in order to give the student an incentive to reach his normal weight.

DESIRABLE WEIGHTS°

Weight in Pounds According to Frame (in Indoor Clothing)

Height (with Shoes on) 1-inch Heels Feet Inches	Small Frame	Medium Frame	Large Frame
Men of ages 25 and over.			
5 2	112–120	118–129	126–141
5 3	115–123	121–133	129–144
5 4	118–126	124–136	132–148
5 5	121–129	127–139	135–152
5 6	124–133	130–143	138–156
5 7	128–137	134–147	142–161
5 8	132–141	138–152	147–166
5 9	136–145	142–156	151–170
5 10	140–150	146–160	155–174
5 11	144–154	150–165	159–179
6 0	148–158	154–170	164–184
6 1	152–162	158–175	168–189
6 2	156–167	162–180	173–194
6 3	160–171	167–185	178–199
6 4	164–175	172–190	182–204

[42] Hickman, op. cit., p. 208.

Height (with Shoes on) 2-inch Heels Feet Inches		Small Frame	Medium Frame	Large Frame
Women of ages 25 and over. (For girls between 18 and 25, subtract 1 pound for each year under 25.)				
4	10	92– 98	96–107	104–119
4	11	94–101	98–110	106–122
5	0	96–104	101–113	109–125
5	1	99–107	104–116	112–128
5	2	102–110	107–119	115–131
5	3	105–113	110–122	118–134
5	4	108–116	113–126	121–138
5	5	111–119	116–130	125–142
5	6	114–123	120–135	129–146
5	7	118–127	124–139	133–150
5	8	122–131	128–143	137–154
5	9	126–135	132–147	141–158
5	10	130–140	136–151	145–163
5	11	134–144	140–155	149–168
6	0	138–148	144–159	153–173

* Metropolitan Life Insurance Company, *Four Steps to Weight Control* (New York: Metropolitan Life Insurance Company, 1969), p. 12. Courtesy of Metropolitan Life Insurance Company.

Hazards of Abnormal Weight

1. Sluggishness and tiredness.
2. Short-windedness.
3. Lack of energy.
4. Backache.
5. Vertigo.
6. Heart palpitation.
7. Severe heat discomfiture.
8. Apoplexy.
9. Angina pectoris.
10. Diabetes.
11. Heart strain.
12. More susceptible to cancer.
13. More susceptible to the common cold.
14. More susceptible to arthritis.
15. More susceptible to posture defects.
16. More susceptible to flat feet.
17. More susceptible to pneumonia.
18. More susceptible to menstrual disorders.
19. More susceptible to longer and more difficult labor during childbirth.
20. More likelihood of child-bearing complications.
21. Shortened life.

The twenty-one hazards of abnormal weight can be summarized into the five D's.[43]

Disfigurement.	Disease.
Discomfort.	Death.
Disability.	

One may choose to begin working toward his normal weight upon being convinced of the health benefits, the satisfactions and pleasures of normal weight, the enjoyment of feeling and looking better, and the expectation of longer life.[44]

ABNORMAL WEIGHT PROBLEMS

Overweight in adolescence, according to Dr. Merrill S. Read,[45] tends to carry over into the adult years. Three quarters of those overweight as teen-agers were found—in one study—to be overweight as adults, with serious disease effects. Poor nutritional habits appear to be the cause of most obesity problems. "These poor food habits may have arisen from poor training early in life, a need to satisfy emotional stresses, or rebellion against the authority of parents."

A diet of losing about one pound per week or five pounds per month will have a far more lasting effect than crash dieting. Generally, when one loses much weight in a hurry, he loses stamina, becomes easily fatigued, often gains back the lost weight, and sometimes adds more. Consultation with a physician before one begins dieting is the most important advice he can receive. A doctor may suggest specific medication at the beginning of the diet, may suggest a healthy diet, and may give supervision during the weight-reducing period. Some suggestions that go along with a physician's weight-reducing diet are the following:

1. Eat three balanced meals each day.
2. Decrease intake of fats, rich desserts, and other starchy foods. Eat plentifully of fruits, vegetables, and lean meats.
3. Roast or broil meat.
4. Choose beef, chicken, turkey, smoked ham, lamb, veal, liver, or fish.
5. Remove visible fat from meat.

[43] Hickman, op. cit., p. 209.
[44] Johnson, op. cit., p. 75.
[45] Merrill S. Read, M.D., "Teen-age Nutrition: Foundation for the Future," *Practical Forecast,* 10 (February, 1965), 91.

6. Avoid reducing drugs, which can be harmful.
7. Avoid crash diets.

Moderate exercise is desirable for everyone at all times. Strenuous exercise may cause immediate weight reduction through loss of fluid, but one's thirst will require drinking and often the appetite gained will cause him to eat more. Therefore, for a weight-reducing diet, the inclusion of moderate exercise will help one firm the muscles and generally give him a feeling of vigor.

When being underweight is the problem, there is generally less need to worry. Seriously underweight people, though, should be under medical care. Those with less serious problems often simply need to eat more. Sometimes supplementing one's diet with the necessary vitamins may be of help. For gaining weight, some minor suggestions may be helpful.

1. Have a balanced diet.
2. Drink milk rather than other beverages at meals.
3. Increase meat, eggs, butter, and cream in the diet.
4. Take light snacks that will not spoil the appetite.
5. Eat a snack at bedtime, such as a milk shake or a malted milk.
6. Increase food intake gradually.
7. Get plenty of rest and sleep.
8. Exercise moderately and relax.
9. Avoid
   a. An imbalance of diet through using *too* many sweet and fatty foods.
   b. Stuffing yourself.
   c. Tension.
   d. Overfatigue.

MEDICATION AND DRUGS: THEIR USE AND MISUSE*

by Thomas W. Clark, M.D.

The constant discovery of new drugs and the improvement of older drugs have helped make our lives healthier and longer. In 1900 life expec-

---

* Written for this volume. Dr. Clark is currently Assistant Medical Director of the Methodist Hospital in Peoria, Illinois, with special interests in medical education. His medical degree is from the University of Illinois; his residency training in internal medicine followed one year of internship in Peoria. For five years Dr. Clark was a university physician at Southern Illinois University, Carbondale, where he was one of the developers of and on the Board of Directors of the Drug Crisis Center at the University.

tancy in the United States was 47.3 years. By 1965 life expectancy had increased to 71 years and modern drugs were largely responsible for this increase. With the production of antibiotics, such as penicillin in the 1940's, many serious infectious diseases were brought under control. Pneumonia, which had a fatality rate of nearly 25 per cent prior to the use of antibiotics, now has a fatality rate of less than 1 per cent. The widespread use of vaccines and serums greatly reduced the prevalence of many killing diseases such as smallpox, diphtheria, and polio. Other drugs have made our lives more comfortable. Analgesics lessen pain, and newer drugs used in psychiatry improve the mental state of many patients by relieving anxiety or lifting them from the dark depths of depression. Anesthetics have permitted great progress in surgery. Other drugs, such as insulin and cortisone, restore certain body functions towards normal, while others are used to alter certain normal functions, such as the suppression of ovulation by birth-control pills.

Thus drugs have helped make our lives happier, healthier, and richer. But these complex substances can be very potent agents, and great care must constantly be taken to guard against error and misuse.

All legitimate drugs in current use are manufactured under strict controls, which include carefully regulated research and development, production, and quality control. All drugs are subject to a multitude of tests on a variety of animals before tests on humans are permitted. Then the drug must be used in exhaustive clinical trials for further evaluation before the pharmaceutical company is permitted to produce the drug for the consumer. Great expense is taken in production to ensure that all batches of any drug are identical and have been made with absolute accuracy and uniform quality. After the drug has been approved by a regulatory agency, such as the Food and Drug Administration, its use may be controlled by the requiring of a physician's prescription for its use. These drugs are carefully and accurately dispensed by well-trained pharmacists. Only certain selected drugs, called proprietary drugs, are allowed to be sold across the counter without a physician's prescription.

Medicines may be taken in a number of ways. They can be ingested, inhaled, or applied topically in the form of creams and ointments to the skin or eyes. Other drugs are injected under the skin, into a muscle, or directly into a vein. Some compounds are specially prepared to insert into body orifices such as the rectum or vagina. No matter which route a drug is given, great care must be taken to be sure that the correct form of the drug is being used, that the correct dose is being given, and that the correct person is receiving the drug.

With a few notable exceptions, such as the diabetic, who self-administers his daily insulin, drugs that are injected are given by a nurse or a physician. Special care is required when injectables are used because of the additional dangers inherent in this method. To minimize the risk of infection the skin is first thoroughly cleansed in the area selected for the injection, and then only sterile syringes and needles are used; they are usually disposed of after each use. Failure to use properly sterilized needles could result in the transmission of hepatitis or cause serious infections in the tissues under the skin.

Drugs, then, are a two-edged sword. Unwanted side effects can occur

Figure 5-5. *A modern pharmacy is well stocked and can dispense any drug needed. To guard against the possibility of error the drugs are systematically categorized and stored. Accurate record-keeping is required wherever drugs are dispensed. (Courtesy of the Methodist Hospital of Central Illinois.)*

with almost any drug. Habitual use of aspirin may precipitate peptic ulcers in some people, skin rashes may occur as a result of allergy to a drug, and carelessness or ignorance in the use of drugs may result in tragedy. Drugs produced illegitimately do not have the benefits of careful testing and quality control, and ethical drugs may be misused with tragic consequences. Common-sense rules should be followed to avert these occurrences:

1. Take only the dose that is prescribed specifically for you. The dose may vary according to age, weight, and other individual differences and the physician will take these factors into account when prescribing. With proprietary drugs, take only the dose suggested on the label.
2. Never take a drug when its identity is in question. If the label is lost from the bottle, it is best to destroy the contents. Do not take drugs in the dark, but read the label carefully. Remember that many medicines and their containers look alike.
3. Mark poisons clearly and keep them apart from other medicines.
4. Keep all drugs in a separate place and out of reach of children. Even

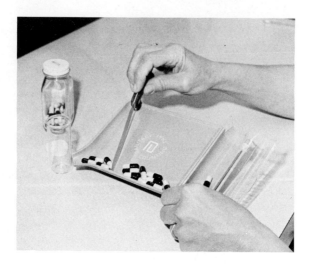

Figure 5-6. *Prescribed drugs are carefully and accurately dispensed by registered pharmacists so that the consumer is protected from taking the wrong dose or the wrong form of a drug. (Courtesy of the Methodist Hospital of Central Illinois.)*

drugs that are not considered poisonous may be fatal when ingested by a small child.

5. Destroy unused medications. Never save a drug with the intention of taking it again when similar symptoms recur. The recurrence of what seems to be the same illness may in fact be something quite different, and even if it were the same ailment, a different form of treatment may be required. Only the physician should make this judgment.

6. Never take a substance of uncertain origin. Drugs that have been produced in illegitimate laboratories do not have the benefits of careful regulation in testing, production, quality control, or accuracy of dosage.

7. Never take a drug for other than its intended purpose. To do so is to misuse the drug, which brings us to the important subject of drug abuse.

Ours is a drug taking society. We have an ever-increasing number of substances to take to lessen pain, to induce calm, to increase energy, and to create euphoria. These drugs are important weapons in the battle to restore health, but the availability of these drugs has contributed to a health problem of new dimensions.

The decade of the 1960's saw drug abuse emerge as a major social and health problem. Smoking marihuana became commonplace among college and high school students, the use of potent hallucinogens such as LSD became common to certain social groups, and addiction to hard narcotics such as heroin may have doubled during this decade. By the end of the 1960's death from drugs became the most common cause of death from the age of fifteen to thirty-five in New York City with over nine hundred deaths due to heroin alone.[46]

But what is drug abuse? Different kinds of people may give different definitions. Most doctors consider using any drug in a way that is not specifically prescribed as drug abuse, as well as taking nonprescription, across-the-counter drugs except as suggested by the manufacturer on the label. Therefore, because marihuana is never prescribed and is not an across-the-counter drug, any use of it at all would be considered abuse.

Other definitions are more liberal, and oftentimes the drug abuser will choose a definition that allows him to feel the most comfortable, such as "drug abuse is using hard narcotics," or "drug abuse is getting high every day." Such definitions, of course, are more rationalizations than anything else.

The reasons that drugs are abused are probably as varied as the number of people abusing them. There is no doubt however that pressure from peers is an important initiating force. Drug abuse may occur as an escape from the pressures of society, school, or family. It has somehow become a part of the so-called youth rebellion against the hypocrisies of parents and our society in general. Often it is a search for pleasure and gaiety; sometimes, a futile search for innovative ideas, productivity, or beauty. Some resort to drugs for added energy, others for sleep, others to fight feelings of desperation, loneliness, or depression, and still others hope for changes in sexuality.

Drug abuse has crept into every segment of our society. It is no longer a product of the ghetto. Families of the rich, the poor, the sophisticated and elite have all been shaken by this malignancy as it spreads into every nook and corner of this land. Prevalence is greatest on the college campus, but high schools are right behind them. Even grade schools, summer camps, and the military services have been invaded. To the dismay of parents everywhere, no child is exempt from this menace.

There is no doubt that there is a significantly higher incidence of personality disorders in those that seek drugs as an escape,[47] but too often these disorders go unrecognized until the people are floundering around in a world of pills, syringes, and needles.[47]

Often the dangers of drug abuse are not appreciated until irreparable damage has been done. In many ways the dangers are related to the particular drugs involved or the way in which they are administered. Often this is obvious, such as the risk of addiction when narcotics are repeatedly taken, or the risk of hepatitis when drugs are "mainlined" (injected into the vein). But, there are more subtle dangers, such as the chance of other infections or the risk of precipitating a long-term psychiatric illness. There is also a very real chance of overdose, especially when illegal drugs are purchased, because the exact dosage is often unknown to both the buyer and the seller. Also, what might be a frequently used dose of a particular

---

[46] Editors of *Medical World News* Staff, "Heroin—The Epidemic Doctors Are Not Allowed to Treat," *Medical World News*, Vol. 11, No. 15 (April 10, 1970), p. 31.

[47] Anonymous, "Diagnosis and Management of Drug Abuse," *Medical Letter*, Vol. 12, No. 16 (May 1970), pp. 65–68.

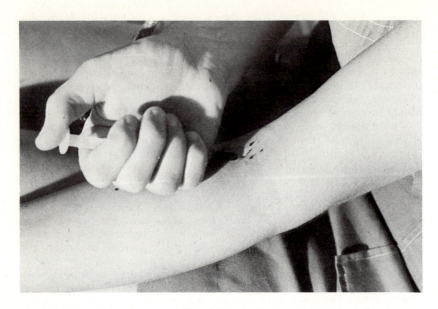

FIGURE 5-7 *The injection of illegal drugs often means using stolen or contaminated needles and syringes and inadequate preparation of the injection site. Hepatitis or skin infections are a probable consequence. (Courtesy of the Methodist Hospital of Central Illinois.)*

drug for one person could be a fatal overdose for another. This is because people vary in their tolerance to drugs. Tolerance to drugs also changes in the same individual. With many drugs there is a lesser effect from the drug after it has been used repetitively. For this reason, to experience the same effect the user progressively increases the dose, that is, his tolerance for the drug increases. As his tolerance increases, he may eventually be taking a dose of the drug that initially would have been far more than a lethal dose. If an unknowing friend were to try this dose for a kick, it would kick him right into his grave.

The real tragedy of drug abuse is often the effect it has on the rest of the family. All too often a previously happy family is disrupted to almost catastrophic levels. In many instances the parents, perhaps out of a feeling of guilt, will allow no sacrifice to be too great to bring the drug abuser back into the family circle. Occasionally younger children in the family are sent to faraway boarding schools to keep them from witnessing the new pattern of family life. This new pattern of family life is likely to be hellish for every member. It probably is safe to say that in most instances, once parents discover that their son or daughter is into drugs the family relationship from that time on is no longer the same.

There are also changes that occur outside the family circle. As drugs become more and more important to an individual, we find that his circle of friends becomes smaller and smaller. Onetime close friends fall by the wayside until eventually the only friends left to him are those that are into drugs to about the same extent as he is. At this point the abuser often labels himself as a member of a subculture, or the "drug culture." This drug subculture may have great influence on its members. An individual's entire life pattern may be completely altered by his drug-using peers. He is now susceptible to pressure from his peers to try different drugs, and for a member of such a group, illicit drugs may now be more easily obtained. It isn't difficult to imagine that under such conditions drugs may become of central importance in his life. And as the importance of drugs increases, the importance of other interests declines. Long-sought goals, such as graduation from college, may be abandoned or forgotten. Productivity on the job or at school declines, and he may desert his family to one degree or another.

Few will disagree that drug abuse is a health hazard. The abuser himself will admit that the evidence is too great to be disputed. The way in which drugs alter the body functions depends upon the particular drug, but all drugs will suppress or excite or alter in some way one or more of the body's functions. In the hands of a doctor these drug-induced alterations can be useful; in the hands of a drug abuser the results can be tragic. Some drugs, such as barbiturates and narcotics, if taken repeatedly will result in physical addiction, which is a state of adaptation to a drug manifested by an extremely uncomfortable, almost intolerable sickness when the drug is no longer available. All drugs, if taken repeatedly, can cause psychic dependence, which is a strong emotional or mental drive to take a drug, either to obtain pleasure or to avoid discomfort. Psychic dependence may be so strong that a person's entire life may revolve around the ingestion or the acquisition of a drug even though that drug is not physically addicting. At this point other aspects of life become less important and there is often general disinterest in previous goals or life style.

Injection of drugs creates additional dangers such as skin infections, phlebitis (inflammation of a vein), and hepatitis (inflammation of the liver). Needles used by another person are able to transmit a virus that is the causative agent of serum hepatitis. It has been estimated that 80 per cent of heroin addicts have evidence of liver damage presumably because of previous hepatitis that may have been unrecognized at the time.[48] Some drugs are able to cause liver damage or even kidney damage because of their toxic effects on these organs. Occasionally these effects are progressive and ultimately result in death.

For reasons not entirely understood we know that any drug can cause changes in the individual's behavioral pattern if taken for a long enough period of time. We have all heard the term *pot head*, which is often applied to a marihuana smoker when changes in appearance and behavior become manifest. However, these changes that may occur are not necessarily due to the drug itself, for many who abuse drugs are seriously maladjusted or suffer from mental disorders before turning to drugs. How many of these changes are related to compulsive drug abuse and how many are related to other social pressures are not known.

[48] P. B. Beeson and W. McDermott, *Textbook of Medicine*, 12th ed. (Philadelphia: W. B. Saunders, 1967).

There are other dangers that have not yet been mentioned but are very real; for instance, impulsive behavior while one is high on a drug, proneness to accidents, and even nutritional deficiencies because of loss of appetite, disinterest in food, or simply not being able to buy a square meal because of the expense of a drug habit.

Any drug can be abused, but generally only those drugs that affect the mind in some way are abused. The generally abused drugs are usually put into one of four categories: narcotics, barbiturates, amphetamines, and hallucinogens. Hallucinogens comprise a broad category of drugs that are not necessarily related chemically but have the common property of precipitating hallucinations if enough of the drug is taken.

MARIHUANA (MARIJUANA, CANNABIS, POT, GRASS, JOINTS, TEA)

Of all the illegal drugs currently in use in our society, marihuana (cannabis) has generated the most popular concern. It is classified as a hallucinogen although it seldom causes hallucinations when taken in the usual amount. Although there is substantial agreement that most other drugs abused are unquestionably deleterious in their effects, there is disagreement, even among well-informed scientists, regarding the degree of threat posed by marihuana. However, more and more reports are being published regarding the occurrence of acute psychological reactions apparently precipitated by marihuana.[49] Paranoia and panic states are known to occur occasionally. Impaired judgment and impulsive behavior may be dangerous effects of the drug, particularly in situations such as driving, climbing, operating equipment of various kinds, or wherever good judgment is important. The chronic user may use the drug to escape stress, and as a result his mental growth is impaired by his not learning how to deal with frustration. Chronic users may withdraw from present realities, lose ambition and drive, and become present-oriented rather than future-oriented.

Even so, the best-informed sources estimate that nationwide 50 per cent of high school and college students have experimented with marihuana to one degree or another. Fortunately, only a few of these experimenters become chronic users.[50]

Typically, a sense of relaxation and well-being follows the inhalation of a "joint." In this state jokes are usually funnier, misfortunes more poignant, and human relations more deeply perceived. The appreciation of food, sex, and, in particular, music is intensified. The user may believe that his thoughts are unusually profound (an impression rarely shared by observers). Visual imagery is increased, feelings of depersonalization may occur, and when one has taken larger doses, colors may shimmer and visual distortions may occur.

Although there is sometimes a desire for repeated use of marihuana,

[49] D. Perna, "Psychotogenic Effect of Marihuana," *Journal of the American Medical Association,* 209:7 (1969), 1085–1086; and J. A. Talbott, "Marihuana Psychosis," *Journal of the American Medical Association,* 210:2 (1969), 299–302.
[50] N. Q. Brill, "The Marihuana Problem," UCLA Interdepartmental Conference, *Annals of Internal Medicine,* 73 (1970), 449, 465.

physical addiction does not occur. And although a causal relationship probably does not exist, various authors have been impressed by the frequency with which chronic marihuana users seem also to be indiscriminate users of other drugs, such as LSD, amphetamines, barbiturates, and heroin.[51]

The legal status of marihuana is the subject of fierce debate. However, the various scientific and medical committees that have studied the matter have come to a surprisingly unanimous conclusion: that marihuana should not be legalized for general consumption but that harsh legal penalties are unwise.[52]

LSD (ACID) AND OTHER HALLUCINOGENS

With the possible exception of marihuana, no drug has stimulated greater public debate than lysergic acid diethylamide or LSD. LSD is the most powerful and dramatic of the hallucinogens, although it shares its properties with mescaline (from the peyote cactus), psilocybin (a mushroom derivative), and dimethyltryptamine, known as DMT. In addition to these, hallucinogens are a score of other agents whose popularity has fluctuated, including STP*, morning glory seeds, and nutmeg. But LSD is the most potent of the hallucinogens, in fact, it is the most powerful psychotropic (mind-altering) drug known to man. The user alleges that the drug augments aesthetic sensitivity and enhances creativity, that it increases the capacity for love and has aphrodisiac effects. Suffice it to say that none of these claims are substantiated by objective data.[53] The facts are that LSD is a terribly dangerous drug and that dramatic and often tragic unwanted reactions are well known. These include acute psychosis, the acting out of sociopathic or homosexual impulses, convulsions, uncontrolled aggression (including homicide and suicide), and overwhelming, ego-shattering panic reactions. Occasionally, users who have had hallucinogenic experiences under the influence of LSD have had recurrences of the hallucinations weeks later. Called flashbacks, these episodes are almost always terrifying and may be brought on by stress or other drugs, such as marihuana.

As with marihuana, there is probably much yet to be learned about LSD. There have been a number of reports attempting to link LSD to chromosome damage and birth defects. There may be an association between LSD and leukemia of the type observed in survivors of Hiroshima and other persons exposed to high doses of radiation.[54]

All in all, LSD seems to be a treacherous drug, and yet it has been illicitly manufactured by amateur chemists, combined at times with other dangerous compounds such as strychnine, and ingested by as many as 5 per cent of the college population.

[51] Anonymous, "Marihuana," *Medical Letter*, 12:8 (1970), pp. 33–35; and Brill, op. cit.

[52] Ibid.

* Dimethoxy-methyl-amphetamine

[53] D. B. Louria, "Lysergic Acid Diethylamide." *New England Journal of Medicine*, 278 (February 1968), 435–438.

[54] K. Hirschhorn, "LSD and Chromosomal Damage," *Hospital Practice*, 4 (February 1969), pp. 98–103.

AMPHETAMINES (STIMULANTS, SPEED, UPPERS)

Amphetamines are central nervous system stimulants and are used medically to suppress appetite and occasionally to combat fatigue. Although amphetamines are not vital to the everyday practice of medicine, vast numbers are produced by the pharmaceutical companies each year and millions of doses somehow are diverted into illicit markets.[55] Benzedrine, Dexedrine, and Methedrine are the most commonly used amphetamines. Although most often taken by mouth, they are occasionally injected intravenously (mainlined).

Abuse often begins when a relatively small dose of an amphetamine, such as Dexedrine, is taken by a student to keep him awake so that he may study late for an examination. However, if abuse continues, the dosage typically increases and ultimately a vicious cycle begins to occur. As large doses of amphetamines are taken, the abuser may experience longer and longer periods of restlessness and jitteriness followed by exhaustion and

FIGURE 5-8. *Eventually drug dependency leads to depression and a feeling of abandonment. The narcotics addict often lives in particularly tragic circumstances because the cost of maintaining the drug habit is so great. (Courtesy of the Methodist Hospital of Central Illinois.)*

[55] S. F. Yolles, *Recent Research on Narcotics, LSD, Marihuana, and Other Dangerous Drugs,* Public Health Service Publication No. 1961 (Washington, D.C.: U.S. Government Printing Office, 1969).

finally sleep. After awakening the amphetamine abuser feels low and depressed, so depressed that he will reach for anything that might lift him out of such a miserable state. For his depression he again takes amphetamines and the cycle begins all over again. Many times the abuser recognizes what is happening and realizes that the cause of his depression is amphetamine abuse, yet his depression is too terrible to allow him to face the world without getting a lift from his drug.

Chronic amphetamine intoxication may lead to psychotic behavior. There is also a high incidence of social and occupational deterioration in chronic abusers, and just recently investigators have shown a possible relationship between amphetamine abuse and a potentially lethal inflammation of the small arteries.[56]

BARBITURATES (DOWNERS, GOOFBALLS, RED DEVILS, YELLOW JACKETS) AND THE DEPRESSANT DRUGS

The best known of the sedatives are the barbiturates. Unlike marihuana, LSD, and amphetamines, barbiturates may be physically addicting. But there are additional factors that make barbiturates and other sedative drugs

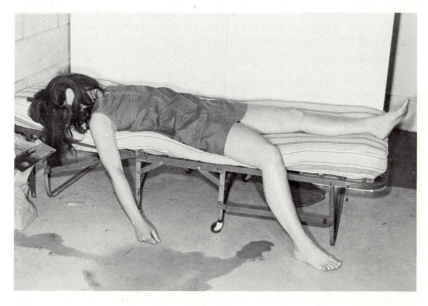

FIGURE 5-9. *The number of deaths caused by drugs have been steadily increasing over the past several years as a result of either unintentional overdose or suicide because of drug-induced despondency and despair. (Courtesy of the Methodist Hospital of Central Illinois.)*

[56] B. P. Citron, "Necrotizing Angiitis in Drug Addicts," *New England Journal of Medicine,* 283:19 (1970).

particularly dangerous. If too much of the drug is inadvertently taken, death will follow because of the depression of certain of the body's vital functions, such as respiration and kidney function. Tolerance occurs, that is, more and more of the drug is required for the same effects to be produced, yet as tolerance develops, the lethal dose remains relatively unchanged and death may occur by unintentional overdose. Other sedative drugs, including alcohol, lower the lethal dose of barbiturates, thus compounding the danger of overdose.

When physical dependence on barbiturates occurs because of repeated ingestion of large doses, a characteristic sickness or withdrawal syndrome occurs when the drug is no longer available. This sickness is not only uncomfortable, but unlike the withdrawal sickness associated with narcotics, it is potentially fatal. If a person has been taking large doses for as long as six to eight weeks and the drug is then suddenly withdrawn, the user for the next two or three days will become increasingly restless and sleep poorly. A state similar to the delerium tremors of alcohol may then follow, which is associated with hallucinations, agitation, and oftentimes by convulsions and even death.

The effects of barbiturates are similar to the effects of alcohol. The abuser under the influence of these drugs is confused, has an unsteady gait and slurred speech, is drowsy, and tends to be poor company. Abusers frequently incur serious injuries from falls or other accidents and may commit crimes and yet retain no memory of them.

NARCOTICS

The opiate derivatives, known as hard stuff, include drugs such as morphine, codeine, Demerol, and heroin. Narcotics are physically addicting drugs, and the addiction occurs after a relatively short time of repeated use of the drug. Although the withdrawal sickness is not as life threatening as is barbiturate withdrawal, it is a rare addict who does not return to narcotics again. Even with treatment, the relapse rate is frightfully high. Over 90 per cent of addicts who undertake withdrawal treatment return to their habit.[57] The development of methadone maintenance programs has been an exciting but controversial recent development. Because methadone maintenance involves the continuous use of a synthetic narcotic on a long-term basis, it has been the object of criticism. However, in selected addicts social rehabilitation seems to be a feasible goal.

At one time narcotic addiction was, for the most part, confined to the ghetto. Now, with the increasing abuse of other drugs, more and more young people are looking for bigger thrills and ultimately are introduced to one of the narcotic drugs, typically heroin. The first response to narcotics is euphoria, sometimes intense. If mainlined the reaction is even more intense and has been described by users as a mule kick, or similar to a hundred orgasms. But after repeated usage the kick becomes less and less, and soon the user realizes that he is no longer taking the drug for pleasure but out of need. He may not admit at first that he has become an addict, but

[57] N. E. Zinberg, "Narcotic Usage," *New England Journal of Medicine,* 270: 19–20 (1964).

eventually denial is no longer possible and his life becomes one of despair and hopelessness.

The cost of narcotic addiction is staggering. In New York City alone over ten million dollars a day are lost because of narcotic addiction and its associated crimes.[58] The cost to the individual is also staggering; it costs the average addict in New York seventy-five dollars each and every day to maintain his habit. To support such a habit the addict is forced to resort to a daily life of crime. Spending everything they have on drugs, addicts eat so poorly that they frequently become emaciated. Needle marks over the veins of the arms and legs are apparent to a careful observer. Usually the addict has left his family, friends, and job, and unless he can be rehabilitated he is lost as a useful member of society.

Making Health Rules a Practice

Nature has kindly freed our minds for larger thoughts and tasks by assisting us to do the daily routines of life by the help of habits. Habits grow gradually and become a part of an individual's life and character. Good habits are the foundations of permanent physical and mental health.[59]

Because habits have been greatly responsible for determining one's quality of life, developing them becomes equally important to the understanding of physical health. Habits cannot be learned but are developed through practice in daily living. In some of the preceding sections material has been presented openly with alternative choices of approaches to problems and with pertinent facts for deeper understanding. In this section the choice of the student is not so much between alternatives of response as between developing the response or not.

The fact that we assume that "If one is a reasonably healthy person, he can expect to remain so if he continues good health habits . . ."[60] strengthens the reasoning that one will either accept or reject the material on health habits, which is written as rules, not as choices.

You can recognize good physical health in yourself and others by various physical indications. Some of these are (1) vitality and a feeling of well-being, (2) a bright facial expression, (3) a well-developed body, (4) a healthy color of skin, (5) glossy hair, (6) bright, clear eyes, (7) correct posture, (8) good teeth, (9) good digestion, (10)

---

[58] S. F. Yolles, "Recent Research on Narcotics, LSD, Marihuana, and Other Dangerous Drugs," Public Health Service Publication No. 1961 (Washington, D.C.: U.S. Government Printing Office, 1969).

[59] Etheredge, op. cit., p. 11.

[60] Ibid., p. 10.

PHYSICAL RATING CHART

Item	Possible Score	First Rating	Second Rating
Do you			
1. Eat all of the dietary essentials daily?	10		
2. See your dentist at least once a year?	5		
3. Brush your teeth after every meal or at least twice a day?	5		
4. Have at least one health examination every year?	10		
5. Get the amount of sleep regularly that permits you to function efficiently? (Eight hours are needed by most people.)	10		
6. Have good posture in walking, standing, sitting?	10		
7. Care for your eyes by studying and working in such a position that sufficient light is on your work and not on your eyes?	5		
8. Have your eyes tested periodically?	5		
9. Have one hour of physical activity daily? Have one hour of social recreation daily?	10		
10. Avoid using hallucinogenic drugs, excessive alcohol, and cigarettes?	10		
11. Have regular elimination without the use of laxatives?	10		
12. Have good health? Surplus energy? Never feel too tired?	10		
Total	100		

regular bowel movements, (11) restful sleep, and (12) a normal appetite.

In order to pretest further your own physical health, fill out the "Physical Rating Chart" in the column titled "First Rating." After you have read the chapter and practiced the habits, you will want to take the test a second time and compare your results.

The first minimum rule of "good" physical health is *Eat regularly the food required for optimum health.* All of the previous section dealt with the dietary needs, the important functions, and problems of deficiencies. A separate section was written on this minimum rule, because it is probably the most important. The remaining eleven follow.

The second rule is *Take a bath every day*. Bathing cleans the skin and gives it proper tone; it is used to stimulate the body, to relax after strenuous exercise or before retiring, and to relieve congestion. "A bath," it has been said, "is the beginning of a feeling of physical fitness and well-being."[61] What kind of bath one takes will depend greatly upon the individual. For some, cold baths can be stimulating, but not all can accustom themselves to these. Warm baths can be relaxing and hot baths (from 110° F. to 120° F.) can again be stimulating. Certain precautions[62] should be taken in bathing: (1) If a cold morning shower causes shivering and discomfort, a moderate temperature will be better. (2) If the heart is weak, medical advice should be followed in bathing. (3) For stimulation and hygiene a shower bath is preferred to a tub bath. (4) Oil should be used on the skin for those with naturally dry skin. (5) Vigorous towel drying should come after a cold bath.

Brush your teeth after each meal or at least twice a day. It is advised that one have two or three tooth brushes, so that one brush will always be dry. If a brush is allowed to remain in a closed dark place, the dampness will provide a thriving home for bacteria. Therefore hang the brushes in fresh air, away from other brushes to avoid bristles touching. Remember to discard a brush before it becomes ragged. Cold water should be used in brushing teeth, because warm water softens the bristles, thereby making the brushing of the teeth and gums less effective. There is a technique to brushing teeth.

The technique of brushing is important. Do not brush too vigorously; this may injure the enamel and push the gum away from the tooth. Brush down on the upper teeth; brush up on the lower ones. Hold the toothbrush so the bristles point away from the biting edge of the teeth and towards the gums at a forty-five degree angle. Enough pressure should be exerted to force the sides of the bristles between the teeth. Brush only a few teeth at a time, inside and out. Brush the biting surface by applying the brush directly and rotating it around. The gums should be massaged also in your brushing. Dental floss or dental tape is useful in removing food from between the teeth.[63]

After brushing, the mouth should be rinsed out with cold water, thus invigorating the gums and removing stray particles of food and toothpaste. The crevices should be cleaned with dental floss rather than

[61] Stearn and Stearn, op. cit., p. 155.
[62] Hickman, op. cit., p. 85.
[63] Ibid., p. 238.

tooth picks because of the floss's softness and less possibility of irritating the gums. An examination of the teeth should be scheduled for twice a year. A final consideration to remember in the care of teeth is that hard chewing is necessary for teeth to be strong and for tartar deposits to be avoided.

The fourth minimum health rule is *Care for skin and hair.* Healthy skin requires (1) good general health, including a balanced diet, freedom from constipation, a well-regulated blood system, and freedom from organic and infectious diseases; (2) exercise in fresh air, sunshine, and change of temperature for skin tone and conditioning and cheerful emotions; (3) cleanliness for proper functioning of the skin pores (the amount of soap should be limited with dry skin. Gentle soapy lather should be applied to the face, the soap washed off with hot water, and the face then rinsed with cold water.); (4) avoidance of harmful overexposure to sun and wind; (5) understanding of the condition of your skin—oily or dry, rough, scaly, or smooth—and its blemishes; (6) only minor concern about cosmetics; and (7) consultation with a physician when a skin disorder occurs.[64]

Some believe that caring for the hair is the primary item in being well groomed. Whether it is primary or not is inconsequential, but it is one of the first aspects of one's person that is noticed and it does reflect general nutritive health. Daily brushing, with a brush of medium-soft bristles, distributes the oil smoothly over the hair and stimulates the scalp. Daily care also should include a massage of the scalp with the fingertips. The frequency of shampoos depends upon the oiliness or dryness of the skin and exposure to dust and dirt. Using soft water is preferable for a full hair luster. Soap should be thoroughly rinsed away after a shampoo. Thus, because the rinsing away of the lather of cake soap is so difficult, cake soap should be avoided or hair luster will be lost. For very dry hair a small amount of olive oil may be rubbed into the scalp and hair. Dandruff is usually caused by a lack of one of the three daily needs of the hair: cleanliness, brushing, and massage.

Rule five, *Sleep at least eight hours daily in fresh air.* According to Harry J. Johnson, M.D., sleep is one of the most important factors of sound physical and mental health.

Adequate sleep is vital to good health. . . . Just as the body must have activity to live, it must also have adequate rest to live at its best. . . . For

---

[64] Ibid., pp. 84–85.

without sleep, you experience fatigue. . . . You can be completely freed of organic troubles, yet if you experience fatigue you are robbed of a sense of well-being. You lose your zest, your ability to think straight, your feeling of cheer. You find the hours dragging and your attentiveness to conversation dragging.[65]

The amount of sleep needed depends on many factors, but Johnson says that nine out of ten adults should have no less than eight hours of sleep per night as an "irreducible minimum." The average college student requires eight hours of sleep in order to finish his course of study successfully. Regular habits of sleep are preferable to making up for the lack of sleep. Sleep is required to a greater degree by persons who are highly nervous, anemic, underweight, or overly active, who tire quickly, and who have been acutely ill.[66]

Simple mental work can be done after a short night of sleep, but more difficult work can be done with less effort and more efficiency when one has slept longer. However, too much sleep will not add to one's efficiency. The amount of sleep necessary for an individual depends upon his age, his work and worry and his physical condition. . . . The amount of sleep necessary decreases until about the eighteenth year, when an average of about eight hours a night seems to be required for complete alertness. A sufficient amount of sleep should be taken to give the body a chance to recuperate from the work of the previous day. If one continues to draw on his bank account of surplus energy without sufficient deposits of sleep, he will soon find his fund of strength exhausted.[67]

For regular nightly sleep, these rules are adapted from Hickman.

1. Form the habit of sleeping a regular number of hours.
2. Plan study hours carefully: make an effort to study during the day or early evening and reserve the time from 11 P.M. to 7 A.M. or 12 P.M. to 8 A.M. for sleep.
3. Plan a few minutes of physical exercise to increase blood circulation and bring greater mental alertness.
4. Avoid the many factors causing sleeplessness, such as not enough exercise, overeating, worrying, tenseness, and the excessive use of stimulants.
5. Remember, physical surroundings should promote sound, healthful sleep. Ventilation without drafts, sounds reduced, darkness, a com-

---

[65] Johnson, op. cit., pp. 4–7.
[66] Etheredge, op. cit., p. 35.
[67] Ibid., pp. 34–35.

fortable and flat bed, a firm mattress, and light but warm covers are favorable conditions for sleep.

6. Forget the problems of the day and completely relax and rest.
7. Remember, a warm bath, a little exercise, or a hot drink and a small amount of food may bring sleep quickly.
8. Avoid the overuse of coffee. Coffee acts as a stimulant for many people.
9. Avoid the regular use of drugs.
10. Short naps in the middle of the day have been found to be very beneficial to some.[68]

Aching muscles are sometimes an indication of lack of sufficient sleep. Guard against this and other unhealthy effects by making eight hours of sleep daily a habit.

Exercise regularly out of doors with fresh air and sunlight. The sixth rule is an important health habit because it greatly influences the body functions of circulation, excretion, and respiration and of the skin, the nervous system and the muscular system. Being a health habit means that exercise should be steady and not sporadic; it is an every-day need, not for weekends only. Walking is an exercise that most college students find is their most frequent activity; this is a good exercise and one that is not easily overdone, so try to appreciate your opportunity to walk between classes, to the dormitory, or to the cafeteria. Some exercises develop muscles and promote coordination; these include running, gardening, tennis, golf, horseback riding, and housekeeping.[69]

Exercise should give you pleasure; it should afford a change from your everyday occupation; it should be exhilarating to your body but relaxing to your mind; and it should leave you mildly tired but never exhausted. In short, it should leave you feeling good.[70]

The amount of exercise that one needs depends upon his age, sex, and occupation, the climate, and his physical condition. Because diversion and relaxation are so necessary to physical and mental health, the "student will improve his learning capacity by interspersing short periods of physical exercises between class and study hours."[71]

Health rule seven is *Have a period of relaxation at the close of the*

[68] Hickman, op. cit., p. 130.
[69] Stearn and Stearn, op. cit., pp. 175–176.
[70] Hickman, op. cit., p. 101.
[71] Stearn and Stearn, op. cit., p. 177.

day's work. This can be a short daily rest period or an agreeable diversion. Relaxation does not have to mean inactivity. It can be a "relaxed pursuit of a hobby or the serene contemplation of life."[72] Many people have enjoyed sports, television, the radio, and reading for true relaxation. Any change from one type of work to another gives a certain amount of rest to the body.

Maintain a balanced program of exercise and relaxation. The eighth rule suggests the possibility of overactivity or too strenuous exercise. Beginning a program of physical activity too quickly can be harmful. Previously seldom-used muscles stretched too far too soon with a previously lazy heart being worked too vigorously can easily spoil one's health. Overactivity is as detrimental as lack of activity. A balanced program provides sufficient time for both relaxing and exercising, the best possible situation.

Retain good posture by sitting, standing, and walking correctly. Poor posture is a lack of balance in the body parts caused by sloppy

FIGURE 5-10. *Correct posture for standing.*

[72] Ibid., p. 180.

habits, disease, fatigue, or accident.[73] Body curvatures vary and thus good posture must vary, because balance is due to the weight and size of body parts. Hickman describes correct posture for standing.

When you stand, your body parts—legs, pelvic girdle, body, and head—should be in more or less straight alignment when seen in profile. Your weight should rest directly over your ankle bones for easy balance. This position will distribute your weight evenly over your arches, enabling you to lift either your heels or your toes without shifting your position. Keep the

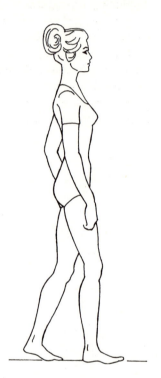

FIGURE 5-11. *Correct posture for walking.*

hip muscles tucked under and the knees slightly flexed. Such a position will prevent exaggerated curves and will be most economical of your energy and less fatiguing for your muscles, for the center of gravity is directly above the base of support, your feet resting on the ground.[74]

When standing, rather than placing the weight on one leg and using the other for a prop, one should let the weight remain equal over both

[73] Hickman, op. cit., p. 114.
[74] Ibid., p. 111.

legs. For a wider base of support, the legs may be spread slightly, or one foot may be placed slightly before the other.[75]

In walking, the head and shoulders should be directly above the pelvic region; the body should be centered over the ankles; hip muscles should be tucked in, taking care of the abdominal bulge; legs should swing like pendulums from the hips; and the knees should be slightly flexed. Arms should be relaxed and able to swing naturally at the side. Toes should point straight ahead and each step should fall directly in front of the last one.[76]

While one is sitting, the space between the chair and the lower back should be closed. The feet should be able to rest easily on the

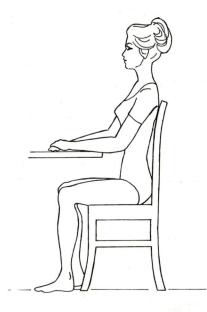

FIGURE 5-12.   *Correct posture for sitting.*

floor. The head, shoulders, and pelvic girdle remain aligned. Bending forward should come from the hips rather than the waist, with the abdomen muscles held tense.[77]

For the sake of appearance, as well as ease and comfort, every woman needs to give some thought to posture in getting into a car. There are only a few steps, easily mastered, which can add to your grace. (1) Stand beside the car facing front. Place the foot that is nearer the car a few inches inside on the floor; (2) until now you have

[75] Ibid.
[76] Ibid., p. 112.
[77] Ibid.

FIGURE 5-13. *The easy way to lift.*

remained in an upright position. Now bend the knees until you are seated, giving a slight push with the foot outside the car; (3) as you straighten up, bring the other foot inside the car. Practice makes it easy and graceful.

Health rule ten is *Wear hygienic clothing.* The requirements for keeping the body at a near-constant temperature and for maintaining one's feeling of well-being dictate the need for hygienic clothing.

FIGURE 5-14. *Getting into a car gracefully.*

Clothes should be considered for their heat-retaining qualities and their ability to absorb moisture. These conditions help the body to regulate heat.

There was a time when clothing choices were limited largely to wool, silk, cotton, and linen. Wool and silk were chosen for cool weather and because they readily absorb, and for a cool feel, cotton and linen were used in warm weather. "More new fibers and fabrics have made their appearance in the last twenty years than in the preceding two thousand years!"[78] This helps to account for the wide selection of fibers and fabrics from which one can choose today. Man-made fibers, blends, finishes, and weaves have multiplied in number. For example, wool is now used in blends and is woven into such sheer fabrics that it can be worn in warm as well as cool weather. Cottons can be treated in such a manner as to give them warm characteristics, and cottons in blends are now worn the year round. Blends, the combinations of two or more fibers, lend great variety and can bring out the good qualities of more than one fiber in the same fabric. The coolness and absorption of cotton and the wrinkle resistance, rapid drying, and "feel" of dacron make dacron-cotton a popular blend today. The finishes applied to fabrics have also extended the choice boundaries of today's fabric selections, giving even more desirable characteristics to the clothes we choose. "Durapress" is a current example of desirable finishes applied to garments that offer comfort, desirable appearance, and easy-care properties. "The suitability of your clothes for the occasion, or their appropriateness, is determined by what you are doing and where you are, as well as by the time of the year and the prevailing customs in the locality."[79] The amount of clothing, too, is important in keeping one's body at a comfortable temperature. The cleanliness, pressing, freedom from need of repairs, and style affect one's feeling of well-being. One may fluctuate from contentment to embarrassment depending upon the clothes he wears and the way he reacts to them.[80] Thus, the choice and condition of clothing have significant influence upon both one's physical and one's emotional health.

Everyone young and old should *Have regular elimination.* Constipation may be due to the lack of thiamine in the diet or the consumption of a too-high-protein diet.[81] Insufficient exercise seems

[78] Mary Mark Sturm and Edwina H. Grieser, *Guide to Modern Clothing* (New York: McGraw-Hill Book Co., 1962), p. 69.
[79] Ibid., p. 11.
[80] Etheredge, op. cit., p. 201.
[81] Stearn and Stearn, op. cit., p. 147.

to be a factor in constipation. Other reasons making regular elimination difficult are a lack of sufficient bulk food and poor posture.[82] Bulk food, which is cellulose and has been previously considered in the section on diet as a need of fiber content in the diet, is found in fruits and vegetables and in the outer coat of ripe grain. Poor posture causes the overcrowding of the abdominal regions and weakening of those muscles. Hickman writes that "One of the most important of all causes of constipation is believed to be the continued use of laxatives."[83] In order to overcome constipation and achieve regular elimination certain rules for correction may be followed.

1. Eat plenty of fruits and vegetables.
2. Drink plenty of water daily.
3. Exercise regularly.
4. Form a habit of elimination at the same time.[84]

The twelfth and final health rule of this section is *Have a periodic health examination.* A periodic health examination can be a "key tool in preventive medicine," emphasizes Dr. Harry J. Johnson. Preventive medicine can be defined "as that practice by the physician which will show a patient the way to better, healthier living, and which will detect the existence of disease at the earliest possible time, so that treatment will be more effective, less costly, and less agonizing."[85]

A simple routine in your doctor's office may take no more than twenty to thirty minutes. It may include an examination of your eyes, ears, nose, throat, lungs, heart, abdomen, and reflexes, a hemoglobin test, and a urinalysis. He [the doctor] may also ask that you go for a chest x-ray. In the absence of specific symptoms, this sort of examination may be adequate for many of you. On the other hand, there are those who need to check into clinics for several days and go through a great variety of complex tests.[86]

Depending upon the individual case the examination may be just a simple consultation, a half-hour routine, a day's tests, or several days of tests and consultation. A regular or periodic health examination means, generally, at least once a year. In this way a doctor can notice changes and thereby detect disease.

[82] Etheredge, op. cit., pp. 74–75.
[83] Hickman, op. cit., p. 225.
[84] Stearn and Stearn, op. cit., p. 147.
[85] Johnson, op. cit., p. 161.
[86] Ibid., p. 165.

6

Developing Good Relationships with Others

You and Your Worlds

With some understanding of one's emotions for seeking healthy adjustment and with a determined effort to develop necessary physical health habits—two personal responsibilities of the college person—we look toward the gaining of understanding in group situations: personal qualities affecting our relationships.

The first aspect considered is "Understanding Some Factors in Personality Development," that is, the developing of personality in respect to getting along with others. Because personal grooming is important to the way others see us, this topic will be included.

Rules regarding correspondence, introductions, dress for the occasion, being a guest, being a traveler, and dating tips will be explored in the section "Recognizing the Importance of Good Social Usage" in the latter part of this chapter. "The Ethical Dimension of a Career" is included for study by the beginning college student. It is believed by the writer that college faculties assume too much in their evaluation of what students understand in the realm of ethics. Although much stems from common sense, it seems that too many students are left without any guidance or help in establishing their bases for action and so must learn by their mistakes. It is hoped that this chapter will help prepare the student for new and recurring situations and help him to avoid making regrettable decisions. Professional ethics play an important role in our relationships with others in college *and* after the college years.

Understanding Some Factors in Personality Development

Education and training are basic requisites for the professions. It has been found, however, that when applicants for a position have equal or similar education and training, the factor that determines who gets the position is most often the personality of the applicant. Research studies also show that more people lose jobs because of personality factors than for any other reason. Whether or not one advances in a position—and if so, how rapidly—is also affected, and often determined, by personality factors as well as by the basic preparation for the position. Because personality can be changed, it behooves the beginning college student to gain some understanding of personality and the factors in personality development, to evaluate his own personality, and then to work assiduously on changing his own personality where changes need to be made.

Personality is an awesome quality. We cannot adequately define it, there is no pat, simple formula for developing it, and it requires constant diligent work to try to better ourselves. Those who define personality have included such ideas as: Personality is a result of everything that has happened to a person, especially the experiences he has with people and things in his environment.[1] Personality is concerned with one's effect on others, his outward appearance, and all of his habits of thought and activity.[2] Personality is the "individual as a whole, his height and weight and loves and hates and blood pressure and reflexes; his smiles and hopes and bowed legs and enlarged tonsils. It means all that anyone is and all that he is trying to become."[3]

There is a vast difference of opinion on the exact components of personality. For our use in considering the developing of personality we shall define it as all of the characteristics of a person, inherited or

[1] William E. Henry, *Exploring Your Personality* (Chicago: Science Research Associates, Inc., 1953), pp. 15–16.

[2] Lillian N. Reid, *Personality and Etiquette* (Lexington, Mass.: D. C. Heath and Company, 1950), p. 168. Copyright 1950 by D. C. Heath and Company. Reprinted by permission.

[3] Karl A. Menninger, *The Human Mind* (New York: Alfred A. Knopf, 1959), p. 23.

developed through his experiences and environment, that are reflected to others in his conversation, appearance, and activities.

One place to look for those qualities sought in a pleasing personality is in the personnel offices of most companies. Personality traits have been enumerated on various employee rating scales. Among them are

ability to present ideas—expression	intelligence
adaptability	interest
agreeableness	judgment
alertness	loyalty
appearance	manners
capacity for growth	neatness
character	optimism
cheerfulness	physical qualities
cooperation	self-confidence—poise
courage	sense of humor
dependability	speech
dress	tact
emotional stability	temperament
enthusiasm	tolerance
friendliness	trustworthiness
honesty	unselfishness
initiative	voice

Primarily the "positiveness" or "negativeness" of one's personality has two effects: that upon relationships with others and that upon one's job successes. A pleasing personality works to build friendships and good marriage partnerships. Occupational success determined by personality characteristics includes both that of getting or not getting the job and advancing or not advancing. The college student will see these job success effects first hand as he tries to get or advance in a part-time job, a summer job, or a professional position as he prepares to leave school.

Personality is not set. Because it is developed through preceding experiences, it follows that it can be modified by anticipatory experiences. With work and a willingness to improve, an individual can change his personality. That fact is basic to this chapter. Without such an acceptance of the idea that personality can change, there would be no need to study the developing of personality.

Steps in Developing Personality

1. Becoming aware of personality problem(s).
2. Seeing reasons for overcoming the problem(s).
3. Wanting to improve.
4. Forming a plan of procedure.
5. Finding encouragement by progress.
6. Never making an exception.
7. Looking at the progress: improved personality—more and deeper friendships and occupational successes.

The remainder of this section will be concerned with improving personality in respect to dealing with both one's attitude and one's appearance—grooming and wardrobe selection. The first step in developing personality is awareness. One method of determining one's own assets and liabilities is by making two lists. Think of the people that you particularly like and list those qualities that cause you to like them, that is, list the outstandingly good qualities. Next think about the people that you do not like. List the qualities that cause you to dislike them. With these two lists in hand go down the list item by item and ask yourself if you have these qualities. Next ask yourself the questions: Are there reasons for changing some of my qualities? Do I really want to change? If the answers to these questions are yes, you are ready to form your plan of procedure, note progress as you keep working on these qualities, and try very hard never to make an exception.

The student should read the following suggestions with personal implications. Agreeableness, manners, and temperament are the three traits concerned most with making friends. Goals for being agreeable include aiming for cooperation and avoiding concern with trifles. Good manners, simply defined, are conduct and behavior that make other people feel comfortable and subtly make them feel important. Good manners are the bases for social usage. Temperament is concerned with emotional control. Probably the best suggestion that can be given here is that remaining quiet when anger has developed will often quell it.

Loyalty, too, is concerned with friendships, but these are the lasting relationships. Loyalty implies that we remember first those close to us and those people we have known. Dependability involves living up to what is expected of us. When one commits himself in any way, he must fulfill that responsibility. These character elements—loyalty and dependability—reflect to others one's personality. Individuals develop a reputation of being "undependable" or "disloyal" to others who see their failures. Once such a reputation develops, it becomes difficult to change, but through a conscious effort, improvement can be made and friendships rekindled.

Ability to express oneself or to be able to join in conversation will be an important factor throughout a college career as well as during professional life and in social relationships. Expression, interest, knowledge, and self-confidence are (at least in theory) the marks of an educated man. Educated men "express themselves well, have many interests, show evidences of intelligence, and, because of their knowledge, possess enough self-confidence not to be embarrassed in their relationships with others."[4]

It is important to be able to talk to another about his occupation, inasmuch as this is probably his main interest; but the more educated one is, the more his interests broaden to other topics, such as current events, literature, music, art, ideas, and ideals. The poor conversationalist is often limited to the weather, local events, and people. The good conversationalist may include these where they have unusual aspects, but in discussing people he is more likely to discuss great people rather than to find fault with local acquaintances or political figures. Religion and politics are best avoided except as ideas and ideals.

Reid describes a good conversationalist as one who "never seems to experience those embarrassing moments when every thought about every single thing in the world has flown out of the window," is "ready with sympathy when another is grieved or hurt," draws "others into the conversation," puts "energy and life into lagging conversation," and, above all, "contributes—not just replies—to lively chit-chat or more serious discussion as the case may be."[5]

A good conversationalist:

1. Is ready with ideas to discuss.
2. Listens as much as he speaks.
3. Has a soothing voice.
4. Speaks clearly and distinctly.
5. Does not use stilted language.

[4] Paul W. Chapman, *Your Personality and Your Job* (Chicago: Science Research Associates, 1944), p. 49.
[5] Reid, op. cit., p. 212.

6. Is interested in people.
7. Talks to shy persons about things they are interested in.
8. Sincerely asks another's opinion.
9. Is sympathetic and shows sympathy.
10. Is understanding.
11. Has a sense of humor.
12. Has the courage of his convictions.
13. Thinks about shared experiences and common activities.
14. Listens for cues to further conversation.
15. Increases his opportunities for experiences and interests.[6]

There are many pitfalls that can defeat the efforts of the conversationalist, unless he is prepared to avoid them. The following should be eliminated or avoided:

1. Profanity.
2. Slang.
3. Errors in grammar.
4. Mispronounced words.
5. Interruptions.
6. Insincerity.
7. Too many details of a story.
8. Petty remarks.
9. Too much exaggeration.
10. Poor voice qualities.
    a. Artificiality.
    b. Weakness.
    c. Shrillness.
    d. Aggressiveness.
11. Personal questions concerning
    a. Age, weight, dress or suit size.
    b. Religion, politics, national origin, or race.
    c. Financial questions.
    d. Details of one's illness, family, or occupation troubles.
    e. Physical or other handicaps.

From Reid comes this paragraph of insight into the similarities of people and conversation.

People are surprisingly alike, and, at the same time, extremely different. They are fascinating for those very reasons. You will feel a warmth toward

[6] *Ibid.*, pp. 212–223.

them when you remind yourself that these people—like you—feel happy, sad, hurt, glad; like you, they mean well but make mistakes sometimes; like you, they have secret longings and aspirations.[7]

Another major personality trait is depth of interests. In order to increase one's interests, it has been suggested that he read one newspaper daily, one good magazine weekly, and one carefully selected book monthly. Discussing an article, book, or other material immediately after its reading aids expression, memory, and the thinking processes. However, flaunting of newly acquired information should be avoided.

Feelings of inferiority or self-consciousness are combinations of thoughts and emotions that destroy confidence, poise, and charm. This is not a handicap that comes upon only a few of us; it is universal. Everyone lacks confidence in himself at times. Realizing that there is a oneness in people's feelings and that others have been able to meet the same difficulties will help you to build confidence in your own powers and abilities. Some have tried to compensate for their feelings of inadequacy by bragging, criticizing others, giving alibis, telling "sob" stories, and overly apologizing. These attempts generally work adversely to the building of good relationships. Consider your telling Jane about Sue's many faults. Jane may think

> If you criticize others when talking to me, I suspect you criticize me when talking to others.[8]

Instead of compensatory activities, one may develop real confidence in himself by:

1. Looking inward:
   Honestly analyze his own feelings.
   Think through his good qualities.
   Realistically see in what other activities he can excel.
   Realize that he can overcome feelings of inferiority.
   Develop a cheery, confident attitude.
2. Looking outward:
   Join a club or group.
   Develop other interests.
   Learn what to do in various situations.
   Try to help others feel at ease.

[7] Ibid., p. 215.
[8] Chapman, op. cit., p. 54.

Using this suggested plan of action will help develop a quiet confidence in oneself. It has been said that "There is a vast amount of difference between self-confidence and conceit. The person with self-confidence grows, while the one with conceit only swells."[9]

A person with tact is one who is often asked to be host or hostess at various activities, because he knows how to mend uneasy situations and avoid many likely ones. He says the right thing at the right time, he mends a thoughtless remark, he refuses a request showing sincere regret, he uses quick forethought, he smooths over social blunders, he sees the other person's point of view, he bolsters courage and confidence, he avoids repeating what is told him in confidence, he avoids snap judgments, he is truthful, and he speaks positively—avoiding anything that may sound like a gripe.[10]

Devices can sometimes be a plan for action. "Five first aids for embarrassing predicaments"[11] can be used as a guide to begin the new attitude of tactfulness. As they are used, the habit of tact will be developed and no further rules will be necessary; the tactful thing will be done or said, because it is the natural thing to do.

FIRST AID, NO. I

The ever-cheering compliment, direct or implied, may entirely counteract a hurt or embarrassment. It is one of the most helpful of the first aids.

FIRST AID, NO. II

Sometimes sympathy or a frank admission of a situation is the most tactful procedure or the most soothing balm to injured feelings.

FIRST AID, NO. III

A sense of humor is a priceless help in time of trouble. (However, to laugh under some circumstances would be the worst possible blunder.) The person who can see the humorous side of situations, make a laughing remark, give a funny twist to the affair, or show the triviality of the situation has at hand a device that will rescue

[9] Maude Lee Etheredge, *Health Facts for College Students* (Philadelphia: W. B. Saunders Company, 1959), p. 26.
[10] Reid, op. cit., p. 255.
[11] Ibid., pp. 256–257.

many a situation by replacing tenseness and embarrassment with smiles and happiness.

At other times an entire change of thought and conversation makes the most effective rescue. However, the change of topic must not be too sudden and too obvious.

FIRST AID, NO. V

A more pleasing interpretation of a motive or a remark may patch up a thoughtless remark.

A sense of humor is a part of being a good conversationalist and it can be used skillfully by a person with tact to ease an embarrassing situation. Humor has many advantages.

It lightens tensions and irritations.
It gives a better sense of proportion.
It views life in a softer, more tolerant light.
It adds to popularity and sociability.
It increases morale.[12]

Humor is probably as impossible to define as it is impossible to put on, like a coat: one can achieve a sense of humor by developing a lighter attitude, not by planning to be suddenly humorous. Reid has described (not defined) humor in a most imaginative way.

Humor is a game in which we tell whoppers, imagine outlandish things, distort the truth, imitate, exaggerate, make faces, pretend, dance and prance, and make wild gestures. We think up all sorts of gags, and puns, and funny-sounding words. We talk utter nonsense. We may even play practical jokes and do silly tricks and pranks. A big parade of fun![13]

Personal Appearance and Grooming

The second major element of personality development is in improving outward appearance. First impressions often come as much from how we look as by what we say or do. We are measured by our look of health, our personal grooming, and the clothing we select. All are important in the presenting of, and the developing of, a more pleasing personality.

[12] Ibid., pp. 268–272.
[13] Ibid., pp. 267–268.

Chapman and Reid both emphasize the fact that the impression of strength or health is one of the things that makes a person appear physically attractive. It gives a look of virility in a man and vivaciousness in a woman. Vitality is the evidence of good health. Some of the requirements of physical health that have been pointed out are eating regularly the food required for optimum health; taking a bath every day; brushing the teeth after each meal or at least twice a day; caring for the skin and hair; sleeping at least eight hours daily; exercising regularly, preferably out of doors with fresh air and sunlight; having a period of relaxation at the close of the day's work; maintaining a balanced program of exercise and relaxation; retaining good posture by sitting, standing, and walking correctly; wearing hygienic clothing; having regular elimination; and having a periodic health examination.

The second need for presenting a pleasing appearance is good personal grooming. Again a questionnaire can help the student to realize where he is and what aspects he will need to improve.

For healthy-looking skin, the body needs a balanced diet, enough sleep, proper elimination, an optimistic outlook, cleanliness, and careful use of cosmetics. The relation between physical health, grooming, and personality is clear at this point. Physical health must come first before special care and makeup for a healthy well-groomed appearance; finally, a person who looks healthy and is well groomed has added to his personality an aspect that brings pleasant reactions from others.

When washing the face soft water is preferable to hard, because the latter contains irritating minerals, causing difficulty in forming lather. The additives in soaps—perfumes and tints—do not add to cleansing efficiency and may be irritating to the skin. Lanolin soap may be particularly helpful with dry skin. A fresh face cloth should be put out at least twice a week, but possibly more often in hot damp weather. To rinse the face, splash warm water onto it until all of the soap is removed. Then splash cold water to close the pores and bring a glow to the skin.

Women should not substitute cleansing cream for soap and water. With slow-acting oil glands or in a dry climate, cold cream may be needed as a lubricant. This should be removed with warm water and soap.

Five basic rules of the use of makeup should be considered before application.

List on Grooming for Men and Women

Do you	*Yes*	*No*

1. Take bath or shower daily?
2. Use deodorant or antiperspirant?
3. Wash hair weekly or oftener, if needed?
4. Wash brush and comb as often as you wash your hair?
5. Brush hair well?
6. Check that you have no loose hair or dandruff on your collar?
7. Check the length of your hair to see if it looks as good from back and sides as it does in front?
8. Manicure nails as needed?
9. Give thought to your posture?
10. Wear clean underwear?
11. Wear clean, well-pressed outer garments?
12. Check shoes regularly for needed polishing and repairing?
13. Check for needed repairs to garments when you remove them and repair before laundering?
14. Check for spots and stains on garments?

---

1. Apply make-up only to an absolutely clean face. Soap and water are your best friends when it comes to having a lovely complexion.
2. Always remove make-up before going to bed. A cleansing lotion, followed by your soap and water, does the best job. Oily skins respond well to soap and water alone.
3. Use a light touch in applying make-up. You defeat the whole purpose of make-up—to look naturally pretty—if you look "made up."
4. Keep your make-up to a minimum for school and other daytime occasions.
5. Cultivate nice make-up manners. Touch-up of powder and lipstick are out of order in the classroom, church, and the middle of the dance floor. When you must refresh your make-up in public, do it as quickly and inconspicuously as possible.[14]

One of America's top make-up artists once told a college class, "Powder, lipstick, eyebrow pencil, and foundation cream are like oils used by a painter. The technique is everything. I can make a girl glamorous with make-up, but I can also transform her into one of the witches in *Macbeth* with the same equipment."[15]

[14] "A Girl's Guide to Good Make-Up" (New York: Avon Products, Inc.), p. 1.
[15] Mary Mark Sturm and Edwina H. Grieser, *Guide to Modern Clothing* (New York: McGraw-Hill Book Co., 1962), p. 8.

A grooming aspect important to both men and women is caring for the hair. For women such care includes shampoos, brushing, and possibly permanents and hair styling. For men the hair cut, washing, and caring for dandruff are the important hair needs. "Shampoo soap should be free of alkali, liquid in form, and lather freely."[16] The application of soap, lathering, thorough massaging, and several rinsings are necessary for removing all of the dirt, oil, and soap. The comb and brush should be washed at each shampoo time. Thus, a clean comb and brush will be used on clean hair.

A hair brush for a man should be just as essential a grooming item as it is for a woman. Daily brushing promotes circulation in the scalp, cleaning of the hair, and freedom from dandruff. Taking frequent shampoos, treating the hair with a special lotion, brushing the hair daily, washing the comb and brush, and massaging the scalp should be productive in freeing the hair from dandruff. If not, a physician specialized in scalp conditions should be consulted. One of the most successful ways to achieve a slovenly and ill-kept appearance is to neglect a haircut.[17]

Not all are fortunate to look becoming in straight hair, nor do many have naturally curly hair. Many use a permanent to give their hair body in holding a set or wave. A permanent without harsh materials will not be unduly hard on the hair. An important point to be remembered by both men and women is that you are an individual with unique features and personality. You can profit as an individual by styling your hair to emphasize your good features and play down your bad and by choosing a style that also emphasizes the type of personality that you have or would like to have. Do not make the mistake of blindly following a fad.

The following material emphasizes shape of face for hair style for women.

THE GREAT DISGUISE[18]

by the Gilette Company, Personal Care Division
THE SHAPE OF YOUR FACE, THE STYLE OF YOUR HAIR

Your hair can do more for your beauty rating than almost anything else imaginable, because hair is one of the great things girls are all about! It's

[16] Reid, op. cit., p. 185.
[17] Ibid., p. 205.
[18] From "Top Secrets from Toni" (Chicago: The Gillette Company, Personal Care Division, 1967), p. T.S-5.

what makes you pretty and feminine because it frames your face with softness. Properly styled, hair can even "re-shape" a girl's wayward features, and help her create the illusion of a more nearly perfect oval—the ideal face shape. If you are like most girls, you will have to be knowledgeable and work for that perfect look; use some wily camouflage. It's simply a matter of playing up your best feature—playing down the one that missed. If you have more than one problem, disguise the one you feel is most prominent.

If you're not quite sure about your particular face shape, pull your hair back from your face and draw its outline on the mirror with a bar of soap or a felt tip pen (it washes off easily!). Then, select the hairstyle that is most becoming to you!

FACE SHAPES

HEART:

A broad brow, high temples tapering to a pointy chin. Avoid styles that make you appear "top heavy," like back sweeps or hairdos tall at the crown, fluff at the temples. Wear hair smooth at the temples and full at the chin. Flips and pageboys are great. Show off a widow's peak if you have one! Length: medium to long.

FIGURE 6-1. *The heart shape. (Courtesy of The Gillette Company, Personal Care Division.)*

ROUND:

A round hairline, full cheeks and softly pointed chin. Avoid width at the ears. Avoid too, center parts and broad, flat bangs (unless you add height to crown and have sides sweep over the cheeks).
Wear height at the forehead, off center half-bangs, a side or slanted part.
Length: medium short to medium long.

297

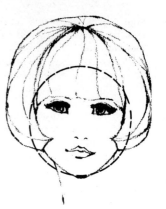

Figure 6-2. *The round shape. (Courtesy of the Gillette Company, Personal Care Division.)*

TRIANGLE:

A narrow forehead, wide jaw and chin line.

Avoid extremely long styles or pageboys, flatness at the temples, fluffiness below the ears and a center part.

Wear fullness across the top of your head to balance jaw width, an off-center part (or no part at all) and keep hair softly waved or curled, back behind ears or curved deeply in on jawline.

Length: short to medium.

Figure 6-3. *The triangle. (Courtesy of the Gillette Company, Personal Care Division.)*

298

RECTANGULAR:

A long face, roughly rectangular, with the jaw almost as wide as forehead and cheeks.
Avoid severe details, upswept hairdos and extremely long or extremely short hair.
Wear width at forehead, fullness along cheek and brow line, softness over ears.
Length: medium to medium short.

FIGURE 6-4. *The rectangular face. (Courtesy of the Gillette Company, Personal Care Division.)*

SQUARE:

A straight hairline, angular jawline, forehead as broad as the chin.
Avoid severe, straight back styles, center parts and hair that flares out along neckline.
Wear height at forehead or curvy bangs, or half or slanting bangs, a high side or slanted part.
Length: short to medium.

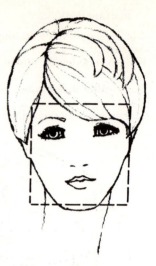

FIGURE 6-5. *The square face. (Courtesy of the Gillette Company, Personal Care Division.)*

OVAL:

A high brow, slightly full cheeks tapering to a softly pointed chin.
This is the perfect face shape, and can wear almost any style. However, if a wayward feature is your special problem, follow our special eye-distracting tips for these less-than perfect features.

FIGURE 6-6. *The oval shape. (Courtesy of the Gillette Company, Personal Care Division.)*

Feature Problems
  Cheeks and Jaws
    Broad—Keep hair away from these broad features. Balance with a soft wide hair arrangement at the forehead. Fancy details should be reserved for the crown and forehead area only. Avoid tight curls.

300

Narrow—Do create softness on top with deep waves or fluffy bangs. Add fullness over ears with soft waves to add width. Above all, avoid a flat top look. Hair length for these features should be short to medium.

Chins

Double—Do keep width back and away from face. Any neckline design should be kept soft and delicate. Above all, chin up and stand straight and tall.

Long or Protruding—Balance this with hair interest on top and front. Choose soft forward waves. Keep neckline arrangement soft too, with back hair higher than chin level.

Short or Receding—Do keep hair interest back from face. Other ideas, keep hair fluffy and short or in a brush-up style.

Square or Heavy—Detract by adding width at forehead with soft waves or curls. Keep hair higher than chin level.

Foreheads

High, wide, narrow or uneven—camouflage with bangs. Choose a side or slanted part. If forehead is low wear bangs that start back near the crown of your head and sweep forward. If forehead is high, wear bangs straight or swept to one side.

Height

Short girls should wear short to medium length hair. Keep it contoured and fairly close to your head. Lift top hair for added height. Avoid long, face hugging curls and styles.

Tall girls should keep top hair flat, side soft and full and tapered toward the back. Choose medium length styles and avoid the too little hair "look"—it will make you look out of proportion!

Necks

Long and thin necks look shorter if hair is worn in medium long, fluffy styles. Avoid straight or severe hairdos and short, curly ones. Short and chubby necks slim down if hairdo is kept short, fluffed up and away from the neck. Avoid long styles.

Noses

Short—Dramatize your profile by gathering hair up at the back of the head or swirling it into a French twist. With short hair style should be simple at the face with interest such as bangs at forehead.

Large—Minimize length by choosing a full hairdo that curves toward the face. High bangs add softness, too.

Long—Wear hair smooth on top with fullness directly opposite nose in the back and at the sides. Avoid fullness at forehead and temples.

Weight

Too Plump—Choose a head hugging, short style that has height at top. Keep hair up and off neck.

Too Thin—Choose a medium to a medium-long style with fullness at the sides and back.

Hair Styles and Glasses

Go together best if hair styles and frames are kept simple. Select a softly rounded 'do with hair lifted up and away from the face. Deep bangs accentuate glasses, so keep them wispy, softly waved, or side sweeping. If bangs are a must—wear smaller frames than you might otherwise choose. Make sure your hair style covers the place where the temple-part of the glasses meets your ears! All our rules are just guidelines—the most important consideration is how you look and feel in the frames you select.

One of the remaining grooming aspects is the regular use of deodorants. Two kinds of deodorants that may be needed are one that stops perspiration and one that counteracts a slight odor. Individual need determines the frequency with which one should apply deodorant. Women need to remove superfluous hair from both beneath the arms and on the legs. This needs to be done as often as every other day or as infrequently as once a week, depending again upon the individual.

A few other simple rules to add to our section on grooming include keeping

For both men and women
   the heels of your shoes straight.
   your shoes polished and shining.
For women
   your stockings smooth.
   your purse from bulging and in proportion with your size.
   your hands soft and moist by massaging to encourage the lubrication by the natural oils of the skin or by applying a lotion.
For men
   your feet clean daily. A deodorant used on the feet avoids odor permeation of the shoes.
   your face clean-shaven.
   your shirts, underwear, and socks changed daily.

Inasmuch as little has been written about men's grooming in specific, a suggestion for minimum grooming items may be helpful as a starter. These could include:

Two tooth brushes and tooth paste or powder.
Shampoo, hair dressing or spray, hair brush, and pocket comb.
Deodorant.
Razor, shaving cream or soap, after-shave lotion, and talcum powder.
Nail file.
Shoe brush and shoe cream or polish.

Clothing brush.
Spot remover.
Clothing hangers for coats and trousers.
Tie rack.

Men as well as women should plan their wardrobes to some extent in order to give style, to give the look of a complete outfit, to avoid antagonizing colors, and to have accompanying accessories.[19] More information is now available on the prevailing styles of men's clothing: the materials used; the selection of suits; sweaters, ties, and shirts; and the use of color in men's ensembles.

The first requirement in wardrobe planning for both men and women is the determination of figure type. Not only correct fit but also clothing style will depend upon figure type.

Men's figure types fall roughly into the following types: tall (6 feet and over), average (between 5 feet, 5 inches, and 6 feet), and short (5 feet, two inches, and under). To describe the type more accurately, however, you must consider whether the build is slender, average, or fat.

Women's clothes and patterns for clothes are ordinarily described as "Women's," "Misses," or "Junior." In actual selection, however, one must also consider height as well as any other figure differences. Tall is considered to be 5 feet, 8 inches, and over; average is between 5 feet, 3 inches, and 5 feet, 8 inches; short is 5 feet, 2 inches and under. Other figure differences that would affect selection could be large hips, narrow shoulders, and so on.

Anne R. Free has suggested some rules in the purchasing of clothing by men that depend upon figure type.

1. In buying your suit, remember that men's fashion designers pattern their styles on an ideal figure. At points where you differ from the ideal, your suits may not fit well.
2. Vertical lines lend height; horizontal lend width. Pin stripes are height suggesters, but broad stripes give more width than height. Plaids emphasize, and suggest, bulk.
3. Padded shoulders broaden and fill out the shoulder line. They also add bulk to the already bulky figure.
4. Fitted, closely tailored coats and suits emphasize height and de-emphasize bulk. Loose-fitting, boxy coats and jackets de-emphasize height and emphasize bulk.
5. Nappy materials, rough prominent weaves, and shiny materials all add to the appearance of bulk and detract from the appearance of height.

[19] Reid, op. cit., p. 200.

6. High-waisted pants, long jackets, cuff-free trousers all lend height. Cuffs, broad coat lapels, coat belts, all cut the figure and lend width.[20]

The following questions are asked so that the student may begin to study his own figure in relation to dress, learn a few ways to select more becoming styles for his own figure, and learn a few ways of creating a more pleasing figure by covering figure faults and by attracting the eye to the best features.

Do all vertical lines make you appear slender? A careful study of the foregoing list indicates that if you wish to create an illusion of slenderness you should select a narrow, vertical stripe; the width of the stripe makes a difference.

Who wears horizontal stripes? Where? You will note from the list that horizontal stripes generally tend to add the appearance of width and to have a shortening effect. Place the horizontal line where you wish the effect of width.

How does color affect the appearance of size? How does texture affect the appearance of size?

Certainly all of the foregoing points could be elaborated upon at great length. It is hoped that these points have aroused your interest and that you will refine these ideas in clothing selection and construction courses.

The use of color by men and women may best be illustrated in tabular form for contrast and similarity.[21]

Women's clothing is more varied than men's. The basic dress with many combinations is one of the important essentials for the wardrobe. The dress worn with tailored accessories outfits a woman for business and school, whereas with dressy accessories it can be worn for other occasions. Separates should be carefully chosen, so that they can be mixed and matched. These separates will include sweaters, shirts, pants, and skirts. Avoiding too sporty or too dressy separates will help to make a practical wardrobe for all occasions. A tailored or conservative suit will be suitable for job interviews and other business

---

[20] From: *Social Usage* by Anne R. Free. Copyright © 1960 by Appleton-Century-Crofts, Inc. Reprinted by permission of Appleton-Century-Crofts, Division of Meredith Corporation.
[21] Ibid., pp. 14–15.

COLOR USE BY MEN AND WOMEN

Color	Men	Women
For effect	should be contrasted.	should be harmonized.
Chosen mostly for	preferences, climate, season, and fashion.	complexion.
For light hair, fair skin, blue or green eyes	wear darker colors in ties and sport shirts. Dull whites, blacks, and extremely light tans and grays should be avoided.	avoid dull colors. Use bright but not overly showy ones.
For brown hair, brown or gray eyes, medium complexion	wear neutral or intense colors. Intense colors are the current fashion.	wear your own preference.
For dark hair, eyes, and coloring	contrast colors. Avoid dull colors. Use vivid colors in ties and sport shirts.	Avoid dullness. Wear vivid colors.

occasions. Comfortable, conservative pumps harmonizing with a costume are good for school as well as business.

For simple dates that type of clothing worn to classes is most acceptable. For dressier occasions, heels and gloves and fine accessories can make an ensemble. A frequent fault of college women is the borrowing of clothing. Irene Pierson from the University of Illinois comments that men "object when girls borrow dresses in order to have a different dress each time. They can usually notice a difference in the way borrowed dresses fit. If they like the dress you wore when they met you, or at a special party, they like to see it again and again. If a man is looking at you as a marriage prospect, too large a wardrobe may make him dubious of his ability to support you."[22]

Men indulge in less variety in clothing than women, with the exception of color. The shirt color is generally lighter than the suit. Tie color should be close to that of the suit, yet a contrasting color may be appropriate with tweed or with sport clothes. Although conspicuous designs are seldom worn, small figures or stripes generally are in good

[22] Irene Pierson, *Campus Cues* (Danville, Ill.: The Interstate, 1962), p. 24.

taste. The color of the handkerchief also should be closely related to the suit. Socks should not be highly contrasted. Accessories in general should be kept simple, conservative, and in harmony with the costume. The man who really enjoys wearing exciting colors might reserve this pleasure for sports clothes rather than business; for example any golf course today resembles the Easter parade with bright and colorful men's golf clothes.

Some points to emphasize on appearance are that (1) figure faults can be minimized by correct choice of style, color, or fabric in clothing and by correct choice of hair style and color in makeup; (2) one should choose fashions in the style and color that enhance one's own figure, face, and general appearance rather than blindly following the fashion; (3) suitable dress and makeup for the occasion comprise one of the surface indications of a well-educated person.

Recognizing the Importance of Good Social Usage

The home economics student should be aware of the importance of acceptable social usage, develop an understanding of its basic principles, and develop adaptable skills for social situations. You should not regard lightly the surface evidences of culture. Using acceptable social forms is no less a necessity than is a good personality. Good or acceptable social form and etiquette mean respect and concern for the other person. Most of the so-called rules have been developed by convention through consideration for others, which is the basis of "good social usage."

Social usage is the manners of society—our ways of interacting; etiquette is the acceptable code of manners in social or official life required by good breeding, convention, or authority. These manners may be affected by environment. Because they change, although change comes slowly, some rules of social usage are discarded and others added over a period of time. "The term 'social usage' refers to the routines, conventions, etiquette (all modified by courtesy and the exercise of good taste and consideration for others) to which we conform in order to have harmonious relations with other people."[23]

The term *social usage* implies immediately the use of manners and etiquette in those situations in which two or more persons react to each other. A few of the social situations most encountered by college

[23] Free, op. cit., p. 2.

students are correspondence; dinner engagements; any time when one is a guest, a host, or a hostess; dates; and traveling. These are the situations considered in this section.

Dress for the Occasion

Among the early concerns of the entering college student is what to wear for various occasions. Most college students come with too many clothes, which gives them less opportunity to add to their wardrobe.

Dress, like morality, is something that one has to determine for himself. He has to learn that dress is a personal thing and that he can not be too easily influenced by his peers. Figure types and color were briefly discussed in the previous section on appearance. If you learn to select line, style, and color for yourself as an individual, you have taken the first step in being well dressed. The suitability of your dress for an occasion demands knowledge of your inner self, of your outer self, of your world, and of your audience. By starting to think about and study the matter now, you can sharpen your sense of perception until you achieve the aesthetically pleasing consonance of person, personality, dress, and occasion. Assuming that you have determined by your own color tones, your own general lines for clothing, we chart hereafter some suggestions for dressing for specific occasions that will, in the writer's opinion, be in good taste—acceptable on any campus or in any campus environ.

FOR CLASS AND CAMPUS

Women students: skirts and sweaters or shirts, tailored dresses or tailored suits; low or medium heels; conservative jewelry or none. On some campuses pants and shorts appear to be the fad.

Men students: slacks and shirt or sweater, coordinated jacket if weather or inclination indicates, or suit. Ties are usually not worn but if worn should contrast with or complement the other apparel. Shoes may be casual or business but preferably not sandals. Again, on some campuses shorts are the fad.

FOR SHOPPING

As for class and campus, except for shopping in the city, where the tailored dress or suit is more appropriate. Here, too, men wear ties.

FOR CHURCH

Women students wear tailored dresses or suits. If an afternoon dress is worn, it should not be low-cut. Shoes with heels, high or medium, are appropriate. Jewelry should be conservative.

Men students wear business suits or conservative, coordinated trousers and jacket, with coordinated or contrasting shirt and tie. The dark suit is always in good taste.

FOR SPECTATOR SPORTS

For women: as for class except, perhaps, somewhat dressier. Medium, high, or even low heels may be worn.

For men: as for class except that ties and jackets or coats are worn.

(The author's purpose in this section is to outline the acceptable on any campus or campus environ. For example, we recognize that wool slack suits might be acceptable for football games in New England and the shorter spectator sports clothes for tennis and golf in the warmer South.)

FOR EVENING WEAR

Dances, Dinners, Receptions
The more formal:

For men. This means formal or very formal—tuxedo, or, rarely now, tails. "Black tie" on an invitation means tuxedo; "white tie" means tails. If you are in doubt as to the appropriate dress for any occasion, always ask. Business suits and immaculate grooming will often serve where tuxedo (dinner jacket) is indicated. If your formal invitations are very rare, don't hesitate to rent a suit. Many men do so. Wear your regular topcoat or overcoat in winter; your business hat, or, if you can do it nonchalantly, a bowler; white or light gray or tan leather gloves; dressy black shoes perfectly polished.

For women. Evening wear includes the formal dinner dress and the evening dress. The dinner dress is suitable for many evening occasions as well as for the formal dinner. It goes to the opera or theater and to weddings as well as to many dances. It differs from the evening gown more in degree than in kind. If long gowns are in style, the dinner dress will be the shorter of the two. If bare shoulders are in style, the dinner dress may have shoulder covering. The dinner dress is worn appropriately wherever a man wears his tuxedo. The evening dress also goes with the tuxedo and with tails.

Dressy jewelry may be worn with both evening and dinner dresses, as may elbow-length gloves. Gloves must always be removed at the dinner table. Shoes with the evening dress should be of gold, silver, or colored satin, matching or contrasting with the dress. The corsage may be worn in any position—there is no wrong way. Make sure it does not clash with your color scheme.[24]

The more informal:

For women: The dressy or "cocktail dress," with heels, gloves, and accessories appropriate to the degree of informality. The fashion today also includes the dressy pant suit.

For men: The business suit or coordinated jacket, trousers, shirt, and tie.

FOR THE MOVIES

Classroom or street dress or pant suit.

FOR BOWLING

For women: full or divided skirt or pants with coordinated sweater or shirt.

For men: slacks and coordinated shirt or sweater.

FOR TEAS, COFFEES, AFTERNOON RECEPTIONS

For women: a day-time dress with gloves and heels.

For men: business suit or conservative coordinated trousers, shirt, jacket, and tie.

NOTE AND OBSERVE PLEASE!

You will probably see other students, both women and men, in class and on the streets in shorts, and some women students in pants. This is *not* good taste in dress and is offensive to many people. In the writer's opinion this falls in the same category as chewing gum and wearing hair done up in curlers in public. These are all surface evidences of lack of culture. You should start *now* developing at least positive surface evidences of culture.

[24] Ibid., p. 21.

Correspondence

Letters of all kinds become necessary or are already so in the life of a college student. Business letters include those first letters to the college registrar seeking information and, later, the application for admission. There may be letters seeking information about part-time and summer work, and, later, many letters seeking information and interviews for career employment after graduation. Knowing and using the accepted form will facilitate positive attitudes by the receiver.

First, consider carefully the choosing of writing paper. White is acceptable for all letters and is a must for the business or formal letter. Always type a business letter. Many informal letters may also by typed. Sympathy letters and other very personal correspondence, such as invitations and replies, thank-you letters, and congratulatory letters, should never be typed.

The *heading* on a business letter may require the firm name and address at the top. There should be no abbreviations or punctuation at the end of a line. The date appears at the top center or top right of business correspondence; it may come at the lower left in social letters. The year is always included in business letters but need not be in social letters.

The *salutation,* at the upper left, includes both the name and address of the person written to as well as the formal greeting in a business letter. Only the greeting is used in the social letter. The greeting will reflect the acquaintanceship. This means that a business letter will seldom have the first name of the person receiving the letter in the greeting. If the name is unknown, *sir, madam,* or *gentlemen* will be used; when the surname is known, it is used as "Dear Mr. Johnson." According to convention, the greeting in a business letter is followed by a colon, in the social letter by a comma.

The *closing* to a letter is a parting remark, more formal in business, friendly in a social letter. Business letters will use "Sincerely," "Sincerely yours," "Yours truly," or "Very truly yours." These same closing remarks may be used in social letters, but here is one's chance to use more individual and friendly phases, such as "Affectionately," "Cordially," "With love," or "Devotedly."

The *signature* is always hand-written, whether it is on business or social correspondence, whether the letter is typed or handwritten. Only the first and surnames are used, never the titles, as Miss, Mrs., Ms., Mr., or Dr. The title may be used in parentheses with the name repeated in type below for business use or in social use for clarification.

Invitations and replies range from the most formal engraved request to the invitation by telephone. The formality of the request will depend upon the formality of the occasion. Anne R. Free[25] suggests some basic rules to follow in writing invitations and replies.

First, *the invitation should state definitely the day, date, beginning and ending time, and the type of occasion.* This will ensure clarity of the date, certainty of when to arrive or leave, and understanding of the formality of dress.

Appropriate stationery will depend entirely on the formality of the occasion: name cards, commerical invitation cards, formal cards suitable for engraving, printing or hand writing, or informal note paper.

Name forms should be stated correctly, using title, first and surnames. A married woman, unless divorced, always uses her husband's first name, rather than her own, when her title, Mrs., is used. Therefore, Mrs. Arthur Surge is correct, as is Miss Jane Ann Thornton, Mr. Paul Phillips, Jr., and Dr. and Mrs. Stephen Anthony.

R.S.V.P. is an abbreviation for the French phrase, *répondez, s'il vous plaît,* meaning "Answer, please." *Such a request,* if desired, *is placed at the lower left margin of the invitation.* Other acceptable forms of requesting a reply are the words, "Please reply," or the hostesses' telephone number placed in the same place as *R.S.V.P.* would appear.

Sample letters are given in the following illustrations. These were written by students in a home economics course in the Department of Home and Family at Southern Illinois University. The class was taught by Miss Thelma Malone, instructor in that department.

BUSINESS LETTERS

All business letters should be typed on a good grade of bond stationery. They should be concise, pertinent.

[25] Ibid., pp. 137–138.

114 South Wall Street
Carbondale, Illinois
July 20, 1967

Mr. Jim Jones
Midvale Central High School
101 Canal Street
Midvale, Illinois

Dear Mr. Jones:

Today Mrs. Jennifer Warren, Chairman of the
Home Economics Education Department at Southern
Illinois University, informed me of a position in
the Clothing Department of your high school. The
opening for Clothing teacher in the Midvale Central
High School is of great interest to me. I should
like to apply for this position.

I have enclosed a data sheet giving information
concerning my education, experience, personal information and references.

I hope that when you are filling the vacancy
for clothing teacher you will consider seriously
and favorably my qualifications and my desire to
work in your high school.

May I come for an interview with you at your
convenience? My telephone number is 673-0218.

Sincerely yours,

Judy Osman

Judy Osman

FIGURE 6-7. *The letter of inquiry.*

Personal Data Sheet

Judy Osman

Personal Information
    Age: 21 (as of February 26, current year)

    Address: R. #1, Trailer #4 Jackson Trailer Court Carbondale, Illinois

    Telephone: 673-0218

    Health: Excellent

    Height and Weight: 5 feet 3 1/2 inches; 120 pounds

Education
    University: Southern Illinois University

    Degree Received: Bachelor of Science Degree

    Major: Home Economics Education

    Grade Average: B (upper 1/2 of graduating class)

    Home Economics Subjects: Food and Nutrition 105, 206, 321, 335; Home and Family 237, 227, 341, 345, 360; Clothing and Textiles 135, 127, 235, 314; and Home Economics Education 111, 235, 320, 333.

Practical Work Experience
    Teacher's Assistant to: Mrs. Roy Jackson

                          Graded papers, typed out tests and mimeographed material, assisted in class.

    4-H Work: Junior leader for three years, helped girls learn to sew and with other projects.

References
    Mrs. Jean Anderson   Mrs. Guanda Reynolds
    Head of Clothing and Textiles County Extention Agent
    Southern Illinois University   404 Makanda Street
    Carbondale, Illinois   Jonesboro, Illinois

FIGURE 6-8. *Personal data sheet.*

Home Management House
Carbondale, Illinois
July 6, 1967

John D. Smith, Superintendent
Twin County Community High School
District 303
Applegrove, Illinois

Dear Mr. Smith:

    I wish to thank you for the interview Saturday.
I realize how busy you are and appreciate the time you
spent discussing your school system with me. I enjoyed
talking with you and hope to hear from you soon.

                Sincerely,

                Shirley Gehrig

                Shirley Gehrig

FIGURE 6-9. *The thank-you letter after an interview.*

PERSONAL LETTERS

Formal invitations and replies are written in the third person. If
handwritten, they should be written with black ink on a good-grade
formal card. Note the punctuation and wording in the invitations
shown.

Personal letters are best if handwritten. Thoughtfulness of the
other person and sincerity are of prime importance in these.

Dear Faye,

I am hoping that you will join me for dinner at six o'clock Friday, the twenty-first of this month.

I am looking forward to seeing you and hearing about your trip to New York.

Affectionately,
Vicki

FIGURE 6-10. *Informal invitation.*

July 13, 1967

Dear Vicki,

I am delighted to accept your invitation for dinner at 6 o'clock Friday, the 21st of this month.

Thank you for your thoughtfulness.

Sincerely,
Faye Kimble

FIGURE 6-11. *Reply to an informal invitation.*

315

Miss Nancy Cazel
requests the pleasure of
Dr and Mrs. John Ray's
company at dinner
on Tuesday, the first of July
at eight o'clock

R.S.V.P.

FIGURE 6-12.   *Formal invitation.*

Miss Carole Claxton
accepts with pleasure
the kind invitation of
Miss Nancy Cazel and
Mrs. Margaret Paulson
for Thursday, the twentieth of July
at eight o'clock

FIGURE 6-13.   *Reply to a formal invitation.*

December 29, 1967

Dear Aunt Sue,

It was wonderful of you to send us the beautiful silver candlesticks for Christmas. They add that "something special" to our dining room table. Don and I both want to thank you.

Sincerely,
Margaret

FIGURE 6-14. *A thank-you letter for a gift.*

February 18, 1967

Dear Donna,

It was so good of you to take time to show my mother and me around Los Angeles. We enjoyed and appreciated all your kindness to us.

We hope you will be coming to the Midwest soon and we may have the pleasure of seeing you again.

Thanking you for your generous hospitality and with kindest regards to you,

Very sincerely,
Nancy Cazel

FIGURE 6-15. *A bread-and-butter letter.*

May 11, 1946

Dear Mrs. Watson,

It has been several months since I had seen Carol, but it was with a real sense of loss that I heard the news. We were very close at college, as she may have told you, and we had corresponded since graduation.

I hope when I am in Chicago again that I may come to visit you, and, if possible, be of some help.

Most sincerely,
Bonnie DuMontelle

FIGURE 6-16. *A letter of sympathy.*

Introductions

Many college freshmen and even some college graduates find themselves feeling awkward or ill at ease when making introductions. There is little excuse for this ineptness because there are only a few basic rules. Some study *and* practice are necessary, however, if one is to be spontaneously correct and relaxed in business and social situations in which introductions are expected or necessary.

Whom? All guests whom you bring into your own home should be introduced to all members of your family that are present. Any guest that comes to your dormitory or other living quarters should be introduced to the housemother, the head resident, or the supervisor if they are present; these guests include young men calling for ladies on a date as well as dinner or dance guests. Your partner should be introduced to the chaperones at a dance or party. All guests should be introduced to a guest of honor and all guests should be introduced at a house party. Friends who come up to speak to you at a party or dance or other small gathering should always be introduced to those in your group. Any guest whom you take to a class or to a meeting should be introduced to the instructor or the person in charge. Introduce yourself to those on each side of you and across from you at a banquet; also introduce your dinner partner to them. At a large tea or reception you may also find it necessary to introduce yourself to others at the party because it is virtually impossible for the hostess, host, and helpers to do this; include your guests or partner in such introductions; it is not necessary to meet everyone at a large gathering, but remember that the basic purpose of teas, receptions, and cocktail parties is to acquaint and greet people of similar interests.

How? The basic, simple rules are that people of distinction are named first, the woman is named before the man, the older before the younger. After this, you consider the formality or informality of the situation. For example: "President Morris, may I present my parents, Mr. and Mrs. Bankroll" or "Mr. Distinguished, may I present my roommate, Janet Cottonpicker"; "Mother, this is my roommate, Phyllis Goneway"; "Mr. Aging, may I introduce Miss Sixteen"; "Mrs. Smythe, may I introduce Miss Comelately"; "Mrs. Guest of Honor, may I present Miss Anxioustomeetyou"; "Janis Land, this is Barbara Ernst"; "Mr. Sixty, Miss Eighteen."

Other *remembers:*

1. Try to give some identification in introductions. This may follow the introduction or be a part of it. For example: Jane is my roommate; Tom is from my hometown; John is in the Honors Program; Howard has just returned from Europe.
2. If a relative's name is different from your own, that name should be included in the introduction. For example: Mr. Famous, may I present my mother, Mrs. Luring.
3. When introducing a person to a small group, do so in the order in which they are standing: Miss Newcomer, this is Betty Freshman, John Smiley, Rosie Turnipseed, and Mrs. Turnipseed.
4. Always stand when being introduced to someone.
5. Men always shake hands when being introduced to other men. A woman may shake hands with men or women her own age, as she chooses; if you are a young woman, you wait for the older woman to offer her hand to you. The man waits for the lady to offer her hand.
6. The standard and always acceptable acknowledgement to an introduction is "How do you do, Miss Name." It is correct to say, "I'm

very glad to meet you" or "I have looked forward to meeting you." Repeating a person's name helps you to remember it, and a cordial acknowledgement, if true, makes a good impression.

7. When leaving a new acquaintance you may simply say "Good-bye"; or, if you mean it, you may say "I hope to see you again soon" or "I'm so glad to know you."

Some *nevers:*

1. Never say: "Mr. House, meet Mr. Gate"; "Mr. Black, shake hands with Mr. Blanco"; "Mr. Lark, meet the wife"; "Joe Bloke, I want to make you acquainted with Timothy Timid."
2. Never acknowledge an introduction with "Pleased to meet you"; "Hi"; "Glad to know you."

Dating

Dating customs vary greatly from country to country; they vary in different regions in our own country and from campus to campus. Usually we think of a date as an opportunity to enjoy the company of someone of the opposite sex, which usually implies no serious long-term plans. The college student would do well to look upon dating also as an opportunity to get acquainted with and know members of the opposite sex so that he may have a basis of selection for marriage. This implies a necessity for less steady dating than is the custom on many campuses, for when one limits himself to dating only one person, there is little or no basis for comparison. Johnny Brash may not wear so well for the lifetime of marriage as would Timothy Lessaggressive. How do you know?

Young people should spend some time and thought in consideration of the reasons for our social standards. Even though you are living in an era when it is "the thing" to demonstrate against many of the rules or regulations established by others through tradition, you must examine your own values and principles. Perhaps in the dating situation it takes more courage, more character, to abide by your own principles than to go along with the crowd. A young person's good name, social, and moral reputation are attributes to be protected and are essential for long-range happiness and a good marriage. A person of pride and character conducts himself in dating situations with poise, self-confidence, and self-respect as well as courtesy and thoughtfulness for his date.

When asking for a date, be specific on plans. When asking, say, for example, "Will you go to the Valentine dance with me on Friday night?" If one is not definite, the girl is in an awkward situation. If one simply asks if she is busy on Friday night, her pride may be hurt to say no but if she says yes, she has lost her chance for a date with you and perhaps she really wants to go to the Valentine dance. Have some plan in mind, something you think that she would enjoy, before asking for the date; it may be, for example, to play tennis, to go to the pep rally, to study in the library, to bowl, to attend the movies. Also, knowing what is planned helps the girl in deciding what to wear. The girl accepts the date invitation with a gracious "I'd like that very much, thank you" or "I shall be happy to go with you, thanks." On the other hand, if she cannot accept, she varies her answer with the degree of her regret. These answers may range from "I have already made other plans. I hope you'll call me again" to "We have other plans. Thank you for calling." A definite time is set during the conversation when the young man will call for the girl. Both are prompt unless there is an unavoidable delay; the day has passed when a young lady keeps the man waiting.

A DATE FOR THE DANCE

Even with difficult parking problems, the gentleman goes to the house to call for his date. He never honks the horn for his date. If the dance is one at which corsages will be worn, he ascertains the color of the girl's dress before ordering the corsage. She will feel that she has to wear it even if it clashes with her dress. Therefore, the money is better spent on the color of flower that enhances the dress.

The gentleman assists the girl out of the car at the dance building unless there is a doorman. She waits inside while he parks the car. Introductions are always made to the chaperones, or if there is a receiving line, the couple goes immediately there.

The man asks for a dance by saying, "May I have this dance?" The girl may smile and nod as she gets up or say, "Certainly." If the dance is a cutting-in dance, the stag goes up to the girl and puts his hand on her partner's shoulder saying, "May I?" Actually, the couple cut in on have no choice, inasmuch as those who object to sharing dances should not attend mixer dances. The man who has been cut in on thanks the girl, smiles, and finds another partner or returns to the stag line. At any other dance, not a mixer, the girl may refuse to dance with a man by saying, "Thank you, I do not care to dance now," but she sits that dance out unless she was able to say truthfully, "I promised this dance to Jack." If the dance is not a mixer, couples should trade dances.

IN THE RESTAURANT

The couple waits for the head waiter to seat them. If there is no head waiter, the young man leads the way to a table, where he seats the young lady in the most advantageous position. He asks the young lady what she would like to order and may make suggestions. He gives both orders to the waiter. The girl has governed her own request by her estimate of the man's affluency. At the end of the meal he leaves a tip of approximately 15 per cent. This may be dependent upon the quality of the service and the type of restaurant. The young man leads the way out of the restaurant, securing the girl's wrap from the check room or wrap stand. He always assists in removing and putting on wraps.

AT THE THEATER

If there is an usher, the couple wait to be led to their seats. If there is no usher, the young man leads the way. He says, "Excuse us, please" if others must rise to allow them to enter. The couple do not converse while the play or show is in progress. The man leads the way out of the seat row and out of the theater.

IN GENERAL

1. The gentleman always opens doors for the lady and she waits for him to do so.
2. The gentleman always assists the lady into a car. She waits for him to do so.
3. The gentleman always assists in removing and putting on wraps and she waits for him to do so even to the point of handing him the wrap if necessary.
4. The gentleman never honks the horn of the car in calling for a date. He parks and goes to the door. The girl is prompt in being ready; it is not in good taste to keep another waiting unless it is unavoidable.

322

5. Do not break one date to accept another.
6. The gentleman always assists the lady with her chair in the dining room or restaurant.
7. The gentleman always stands when ladies enter a room and does not seat himself as long as they are standing. He also stands for an older man and when being introduced to anyone.
8. The young lady always stands when an older woman enters the room and remains standing until she is seated.
9. Young ladies do not call men friends on the telephone unless there is a good reason. Although such calling is now accepted, it is not good taste and the young lady may appear too eager.
10. The young man always thanks the girl for the date when he returns her. She replies graciously but honestly; there is always something pleasant about the evening.
11. Do not try too hard to make an impression. Be thoughtful of the other person, be friendly, smile, and be your natural self. Be interested in the other person and others whom you meet.
12. The gentleman does not take a young lady to a place of questionable reputation.
13. Analyze yourself on such personal characteristics as dependability, honesty, concern for others, enthusiasm, cheerfulness, and good grooming.
14. Both the gentleman and lady have the courage to live and behave by their principles even though others in the group may have different values.

Being a Guest

Is it an open house, a coffee or tea, a reception, a picnic, or a dinner? Even though attendance at some of these may be mandatory, make up your mind to have a good time and others will enjoy your company. So decide on the correct dress for the specific occasion and enjoy yourself.

Open houses, coffees, teas, and receptions are certain to be on your list of activities on any campus. Coffees are more usually held in the morning, teas in the afternoon, and receptions in the evening. Any may involve large groups of people, for example, the sorority or fraternity open house at Homecoming, the tea or coffee for that visiting VIP, the president's reception for seniors. Invitations to any of these are the only written invitations to occasions at which food is served to which you do not need reply. However, if you cannot go, it is always

FIGURE 6-17. *Diagram of a tea table showing service on both sides.*

courteous to mention your regret to the hostess when you see her; this may be before or after the event.

You arrive, correctly dressed and well groomed, not later than twenty minutes before the last hour mentioned in the invitation. You go directly to the hostess or to receiving line, if there is one. If you do not know the first person in the line, introduce yourself. Usually there is someone at the end of the line whose duty it is to take you to the table and/or to introduce you to some others whom you may not know. If there is a long line, or even a short one, at the serving table, wait until there are fewer. Remember that you came primarily to visit, see friends, and get acquainted with others. So, no breadlines, please! You proceed around the serving table to the right. You stay at least twenty minutes and do not seat yourself but move around in order to be sociable and visit with more people.

FIGURE 6-18. *Diagram of a tea table showing service on one side.*

324

You are not expected to say good-bye to the host and hostess if it is a large affair and if they are still receiving guests. If they are *not* busy when you leave, do find something gracious to say to them as you leave.

You have received your invitation two weeks ahead of the affair and have answered promptly. Your answer is formal or informal according to the invitation and always restates the date and hour.

You arrive, promptly and correctly dressed. If you are unavoidably detained, courtesy requires that you telephone the hostess telling her that you will be late and why you will be late, and ask her not to wait for you. If you then arrive after others have been seated, go directly to your hostess, apologize, and take your seat.

If it is a large dinner party, the name of your dinner partner is given to you when you arrive. The man introduces himself to his partner if he does not know her, offers her his right arm, and takes her into the dining room. After the hostess is seated, he pulls out the chair for his dinner partner, who will be seated on his right; he stands so that she may sit down from the left; and pushes the chair forward once after she is seated. The man guest of honor is always seated on the hostess' right; the host is seated at the opposite end of the table and the woman guest of honor on his right. Husbands and wives are not seated next to each other.

You always wait until the hostess has picked up her napkin before taking your own, and the hostess always "lifts her fork" first. At a large dinner party or banquet wait until those on each side of you have been served before starting to eat. The dinner napkin is unfolded halfway on your lap and is not tucked in. At the end of the meal you wait for the hostess to replace her napkin and then leave yours, semifolded, on the left side of your plate. If called to the telephone during the meal, ask the hostess to be excused, and leave your napkin on your chair.

The connoisseur of food is one who knows and likes many different foods. It is better to take food that is offered or served; try to eat and like it. If some food is outstandingly good, tell the hostess and she will be pleased; otherwise, do not comment on the food.

In general, the silverware is placed in the order in which you will use it, from outside in. If in doubt, follow the lead of the hostess.

Study the following suggestions and make their use a habit. They are acceptable wherever you may go.

1. Responsibilities of the guest
   a. Replying to the invitation with acceptance or regret.
   b. Arriving promptly.
   c. Being pleasant and attempting to help make the party successful.
   d. Speaking to the host and hostess when leaving, expressing pleasure at being invited.
   e. Sending a book, flowers, or some other small gift, when it is impossible to return the entertainment.
   f. Sending a note expressing thanks.

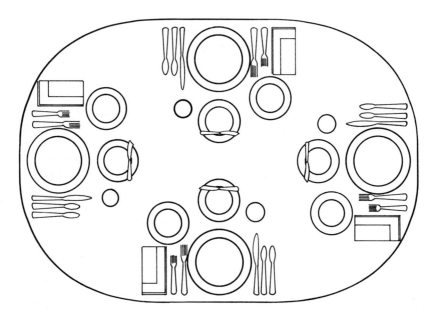

FIGURE 6-19. *Diagram of the home dinner setting.*

2. Entering the dining room
   a. If place cards are used, when the meal is announced, the host leads the way to the dining room with the woman guest of honor. The hostess comes last with the man guest of honor.
   b. On less formal occasions the hostess enters first to direct the seating of guests.
   c. Names of the gentlemen's dinner partners may be given to them on arrival, and in that case each escorts his partner, offering her his right arm. (The lady on his right is considered his partner.)

3. Seating
   a. Guests stand behind their chairs until the hostess sits down.
   b. The chair should not be moved unless necessary in sitting.
   c. Everyone sits down and rises from the left side of the chair.
   d. A gentleman seats the lady on his right, pulling the chair out by its back and pushing it in once.
   e. If no gentleman is on the other side of the lady on his left, and she has not already seated herself, he seats her also.
   f. When seated, sit upright in the chair, *keeping one hand in your lap while eating.*
4. The napkin
   a. The napkin may be placed to the left of the plate or in the center of the plate when the table is set.
   b. Napkins should be placed with open edge toward the plate, and the open corners at the lower right.
   c. Open the napkin by grasping the open corners with the right hand and pulling it onto the lap, at the same time unfolding it halfway.
   d. Napkins should be unfolded only halfway, whether dinner or luncheon size.
   e. At the end of the meal, the napkin should be replaced to the left of the cover, loosely folded (it should be refolded neatly if you are a house guest and expect to dine there again).
5. When to begin eating
   a. Follow the hostess' example in all questions of etiquette. Don't begin eating until she does.
   b. At a small table wait only until all are served at that table to begin eating, even if there are others in the room. At a large banquet table it is necessary to wait only until those on both sides of you are served before starting to eat.
   c. The hostess should continue eating until all guests are finished.
6. Conversation at the table
   a. Conversation should include dinner partners on both your left and your right; it may also include those across the table, if they are near enough.
   b. Conversation subjects should be general enough to interest everyone and should be pleasant and uncontroversial.
   c. Usually the food should not be discussed. However, if some dish is outstanding or is a favorite of yours, the hostess may be pleased if you mention it.

327

    d. If asked to express a choice of food, do so at once; otherwise take what is served without comment.

    e. Contribute to the conversation but do not monopolize it.

7. In case of accidents

    a. When something is spilled, apologize briefly to the hostess.

    b. If silverware is dropped, ask quietly for another piece.

    c. If a bit of food is dropped on the tablecloth it is probably better to leave it there unless it can be retrieved inconspicuously.

Traveling

As a college student you will be traveling to a variety of places— to and from home or other places for vacations or as a member of some group such as a theater group, an athletic team, or a club group. Remember that you will be judged by your public conduct and that your university will also be judged as long as you are a student of that university.

Be well groomed and appropriately dressed. Be considerate of your fellow travelers. Talk with other people if you and they desire it but keep all casual relationships impersonal. Be friendly but respect the privacy of others. Do not permit casual acquaintances to pay for your meal, hotel, entertainment, or taxi; this may imply an obligation on your part. Although this is particularly important for women travelers, it also applies to men.

Do not make derogatory remarks about the food, the country, the city. You may spoil the enjoyment of someone else who might have enjoyed them.

Do not take souvenirs from hotels, restaurants, or other public places. To the owner of the article, whether it be an ashtray, a towel, or what-not, it is theft. It also implies theft to most people who see them after you return home. So buy your souvenirs if you want something typical of the place.

Carry a limited amount of luggage.

Do write prompt thank-you notes to those whom you have visited, who have given you a going-away or other party, who have given you a gift, or who have gone to the airport, station, or dock to see you off.

Tipping is expected in many situations and in most countries. Even in the Soviet Union, gifts are expected and accepted in lieu of money. The tip is supposed to make up the difference between the base pay and what may be considered a living wage. If you are traveling in a foreign country, any good travel book will indicate when and where to tip and gives an indication of the amount in the coin of the country. Do not tip where there are signs indicating "no tipping." If service is slow, inadequate, or discourteous, you may tip less or not at all. On the other hand, you should tip more for extra and/or excellent service. Always keep a pocketful of change. In addition, a smile and a "thank you" or "everything has been very nice" is always the courteous thing. Learn the approximate amounts to tip and thus avoid being ostentatious or gauche.

7

The Ethical Dimension
of a Career* *by Willis Moore*

It is generally granted that to be successful in any kind of career
a person must know the facts related to his field of work and be
skillful in their use; but it is not always clear, particularly to one
who is just preparing himself for his life's work, that facts and skill
alone are not enough to make him a worthy member of his profession and of society. A little reflection should remind all of us,
including the beginner, that technical knowledge and skill, which
necessarily loom so large in professional education, may be used
for better or worse ends, for the improvement of man's life or for
antisocial purposes. Where these phases of professional training are
used for the maintenance or betterment of the desirable aspects of
our human world, as they are with most people, we judge that career
to be a socially worthy one and an honor to the profession exemplified.
From time immemorial every tribe, community, and nation has had as
its heroes those individuals who have used their special knowledge
and skill in an unusual degree in the interests of their fellowmen.

History, however, records enough examples of persons who have
put the education provided by society of selfish, antisocial, and
even criminally destructive uses that we must take account of them
and attempt to determine the nature and operation of the factor
in terms of which their careers differ from those of people we
applaud. Unfortunately we do not have to turn to ancient history
to find these bad examples. The daily press presents us with frequent instances of the well-trained lawyer who is using his knowl-

* Written for this volume by Professor Willis Moore, Chairman of the Department of Philosophy, Southern Illinois University, Carbondale. He is the author
of many articles on social philosophy and value theory.

edge to defeat the ends of justice, the clever bookkeeper who through his skill has been able to hide a theft for years, the salesman using applied psychology to sell shoddy or dangerous products, or the politician who by means of his forensic or writing proficiency knowingly persuades the voting public to act contrary to the general good. The difference between these misdirected careers and the honorable ones described earlier lies not in degree of technical proficiency but in what we shall call the moral dimension of their respective patterns of life.

Is a Discussion of Ethics Appropriate in an Educational Context?

Some educators who admit that all of a person's life, including his professional activities, has this moral dimension would still argue that a textbook introductory to professional training should deal only with those facts and skills essential to technical success. Evidently the leaders in home economics training quoted in earlier chapters of this textbook do not agree with such educators. On almost every page of these chapters there is some allusion to moral and other values. We are told that the profession of home economics is "service-oriented," with the goal of trying to improve the quality of living . . . (p. 42) and to "establish values which give meaning to personal, family, and community living . . ." (p. 11). The student is frequently reminded of his duty to help others, to be sensitive to their needs, to serve humanity, and so on. These descriptions and reminders recognize the equal importance of the technical and moral aspects of a career. In taking this position these leaders in the profession of home economics place themselves in a large and growing company of educators who believe that no program of training in the professions is complete without recognition and discussion of the ethical or moral and other values involved.

The remaining sections of this chapter focus attention on this moral factor in life, especially in a professional career. They will deal with a number of problems brought to light by social scientists and philosophers who have studied morality and will attempt to outline an emerging theory of general morality that may provide a framework for the ethics of the profession you expect to enter.

How Does A Person Become Moral?

One of the basic questions raised by students of moral values has to do with the way we come by this moral factor in life. It was once widely believed that we are born with a moral code "written on our hearts." Modern social psychologists reject this theory in favor of the view that we somehow learn right from wrong after we are born. They hold that this does not come about automatically; but they and the philosophers are still studying and debating just how this learning takes place.Certain of the conditions under which moral learning takes place have been known since the days of the Greek philosophers, whereas others are still being uncovered and studied by social scientists. We have long known that young people tend to make prestige persons their models in behavior and also in the matter of choices. In some manner this process of imitation leads into similarity of moral attitudes and decision. Educators have for centuries taken advantage of this tendency in students by using selected hero models to induce modifications in their moral attitudes. Today we often deplore the prevalence of the wrong types of heroes in literature, on the radio, and in television programs because of their pernicious effects on youthful audiences. We also know that moral character is shaped in terms of activities carried on in playground situations, in clubs, in gangs, and in all sorts of institutional practices. Under certain circumstances, argument and other forms of persuasive discourse, used by parents, religious leaders, teachers, and other prestige persons, admittedly help shape moral growth. Finally the exposure of the individual to imaginatively or experimentally presented long-range consequences of behavoir patterns may help the individual, in the light of these experiences, to mold himself morally.

Should We Leave the Job to Home and Church?

It seems reasonable to suppose that the schools in general could, as they evidently think they have been doing, affect the moral development of youth by taking advantage of a number of the previously described possibilities; but some people have objected to any such planned program for the schools on the ground that the teaching of morality belongs not to the schools but to the home and the church. There is a growing realization today that these early influences on the child are no longer adequate, at least under contemporary conditions. Perhaps parents do not take the time and trouble to inculcate morals as elders once did; perhaps the church is not reaching youth as it once did. One possible explanation of the failure of home and church to exert the influence they once did in this matter is that the conditions and circumstances in terms of which youth live are today so different and so much more complex than they were when the customary and traditional moral code taught in home and church was developed that it no longer seems relevant to young people. Perhaps only in schools, which are not so tradition bound as other institutions, can the valuable portions of these codes be made relevant to today. Regardless of the reasons, it is becoming increasingly clear to educators that they are expected to carry a much larger portion than they once did of the burden of seeing to it that the moral dimension develops alongside the intellectual and the operational potentialities of the learner.

Is the College Age Too Late for Moral Learning?

It is often said that long before a human being reaches the college age his patterns of moral behavior are so firmly molded that nothing further can be done to modify them. Some people have even set this terminal date for moral learning at the beginning of the grade-school period. The better knowledge now available of the nature of the moral factor in experience and its modes of operation in life tends to discount this old idea. For one thing, we know that knowledge plays a part in the moral decision and that persons are still capable of discarding, acquiring, and modifying knowledge items during the college years. If they were not, college would be a waste of time. We know that the opening up of new areas of experience during this period has a shaping effect on moral patterns. Parents often take it for granted that college can change such patterns for the worse. Why do they not acknowledge that change can take place for the better? The college age is one of critical reflection on what has previously been learned in every area and by whatever method. It is the age of reassessment, evaluation, often of reaffirmation, and occasionally of rejection, even down to the level of childhood beliefs, attitudes, and values, all elements involved in the complex we know as the moral dimension. It is a common occurrence that while in college the individual makes a radical shift in direction, sets new goals, and abandons old ones. These changes are at least as often in the direction of moral improvement as of moral deterioration. And college staff members can and should share the responsibility for providing the factors that help the student on to maturity.

College-level treatment of moral matters is seldom a matter of persuasive discourse directed to the student. The whole institutional setup, together with the many subsocieties and subinstitutions contained within it, serve, by means of the behavior they require, to shape the character of the students, and the occasional great teacher or adviser influences by example. The most effective technique of exerting a shaping influence on the moral dimension of college students, however, is by exposing them to an intellectual expansion of moral situations and various argumentative interpretations of the elements of such through readings, lectures, and discussion in courses in ethics and social philosophy and in segments of numbers of the other social studies and the humanities. Most importantly the student can thus be helped to extend the application of generally accepted moral principles to areas of the professional career for which his specialized training is preparing him. The distorted and misdirected careers to which we referred earlier can, in part, be charged to our failure to make it clear to young people preparing for life that a professional career is a continuation of the intimate, personal living experienced in the home and community and is subject to the same general rules of conduct admittedly relevant and necessary there.

But What Is This Moral Dimension?

We have been using this phrase *moral dimension* and *moral factor* rather glibly without attempting to make clear what they mean. The term *moral* is in such common use that the average person would scarcely feel the need to look twice at any phrase containing it; but the philosopher, a part of whose business is to reflect on and clarify the meaning of even common words, sees a need to consider such a term seriously. Studious analysis of language phrases has often led to surprisingly helpful results. We may begin our study of this phrase by asking under what circumstances it is used. In what kinds of situations do we expect to discover the moral factor or dimension?

The Moral Factor Found Only in Certain Decision Situations

Philosophers agree that there is a moral factor only in those situations in which a person is making a choice, a decision. There are plenty of occasions when a person is making no decisions but just watching the world roll by, when he is simply enjoying the panorama of life or moving about in terms of mechanical habit or routine with no call for making decisions. In these circumstances he is neither good nor bad in any degree; but when he has to stop his routine or reverie in order to tackle a problem or take a new turn, he enters a situation requiring a decision, a choice; and here the moral dimension may appear. If the turn in behavior is being forced upon him and he has no choice in the matter, we do not see it as a moral situation; he must be deciding freely. But not every decision thus made freely is recognized as being moral in nature. For a choice to have a moral dimension the anticipated consequences of the alternatives must have a bearing on the welfare of mankind and must differ from each other in this regard. Only if a person is making a choice among possible paths of action, each of which has consequences of good or evil for man with those consequences differing in this regard, is his choice a moral one. Should the paths lead to ends with no consequences for human welfare or should these consequences be equal in what we call value, the situation has no moral dimension.

THE MORAL FACTOR OCCURS IN DEGREES

There are philosophers who argue that every choice we make has at least some slight impact on social welfare, but it seems evident to common sense that in some cases this impact is so small as to be negligible. The choice of which shoe to put on first in the morning can make no significant difference in my future or that of others in my society. Other choices have great importance in this regard, as for instance, what I choose to do when I see my neighbor being attacked by a mob. There are other choices where the anticipated consequences are intermediate in importance for the future of all. The significance for mankind of a student's failing to prepare adequately for tomorrow's examination falls somewhere between that of the two cases previously described.

Organized societies, realizing that decision situations differ in the degree of importance of anticipated consequences of alternatives, see the moral factor as varying similarly in degree and proceed to assess moral penalties and rewards accordingly. Ideally they vary the punishment or reward in accordance with the social seriousness of the chosen consequences. Although early students and administrators of moral matters tended to divide moral acts into black and white categories, more recent theorists, and practicing societies nearly everywhere, are more likely to see this moral factor as occurring in varying degrees of intensity ranging along a continuum from practically zero at one end, as in the choice of which shoe to put on first, to a very high degree when the life of another or others hangs on our decision. In the instance of the more serious decision situations, ones in which societies believe they have much at stake, rules are drawn up for the guidance of relevant behavior and severe penalties are imposed for their violation and attractive rewards offered for compliance. For decisions having little or no social significance no rules are made and no rewards or penalties posted; in cases of decisons of varying degrees of intermediate social importance the rewards and penalties vary appropriately. Toward the lower end of the intermediate sort of choice situation most of the rules are mere customs or conventions rather than laws and the rewards and penalties simple social approval or disapproval.

GROWTH TOWARD MORAL MATURITY

No one nowadays calls a newborn baby's acts morally right or wrong or rewards or punishes him for what he does. The reason for this is that he is making no decisions. His behavior is purely reflex action or what parents and others force upon him. Decisions affecting his life are made for him. Gradually, as the baby advances through childhood toward maturity, the number of decisions made for him decreases and the proportion left to him increases, and his moral life develops correspondingly. This gradual handing over to the maturing youth of the decision-making process does not mean that he is being progressively deprived of guidance. As indicated earlier, in decisions that may have serious consequences for his future life or for others, society provides the sorts of rules we have described, with appropriate rewards and penalties. Furthermore, the growing personal experience of the youth serves to reinforce, or, occasionally, to counter, the judgment of society as to the consequences of decisions made, thus assisting in the maturing process.

By the time young people have reached the college age, provided they have been allowed and encouraged to develop their moral decision-making capacities in the light of inherited social wisdom and a growing personal wisdom generated by their own experience, they should be ready to make most such decisions for themselves. Certainly by the graduation date they should be able, in common, recurrent situations, to make sound moral decisions without having to run to parents and other authorities for orders or advice; in uncommon or rare situations the wisest and most experienced of us may need counsel in moral matters to the day we die. It should be borne in mind, also, that there is no education, no experience, that can make anyone's moral decision making foolproof; not one of us, no matter how well educated in moral decision making or how strongly motivated to do the right thing, can avoid the occasional moral error. No human being is perfect.

SUMMARY

Let us sum up what has been said to this point. There is, over and above knowledge and skill, a moral factor in a successful career. This factor is not inborn but learned and, therefore, theoretically controllable, teachable. Although one's moral character is fairly well developed by the time he reaches the college age it is not so fixed as to defy reshaping under the influence of appropriate educational processes. Not all situations have a moral dimension. We limit the use of this phrase to those in which persons are making choices involving better and worse consequences for society. This moral factor appears in varying degrees in these choice situations, a fact that society recognizes by treating the various choices in terms of corresponding degrees of penalties and rewards. Ideally the human being progresses steadily from a nonmoral beginning to a responsible maturity as older persons hand over to him more and more decisions, and ones of increasingly greater social importance, until by the time of college graduation he is ready to make all but the rarest of moral decisions for himself.

How Do We Tell the More from the Less Moral?

What we have said so far marks off the moral from other situations in which no moral factor is present, but we have not made it clear how we tell the more from the less moral. We have been suggesting that moral choice has something to do with the consequences of that choice for society. There are two major types of approach to a study of how moral decisions are to be understood and justified. One is by taking the perspective of the person making the decision, seeing the whole process from the standpoint of the individual member of society. This begins as a rather subjective outlook upon life and ends with a description of what the individual desires, wants, or seeks as the good life. Early philosophical studies of the moral situation, for the most part, took this approach.

Another approach is more objective, more in keeping with what we have come to think of as the scientific method. This involves standing off from the workings of society and looking at the whole process as we might observe processes in physical nature, from the outside, objectively. This type of approach to the area of morality was used, in part, by Aristotle when he began his ethical studies by listing the various items different groups thought to be the chief objective of life. It is best exemplified today in the descriptions of the moral positions of actual societies as studied and reported by anthropologists and other social scientists. In terms of this approach we tend to see moral codes as the devices societies use to maintain themselves and promote general welfare.

Ideally these two approaches should serve to complement each other, and the most adequate moral theories are those developed in the light of both the subjective and the objective approaches. For various reasons it seems better to look at the matter first from the perspective of the social scientist and then to fill in the picture with the warmer, more intimate data derived through subjective, even introspective, procedures. From the objective perspective we can place the moral factor in the setting of total social process, detecting the role it plays in the ongoing life of human society. This approach helps us to see ourselves as we might be viewed by some outside observer. By first taking this approach we may be able to see our human state of affairs, even in its moral dimension, shorn of some of the prejudices and provincialisms that so often distort our descriptions of it.

The Moral Situation as the Social Scientist Sees It

Anthropologists and other social scientists have made it clear that from the objective viewpoint the moral factor in a human life is society pressing its claim upon the individual, influencing him so to act as to maintain and improve the effectiveness of the cooperative effort that is society. The customs, rules, codes, and laws of which we have been speaking are simply the cumulative wisdom of society as to the patterns of behavior that are helpful, perhaps even essential, in the preservation of social life and effort. These items of wisdom are generated slowly over long periods of time, almost unconsciously and largely by trial and error, until some unusually perceptive individual, a Moses, a Socrates, or a Jesus, brings them into everyone's consciousness by putting them into words.

Anthropologists have noted that, from their objective viewpoint, there is a very considerable difference in degree of importance among these rules or principles with regard to what they do for a society. All societies, the world over, have discovered that in order to exist at all certain broad rules must be followed, and these rules, tabus, or precepts become the basic ones in each society. For instance, universally, everywhere, societies have rules against indiscriminate killing and lying. The reason for these rules is evident. Societies are bands of people working cooperatively and in terms of some kind or degree of division of labor. To be able to do this at all effectively the individuals must be able to trust one another. Trust includes believing that the others will not stab you in the back when you are not looking and also will tell you the truth about what they are experiencing. If lying and killing were allowed to prevail no society could long hold together and the advantages of cooperative endeavor would be lost. There are other rules that are offshoots of these or ones having similar significance for group living.

The anthropologist finds, also, a lot of rules, peculiar to a given society, that seem from our modern scientific viewpoint to have no real use. These have been assumed by the original leaders of these societies to be useful, but the data on which these leaders have based the rules may be faulty or the purposes may have been narrowly selfish. In short, many, perhaps most, of these rules in a given society are not well grounded. This judgment still holds, in some degree, of modern societies, and one of the tasks of the social scientist and the philosopher is to ferret out such useless or harmful rules and expose them so that socially minded citizens may campaign for changes. Unfortunately, most people accept uncritically the mass of conventions and regulations as handed down to them by society, thus perpetuating, along with the basically valuable items, old errors, and outmoded ways. Societies need the critical, independent thinker who has the courage to be a rebel, a radical, with regard to this inherited material, who, through his activities, can make us justify these old rules or, where we cannot do so, modify or discard them. No society can grow, or even hold together long, without the critic and the innovator.

The anthropologist's approach to an understanding of the moral dimension of life rests on the assumption that the survival of the species is the basic drive of man and that social life is the chief mechanism whereby that goal can be accomplished. It is easy to show by means of biological, sociological, and historical data that an essential factor in man's history in the long struggle for existence was his banding together into groups that make possible cooperative effort with all of its advantages over the efforts of individuals working in isolation. From this perspective we can see, further, although the anthropologist does not make so much of this matter as he might, that once bare survival has been achieved these cooperative groupings enable us to make life better and better in many qualitative ways. Leisure time and all the things we can enjoy by reason of it, the mass of goods and activities we call culture, constitute what our group living makes possible over bare survival.

From the viewpoint of the social scientist, therefore, a choice is better than another in the degree in which its consequences are more helpful in preserving the conditions necessary to the cooperative operations we call society. Choices leading to destructive consequences for society, ones hindering or making impossible cooperative activity, would be so low on the moral scale as to merit the adjective *immoral*. A close look at the rules that properly sum up the conditions favorable to cooperative activity reveals that for the most part they have to do with the way we treat one another. Man has discovered, largely through trial and error, that he cannot live in groups unless each and every individual behaves toward others in certain specified ways, hence the rules against lying, stealing, coverting, killing, and dozens of lesser offenses.

Anthropologists have noted that in many societies moral leaders have attempted to condense these rules about our relations to others into one basic principle. Our Golden Rule is one such instance of this attempt: Do unto others as you would have them do unto you. Sometimes this is put negatively, as in the culture of India: Do nought to others that would cause you pain if done to you. Anthropologists call this the rule of reciprocity. The most enlightened and compelling version of the rule of reciprocity in our culture is Immanuel Kant's restatement of the Golden Rule. [Kant, Königsberg, Prussia, 1724–1804]: "Act so that you treat humanity, whether in your own person or in that of another, always as an end and never as means only."[1] Kant, influenced not only by the Christian doctrine of the worth of the individual but also by the anthropologists' requirement of an objective

---

[1] *Foundations of the Metaphysics of Morals* (New York: The Library of Liberal Arts, Bobbs-Merrill, 1959), p. 47.

statement of moral rules, so states the principle as make it apply with equal force to oneself and others. We are to treat humanity, whether in ourselves or others, with the utmost of respect, as the essence of dignity, as something capable of making rational choices, of being moral. We are, therefore, never to use either ourselves or others as mere instruments for achieving material or other ambitions. We should never make an exception of anyone, ourselves or others, when applying any rule. Rules should be applied universally; there should be no favored persons; this is the way nature acts, and we should do likewise. In no other way can we expect people to work together peaceably and effectively in a society. Kant was here enunciating the essential principle of a democratically operating society.

All versions of the rule of reciprocity, including that of Kant, assume that such a behavior pattern would bar all acts harmful to persons: lying to oneself or a neighbor, stealing, slandering, injuring, killing, or any one of the hundreds of behavioral performances that make for weakened interpersonal relations and, consequently, a disintegrating society. Should we accept the rule of reciprocity as a general guide for decisions affecting persons, and, beyond that, the welfare of society, we could say that one act is morally better than another insofar as it shows greater respect for personality, including what we often term the rights of persons, and tends more to preserve and further mutual appreciation and social solidarity. Contrariwise, an act is morally worse than another in the degree that it expresses less respect for personality, veering toward contempt and thus lessening mutual appreciation and possibilities of cooperative activity.

The Moral Situation as Certain Philosophers See It

For over twenty-five hundred years Western philosophers have been mulling over this problem of the nature and function of the moral dimension of life, and although their approach and perspective have usually been quite different from those of the anthropologist their conclusions have been quite similar. For the most part, at least until quite recently, the philosophers have looked at this problem from the perspective of the human individual with a life to live, a subjective or "inside" viewpoint, as contrasted with the scientist's objective or outside perspective. From this subjective starting point we ask: What do men want of life? What kind of life is satisfactory? What elements go to make up a Good Life? Once those questions are answered philosophers go on to determine in rather general terms how men must behave in order to achieve the specified goal. Again we come upon rules, laws, and principles as we do from the objective approach, and the basic ones are much the same as those discovered by anthropologists to have been the guides for actual societies. It should not surprise us that there is substantial agreement between philosophers and anthropologists in their listings of these rules, for, after all, the two groups, from different perspectives, are studying the same area of experience. Our expectation is that, working together as they are beginning to do, the philosophers and the anthropologists, with the help of other social scientists, will develop a more adequate theory than we now possess of what the better life consists in and will discover more dependable means of achieving it.

ARISTOTLE'S THEORY

The philosophers of the Greek period were the pioneers of this subjective approach, and, as we should expect of any pioneering effort, the theories developed differed widely. They all tried to answer the question: What is the goal of life? By the time of Aristotle (born in Stagira, Macedonia, 384 B.C.), there had been enough thinking on the subject, with enough diversity of conclusion, that he felt constrained to summarize and correct what had been said. In a summary that anticipates the objective method of later social scientists he pointed out that various people have held the ideal life to be one of pleasure, one devoted to politics, one of rational activity, a wealthy one, or a combination of one or more of these and morality.

In his *Nicomachean Ethics* Aristotle developed a theory of his own that, with a few modifications, still seems to many people to be an acceptable one. A major error of these earlier theories, he believed, was the contention, in each case, that the goal of life should be some one type of thing. In modern terms we should call these various goals values. Each of these theories is expressive of a very narrow perspective on life, omitting much else that is important. A person who seeks wealth only, or political power and prestige and nothing else, is leading an extremely circumscribed life and, in the long run, an impoverished one. Each of these items, plus many others, has value for man and should not be excluded from life. Aristotle therefore contends that the ideal life is a rich plurality of goods or values. To this wholesome unity of values he gives the name *happiness*. Happiness includes pleasure but is not identical with it, for the total encompasses health, wealth, honor, family life, friendship, op-

342

portunities for exercising our thinking capacity, even good looks and a long life, plus numbers of other items.

This life of plural values cannot be really good, however, unless it be so organized that no one of these items takes so much of a person's time and effort that others suffer. One should not, for instance, focus so much on getting political power and honor that he neglects his family or his health. Nor can life be good should a person use certain of these elements as tools for achieving others, as an ambitious businessman might make friends solely for whatever use they might be to him in business. Although the acquiring of any one of these goods may incidentally help in achieving others, this should not be our motive in seeking them; each ingredient value should be seen as worthwhile in itself.

Reason, thus, must be used as an organizing and guiding power in life to keep our multiple capacities and their distinctive goals in balance. This meant for Aristotle a life of moderate or measured activity in the exercise of those normal physiological and emotional capacities by means of which we achieve these goals. We have a capacity for eating and drinking, for example, and the exercise of this capacity in the proper degree leads to health. If we eat too much we are gluttonous and miss our normal goal of health; if we eat an unreasonably small amount we are ascetic and again miss the goal. The proper amount is a sort of middle ground or what he called the Golden Mean. This Golden Mean, in all such situations, varies from person to person, so each has to experiment and think it out for himself; but does have a Golden Mean that if he is to come close to happiness must be discovered and followed as best he can in the exercise of his normal capacities. Aristotle realized that with all their efforts few individuals are likely to do better than approximate this mean or a well-balanced life, but he insisted, nevertheless, on the worth of the Golden Mean and the well-balanced life as guiding ideals.

The moral dimension of life in terms of this theory appears in the choices we make with regard to the ingredients of life and with respect to the Golden Mean. A person is virtuous in the degree that he approximates the Mean in normal types of behavior, nonvirtuous or vicious in the degree that his behavior departs from the mean. Reasoning in the form of practical wisdom is the activity that enables man to choose properly. Aristotle placed heavy emphasis on the process of building habits of action in this manner so that one, in time, becomes ready or disposed to act virtuously upon the recurrence of a situation to which he has responded correctly before. A person of good habits is one of character, one we can expect to act properly when faced with a moral decision.

Many modern students of ethics would accept much of Aristotle's view but feel the necessity of modifying it in terms of certain findings of social scientists. Thus they would insist that we start with the anthropological and biological observation that man's basic drive, whether he is conscious of it or not, is the survival of the species, a point that is supported by the fact, among others, that occasionally parents and others will actually sacrifice their lives for the younger members of the species. This basic drive usually operates through actions designed to further the life of the individual and, thus, is not consciously noted. At the conscious level appear those needs or drives that Aristotle describes, plus many others, whose objects or values make up what he called happiness or the good life. Much that enters into this pluralistic end or goal is over and above mere survival, serving to enrich or embellish life.

The ideal of a perfectly balanced, well-rounded life, as recommended by Aristotle, is now seen as both too difficult for most people to achieve and of less worth in this modern world of specialization. Aristotle himself singled out two ingredients of the good life for emphasis far beyond any others, thus creating a certain imbalance in the ideal. He made so much of the social factor, particularly as exemplified in friendship, that wealth, health, political prestige, and most of the rest seem to pale into insignificance. Similarly he seems to be saying that only a person who can reason well and at high levels of abstraction can achieve happiness, but if this is the case then the true goal of life is closed to most people. Present-day philosophers would not so restrict the numbers of people who can achieve well-being.

Contemporary philosophers would, as did Aristotle, unbalance his ideal life by emphasizing the social factor. As social scientists have insisted, a smoothly functioning society, or cooperative association, is the primary mechanism whereby relatively weak man has been able to survive and, beyond that point, to build rich cultures. They also point to reason as the unique tool whose use has enabled man to overcome his own weakness and the hazards of nature and obtain the goods he desires. Aristotle felt the importance of these two factors but did not know their key value in man's upward thrust.

For some years anthropologists were inclined to oppose Aristotle's theory that there are universal principles of right behavior, ones that are the same, except for variations in degree due to individual differences, the world over. Influenced by the noted differences in moral rules among societies, many anthropologists concluded that such rules are relative to time, place, and circumstance. More recently, after probing more deeply into these customary rules, they have found what they call cultural universals, samenesses from culture to culture, thus, the rule of reciprocity, the one against indiscriminate killing, and so on. The differences that remain can be seen as being due to local circumstances and errors. Most of the items in the moral codes of actual societies are useless, outmoded, or downright harmful. After all these tabus and rules have been worked out more or less unconsciously over long periods of time by fallible men, so we should expect some erroneous and useless items. Now that we have developed more reliable and systematic ways of gathering, interpreting, and using data we can hope and expect that by means of this universal scientific method, which knows no national, geographic, or even time boundaries, men can develop one unified, well-grounded idea of the better life and one set of the basic rules of the road for all mankind.

An Emerging Ideal of the Good Life

We are now in a position to look at life from the combined perspective of the subjective and the objective approaches and to picture roughly and generally what constitutes a decent, desirable, or acceptable life. Of some of these factors we are quite certain. Where the social sciences and subjective judgments the world over agree on their indispensability for an acceptable life we can list them. As we move on to other factors for which value claims are made we may be sure of them only in varying degrees. Anyway, we must, as men have always had to do, make an attempt at the construction of such an ideal in the light of the best knowledge now available, admitting the necessity of a continuing process of studying and reexamining this ideal as our knowledge of man and his world continues to unfold.

The basic factor in this picture of an ideal life, almost by definition, is that complex set of conditions that make life itself possible. We shall call these the physiological necessities. Conspicuous among these are food, shelter, protection against disease, the provision of uncontaminated water, air, and so on. The list of these items is a long, often interlocking one, including, of course, the means for achieving them with reasonable expenditure of effort. Time was when it took nearly all man's energy and time just to survive at this minimum biological level. Many contemporary psychologists would insist that conspicuous among these basic biological needs is the complex we now call mental health. The social scientist would remind us at this point that we must not neglect any and all conditions and factors requisite to reproduction as a means of the survival of the species.

The second major complex factor in a good life is the social dimension in its many grades and degrees. As already suggested this factor is essential to the survival of the species; and from the subjective viewpoint it is, perhaps, our most pervasive and most demanding need. At its very lowest level it is the simple need to be with others of our kind, sheer association. In those rare situations in which a person is deprived of normal human companionship, he substitutes other animals, even a spider or a sunbeam, for the missing human associate. No punishment is more severe than solitary confinement, which, when prolonged, often results in mental derangement and suicide. Beyond mere association come friendship, love, and family feeling. The more sensitive of human beings experience this need for identification and association with others beyond the family into community, national, and worldwide situations. The rare, poetic soul may thus identify even with other forms of life or with all of reality. The social scientist would describe this complex of needs as the recognition of society's claim on our loyalty to the principle of cooperative activity serving the goal of survival of the species.

Beyond these two basic levels of need, the physiological (including the mental) and the social, we tend to differ in our listings. These differences among us are in part only verbal but in part they represent differences in emphasis. It may well be that cultural factors affect our value judgments in such an ambitious enterprise as the construction of an ideal life. Be this as it may, it is both desirable and possible for us to go ahead with this listing, at least for our culture.

Following on the heels of the social factor and growing out of it is the need of recognition. We mean by this term having a place in the operations of our society, a part in what is going on, a job, a recognized function to fulfill. This means being of some importance in the group and, ideally, being an indispensable element in the total.

346

At higher levels of discussion we speak of this as the need to be treated as a person, a human being, not just as a cog in a machine. Nothing is more damaging to a developing child than lack of recognition by associates, parents, teachers, and other prestige persons. It is almost an aphorism in educational psychology that to be motivated, to be a successful learner, a child must be accorded that kind of attention we reserve for a person of importance. The achievement of recognition by our fellows is the basic type of social security.

Human beings need to be doing something, to be active. The completely idle life is, for all but the rare individual, an empty, boring, unsatisfactory existence. People who by reason of inherited wealth or some other circumstance that either allows idleness or forces it upon them tend to make up something to do. They may substitute social life, games, charity work, or a hobby for what would normally be an occupation. Older persons who retire to a life of inactivity tend to weaken and die earlier than do men who "keep alive" by engaging in a hobby. And this work serves its purpose best if it is recognized by society as useful.

A distinction must be made between *work* as we have been describing it and *drudgery*. Many people identify the two and thus reject work as an evil. By *work* we mean activity with a socially recognized usefulness, effectively under our own control and within our normal limits of capacity. *Drudgery* is activity nearly or wholly under another's directions, unrecognized by society as of importance in its scheme of things, and too difficult, exhausting, or dangerous for our good. It is drudgery, not work, that men shun. Work they want both as an end in itself, satisfying of our need to be doing something, and as a major means of achieving social recognition.

Perhaps as an integral ingredient in work, perhaps as a development out of it, is the need of an opportunity to be creative. People want very deeply to be able to make a real difference in things; they want to leave their mark on the community, something new, uniquely their product. This might be a modest mark written in terms of some good to others identifiable only with themselves; it might, for some, be a work of art, a novel, a reorganization of society, a new idea. Some philosophers believe this urge to creativity to be a universal urge, not just in man but in the whole world. At any rate, we can agree, perhaps, that no person is completely satisfied with life unless it offers him the opportunity to invent or create, that is, to make a unique contribution to man.

A life devoted wholly to activity is, of course, a biological impossibility; persons must also rest. We can give the name *leisure* to all that stretch of time during which we are not pursuing our professional or other duties. Should we use the term that broadly it would include the sheer inactivity we call rest as well as the periods devoted to recreation, including hobbies. Men need leisure of both kinds; no life is good in which its duration is divided into work and rest alone. We need a change of pace within our periods of activity. That is the way hobbies play an important role in life. Even our work duties are carried out more effectively when interspersed among periods of rest and hobby activity.

An essential ingredient of the good life, one we enjoy for its own sake and one that is essential to any creative work, to any kind of development, is freedom. The tiny baby whose bodily movements are cramped or restricted does not develop normally, and an analogous distortion occurs in the realm of moral and intellectual development when a considerable degree of freedom to decide and to think does not prevail. That the child has a basic desire for freedom is shown by his angry reactions to suddenly imposed restriction even on leg and arm movements. We never lose this need to feel free to move about, to think new thoughts, to experiment, and the ideal life makes provision for such freedom.

One cannot look at man's behavior in this world without being struck by the prevalence of activity that seems designed to open up new areas. There seems to be an urge to the encounter with the novel. We can call this the need for adventure. One thing that makes so many kinds of lives seem so dull is the lack of this ingredient in an appreciable degree. Once men achieved adventure in the simple activities directed to the gathering of food through the hunt. Today, in a highly developed culture such as ours this need must be satisfied in more sophisticated ways. Travel, sight-seeing, a wide range of reading, art experiences, and "adventures" of the mind are ways we now use. War, unfortunately, has yet some of the old, old appeal to the adventurous, and if we are going to get rid of it we must provide everyone with some kind of substitute adventure.

The life of thinking answers to a higher need in man, one that is not open to lower animals. The Greeks were so intrigued with this fact that they defined man as *the* rational animal. Thinking is valued both as a tool and as an enjoyable occupation in itself. No one needs to be argued into the position that thinking is a valuable instrument for achieving other ingredients of the good life, but students sometimes think of it only as a necessary evil. As in the case of work, however, when we are thinking freely, for ourselves, to some purpose and not to an excessive degree or on insolvable problems it becomes an enjoyable activity. There is nothing in which we take more satisfaction than a conclusion we have worked out or an intellectual discovery we have made. Knowledge is enjoyable. It ranges all the way up from mere sight-seeing experiences to the great systems of science and philosophy. Life is truly and completely good only where the opportunity for achievement of knowledge is present.

We sometimes speak of another factor, the aesthetic, as providing the color of life, its warmth. From primitive man to the creature who lives in our highly mechanized culture there is a deep-seated need for the factor of beauty in life. We differ radically on what this beauty consists in, but universally we demand it in some form. The demand may range from that for orderliness in dress or home surroundings, up through satisfying color, sounds, or other modality arrangements, to the highly intricate works of art often, unfortunately, exhibited only in museums or on the stage. That this urge to beauty and beautification is a deep-seated one is evidenced in the fact that, given the leisure time and freedom to do so, almost any person or group will resort to decoration or artistic arrangement. They often steal time from their work to beautify their surroundings. Managers of factories have found that where they provide tastefully painted surroundings and soft music the output of the workers tends to go up. Their motivation may be of a low type here but the end result *is* significant.

Every culture we know anything about has had some type of what we call a religious ingredient, an overview of life backed with an emotional commitment to what is judged of greatest value in it. The verbal description of this factor varies greatly among the world's cultures, but each has some such ultimate commitment. This is no place to elaborate on the types of religion anthropologists have noted, so we shall simply insist that the good life, universally, contains some form of the religious commitment, some elaboration of that natural piety that grows out of our contacts with a great world, an unfathomable experience. The wonder, awe, fear, and gratitude that make up that natural piety inevitably generate in any man with the leisure time to reflect on such matters some systematic theory of what it is all about, and that is his religious philosophy.

All these ingredients we have discussed, and perhaps many more, are elements of what we have called the emerging ideal of the good life. We may now turn our attention to some ideas we are beginning to agree on as to how we should live in order to achieve this good life.

Some Emerging General Rules for Living

Social scientists and philosophers have, in recent years, made enough progress in the great task of developing a universal ethic that we can hazard some generalizations as to what it will be. Some of the material for this emerging theory is derived from anthropological studies of human culture. These studies reveal certain basic rules common to all cultures, the observance of which is essential to the maintenance of group activity. Some of the material comes from the findings of sociologists, psychologists, and other social scientists as they gradually present us with a reliable picture of the nature of man, of that cluster of basic needs whose satisfactions constitute the good life we have been talking about, and of the patterns of behavior required for the achievement of those satisfactions.

One general rule, perhaps the most important one for man to follow if he is to survive as a species, is that he must learn to live with his fellowman in peace. Mere survival is impossible under contemporary potentialities of warfare unless we achieve peaceful coexistence the world over. This requirement for group living was discovered long ago, back in tribal days, and the rules against indiscriminate killing within the group and other crimes against persons appeared in practically every list of tribal tabus. As groups grew larger, merging progressively into cities, states, nations, and empires, these rules were expanded correspondingly to ban such behavior in ever-widening areas. What we are beginning to see today is the absolute necessity of making the final expansion of coverage of such rules to the whole of mankind. This last extension of the ban on crimes against persons would mean the institution of law even among nations, resulting in, among other things, the elimination of war as a means of settling disputes, the old, old idealistic dream of genuine world peace.

Many thinkers have insisted that the achievement of peace on earth is basically dependent on underlying human attitudes or feelings toward fellowmen. They have insisted on probing more deeply than the outward behavior described in the rule just discussed. Immanuel Kant, as mentioned earlier, is among those who have seen this clearly. His formulation of a practical working rule for interpersonal relations is a good early example of what such probing can reveal. The basic principle of successful human association, as he enunciated it, will undoubtedly appear as a central item in any future universal moral code. As an attitude it is respect for persons as persons, without regard to nationality, religion, race, or other relatively superficial characteristics. Each and every person is a thinking being capable of making decisions, thus deserving of the opportunity to decide for himself. Kant believed that this rational element in every person makes each one a sacred personality, a being of the highest value. The appropriate behavior of man toward man is, therefore, universal equality of treatment, with oneself included as a member of the group. Universal respect for personality, whether in oneself or others, is, therefore, the general rule. Acting in terms of principle one would never make an exception for anyone, show no special favor and no special disfavor toward anyone. This rule would ban discrimination, segregation, slavery, and every form of partiality or prejudiced pattern of behavior. It would ban disrespect, neglect, contempt, abuse, and any sort of harm to persons. Possibly no other rule for interpersonal relations would be necessary were this one thoroughly understood and completely embodied in practice. Jesus, as one great teacher, saw it this way: Love thy neighbor as thyself; do unto others as you would have them do unto you.

Another facet of Kant's practical rule involves the role of reason in determining social behavior. Inasmuch as the world around us, as our scientists are discovering, is a great rational system, wholly consistent, never contradicting itself, always the same, everywhere, rational consistency is the pattern we should follow in constructing and maintaining our social world. Rules should be universal, the same for everybody, everywhere. Reason, thus interpreted, should be our guide and instrument in building decent, workable interpersonal relations, in engineering the material and feeling base for cooperative living. Kant himself, in this spirit, sketched the conditions he believed to be essential for a lasting world peace. Reason rather than blind feeling should be our guide in decision making from the affairs of daily life to matters of international relations. Kant believed reason in the world to be the workings of God and in man the essence of God. Without committing ourselves to his theology, we can agree with his insistence on respect for personality and appreciation of the rational as against the purely emotional approach to problems. It makes sense to say that in all problem situations, including political, religious, racial, economic, and other disputes, it is better to reason together in mutual respect than to resort to brute force.

A consequence of our taking seriously Kant's practical rule for interpersonal relations would be the ending of economic, political, or other forms of exploitation of man by man. Spelled out for institutional practice this principle would mean democracy in the organization and operation of every functional unit of our society. It would rule out that bitter competition that has cost the human race so much in the values of life in favor of peaceful cooperative activity. It would require men to operate in terms of the motive of service to others rather than selfish advantage.

A universal moral code can be put into a simple sentence or so, as great teachers have attempted to do, as we have shown; but the details of what such a simple statement means in practice will still fill books. The advantage of having the simple version is that we can look back on it, occasionally, as a way of checking on our detailed behavior. When we do thus look back we are sometimes surprised to discover how far we have inadvertently departed from the basic rule. In a period of war or preparation for war it comes as something of a shock when we are forced to realize that somehow we have arrived at this state of affairs starting from the rule that we should love our neighbors as we love ourselves. The shock may start us thinking again.

The Meaning of This Theory for Your Profession

The concept of a profession is closely related to the principles we have been describing as the basic elements in a developing code of behavior for all mankind. A profession is a subsociety within the larger society; it is a group of persons working cooperatively toward a common end. Ideally membership in it is voluntary, and its members operate in terms of rules they work out for themselves. A particular profession is one of several or many similar groups, each performing a specialized function within the larger society. In our society, for instance, we have such well-established groups as the medical profession, the legal profession, and the teaching profession, each serving one of the great needs of the larger society. Each of the professions just named has its own special ethical code, formulated, interpreted, and enforced by its own members. Ideally each such code is designed to influence the behavior of its members in the direction of the welfare of the society it serves.

Professional codes are simply the special versions of the general ethical code required to fit the general rules to the special circumstances under which the profession works. As an example, we who are engaged in the teaching profession have a rule in our code that says we should never take selfish advantages of the teacher-student relation.

This is a special application of the general ethical rule that every person, regardless of status, should be treated with respect, never as a mere tool, that no person should ever be awarded or assessed a special favor. The rule of reciprocity is applicable here, and the code simply renders that rule in terms of a common type of temptation in the professional teaching context.

Most of you will someday be members of the home economics profession and of some subgroup within the larger profession, for example, teachers of home economics, dietitians, journalists, social workers, interior designers, and so on, using your technical training in your chosen form of service. In your specialized capacity you will be helping to improve the quality of life for others in more tasty and nutritious foods, in more attractive home surroundings, in a more healthful environment, in better family relations, and in hundreds of other ways. In working for the goal of a better life for all, for a better world for all, you will be exemplifying the moral dimension with which we have been concerned. As we saw in the first paragraph of this chapter, it is not enough that you have these professional skills the schools can provide. You must also have the will to use them for the good of all and some instruction in how this is to be done. The great thinkers in the area of moral matters can help you discover and understand the broad general rules for living the better way; your teachers and other experienced fellowmen can help you see the application of these rules in the professional work you will be doing.

Further Reading

A. Classics in Ethics

1. Aristotle, *The Nicomachean Ethics* (any edition).
2. Epicurus, *Letters, Principal Doctrines and Vatican Sayings* (New York: The Library of Liberal Arts, Bobbs-Merrill Co., 1964).
3. Kant, Immanuel, *Foundations of the Metaphysics of Morals* (New York: The Library of Liberal Arts, Bobbs-Merrill Co., 1959).
4. Mill, J. S., *Utilitarianism* (New York: The Library of Liberal Arts, Bobbs-Merrill Co., 1957).
5. Plato, *The Republic, Euthyphro, Apology, Crito,* and *Gorgias* (any edition).
6. Tawney, R. H., *The Acquisitive Society* (New York: Harcourt, Brace and World, 1920), especially Chapter VII, pp. 91–122.

B. General Ethics Textbooks and Anthologies

1. Clark, Gordon H., and T. V. Smith. *Readings in Ethics* (New York: Appleton-Century-Crofts, Inc., 1935).
2. Everett, Millard S., *Ideals of Life* (New York: John Wiley and Sons, Inc., 1953).
3. Hill, Thomas E., *Contemporary Ethical Theories* (New York: The Macmillan Co., 1950).
4. Titus, Harold H., *Ethics for Today*, 3rd. ed. (New York: American Book Co., 1957), pp. 1–561.
5. ——— and Morris T. Keeton. *The Range of Ethics* (New York: American Book Co., 1966), pp. 1–418.

Appendixes

Selected References

Part I

BOOKS:

American Home Economics Association, *Home Economics in Higher Education* (Washington, D.C.: The Association, 1949).

Baldwin, Keturah E., *The AHEA Saga* (Washington, D.C.: American Home Economics Association, 1949).

Bane, Lita, *The Story of Isabel Bevier* (Peoria, Ill.: Charles A. Bennett Co., Inc., 1955).

―――― and Mildred R. Chapin, *Introduction to Home Economics* (Boston: Houghton Mifflin Company, 1945).

Beecher, Catherine E., *A Treatise on Domestic Economy* (New York: Harper and Brothers, Publishers, 1859).

Bevier, Isabel, *Home Economics in Education* (Chicago: J. B. Lippincott Company, 1924).

Buehr, Walter, *Home Sweet Home in the Nineteenth Century* (New York: Thomas Y. Crowell Company, 1965).

Cassara, Beverly Benner (ed.), *American Women: The Changing Image* (Boston: Beacon Press, 1962).

Goodyear, Margaret, and Mildred C. Klohr, *Managing for Effective Living* (New York: John Wiley and Sons, Inc., 1965).

Hall, Olive A., *Home Economics Careers and Homemaking* (New York: John Wiley and Sons, Inc., 1958).

Hawkins, Mary (ed.), *The American Home Economics Association, 1950–1954*. Supplement to *The AHEA Saga* (Washington, D.C.: The Association, 1960).

Hunt, Caroline L., *The Life of Ellen H. Richards* (Washington, D.C.: American Home Economics Association, 1958).

Lake Placid Conference on Home Economics, Proceedings of the First, Second, and Third Conferences, September 19–23, 1899; July 3–7, 1900; and June 28–July 5, 1901 (Lake Placid, New York, 1901).

Lake Placid Conference on Home Economics, Proceedings of the

Tenth Annual Conference, July 6–10, 1908 (Lake Placid, N.Y., 1908).

McGrath, Earl J., and Jack T. Johnson, *The Changing Mission of Home Economics* (New York: Teachers College Press, 1968).

Phillips, Velma, *Home Economics Careers for You* (New York: Harper and Brothers, Publishers, 1962).

Sanders, H. C., et al. (eds.), *The Cooperative Extension Service* (Englewood Cliffs, N.J.: Prentice-Hall, Inc., 1966).

Spencer, Lila, *Exciting Careers for Home Economists* (New York: Julian Messner, 1967).

Tate, Mildred Thurow, *Home Economics as a Profession* (New York: McGraw-Hill Book Company, 1961).

U.S. Department of Commerce, Bureau of the Census, *Statistical Abstracts of the U.S., 1971* (Washington, D.C.: U.S. Government Printing Office, 1971).

PERIODICALS, PAMPHLETS, BULLETINS

"Action—Peace Corps, Vista, Service Corps of Retired Executives, Active Corps of Executives, Retired Senior Volunteer Program, The Foster Grandparent Program" (Washington, D.C.: Action, 1972).

Blackwell, Gordon W., "The Place of Home Economics in American Society," *Journal of Home Economics*, 54 (June 1962), 447–450.

Blegen, Theodore C., "Potential of Home Economics in Education and the Community," *Journal of Home Economics*, 47 (September 1955), 479–482.

Byrd, Flossie M., "A Definition of Home Economics for the 70's," *Journal of Home Economics*, 62 (June 1970).

"A Career in Home Economics Extension," American Home Economics Association, 1959.

"Career Opportunities in Government," U.S. Civil Service Commission, 1960.

"Careers in Family Relations and Child Development," American Home Economics Association, 1970.

"Careers in Home Economics," *Changing Times, The Kiplinger Service for Families*, 1729 H. Street, N.W., Washington, D.C. (January 1962).

"Careers in Institution Administration," American Home Economics Association, 1970.

"Careers in Textiles and Clothing," American Home Economics Association, 1970.

Cowles, Millie, "One Front in the War on Poverty: Early Childhood Education," *AAUW Journal*, 59 (October 1965).

Craig, Hazel T., "The History of Home Economics," *Practical Home Economics*, 468 Fourth Avenue, New York, New York, 1945.

Department of Home Economics, National Education Association, "Facts, Facts, Facts" (Washington, D.C.: National Education Association, Fall 1966).

Eagan, Mary C., "The Expanding Service Arena in Home Economics," *Journal of Home Economics*, 64 (February 1972), 49–55.

East, Marjorie, "Family Life by the Year 2000," *Journal of Home Economics*, 62 (January 1970).

"Federal Careers," U.S. Civil Service Commission, Chicago Region Main Post Office Building, Chicago, Ill., 1962.

Hancock, E. P., "Fields and Future of Home Economics," *Journal of Home Economics*, 58 (January 1966).

Handbook on Women Workers, Womens Bureau Bulletin 294, United States Department of Labor (Washington, D.C.: U.S. Government Printing Office, 1969).

"Head Start—A Child Development Program" (Washington, D.C.: U.S. Department of Health, Education, and Welfare, 1970).

Henderson, Grace M., *Development of Home Economics in the United States* (University Park: Pennsylvania State University, College of Home Economics, 1954).

Hilton, Helen LeBaron, "Now That Women Are Liberated," *Journal of Home Economics*, 64 (April 1972).

Home Economics Careers in Health and Welfare (Washington, D.C.: American Home Economics Association, 1965).

Home Economics New Directions, A Statement of Philosophy and Objectives, prepared by the Committee on Philosophy and Objectives of Home Economics (Washington, D.C.: American Home Economics Association, June 1959).

"Home Economists Needed This Summer for the Peace Corps Programs" (Washington, D.C.: Peace Corps, 1965).

Hurt, Mary Lee, and Margaret Alexander, "New Challenges," *Journal of Home Economics*, 61 (December 1969).

Hutchison, C. B., "Goals for Home Economics," *Journal of Home Economics*, 40 (March 1948), 117–19.

Jefferson, Ruth Bryant, "Interracial Understanding: A Challenge to Home and Family Life Education," *Journal of Home Economics*, 51 (February 1959), 87–93.

"Jobs in Professional Home Economics" (Chicago: Science Research Associates, Inc., 1965), Chapter IV.

Kuczma, Rose, "Placing Our Accent," *Journal of Home Economics*, 53 (December 1961), 815–819.

Laidler, F. F., "Work to Be Done," *Journal of Home Economics*, 56 (February 1964).

Lambert, Carroll, and Don Carter, "Impact on Family Life of Project Head Start," *Journal of Home Economics*, 59 (January 1967).

LeBaron, Helen R., "Home Economics, Its Potential for Greater Service," *Journal of Home Economics*, 47 (September 1955), 468–471.

"Minimum Academic Requirements for ADA Membership" (Chicago: The American Dietetic Association, August 1967).

Mobley, M. D., "A Review of Federal Vocational-Education Legislation 1962–1963," *Theory into Practice*, 3:5 (Columbus, Ohio: Ohio State University, 1964).

————, *New Dimensions in International Programs in Home Economics* (Washington, D.C.: American Home Economics Association, 1954).

Nosow, Sigmund, "The Nature of a Profession: Home Economics, A Particular Case," *The Field of Home Economics—What It Is* (Washington, D.C.: American Home Economics Association, 1965).

Olmstead, Agnes Reasor, "Home Economists' Responsibility to the Family," *Journal of Home Economics*, 53 (September 1961).

"Opportunities for Home Economists," *Journal of Home Economics*, 56 (November 1964).

"Opportunities for Home Economists with Farmer's Home Administration," *Journal of Home Economics*, 58 (February 1966).

"Peace Corps, One Part of Action" (Washington, D.C.: Action, 1972).

Practical Forecast, 11 (Spring 1965).

"Project Head Start," *NEA Journal* (October 1965).

Smith, Doris S., Flora L. Thong, and Garrett H. Yanagi, "Home Economist—Homemaker Aide Team Expands Environment Enrichment Program," *Journal of Home Economics*, 57 (November 1965).

Part II

BOOKS:

Allen, Clifford, *Passing Examinations* (London: Macmillan & Co., Ltd., 1963).

Bane, Lita, and Mildred R. Chapin, *Introduction to Home Economics* (Boston: Houghton Mifflin Company, 1945).

Bogert, Lotta Jean, George M. Briggs, and Foris Howes Calloway,

Nutrition and Physical Fitness (Philadelphia: W. B. Saunders Company, 1966).

Carter, Ellen S., and Iline Fife, *Learning Your Way Through College* (Springfield, Ill.: Charles C. Thomas, 1963).

Chambers, Helen G., and Verna Moulton, *Clothing Selection* (Philadelphia: J. B. Lippincott Company, 1961).

Cole, Luella, *Student's Guide to Efficient Study*, 4th ed. (New York: Holt, Rinehart and Winston, 1961).

Etheredge, Maude Lee, *Health Facts for College Students* (Philadelphia: W. B. Saunders Company, 1958).

Free, Anne R., *Social Usage* (New York: Appleton-Century-Crofts, 1960).

Gerken, C. d'A., *Study Your Way Through School* (Chicago: Science Research Associates, Inc., 1953).

Heston, Joseph C., *How to Take a Test* (Chicago: Science Research Associates, Inc., 1953).

Hickman, Cleveland P., *Health for College Students* (Englewood Cliffs, N.J.: Prentice-Hall, Inc., 1964).

Johnson, Harry J., *The Life Extension Foundation Guide to Better Health* (Englewood Cliffs, N.J.: Prentice-Hall, 1959).

Johnston, Betty Jane, *Equipment for Modern Living* (New York: Macmillan Publishing Co., Inc., 1965).

Lass, Abraham, and Eugene Wilson, *The College Students' Handbook* (New York: David White Company, 1965).

Lippeatt, Selma F., and Helen I. Brown, *Focus and Promise of Home Economics, A Family-Oriented Perspective* (New York: Macmillan Publishing Co., Inc., 1965).

Manuel, Herschel T., *Taking a Test* (New York: World Book Company, 1956).

McLean, Beth Bailey, *Meal Planning and Service* (Peoria, Ill.: Charles A. Bennett Company, Inc., 1964).

Nason, Leslie J., *Keys to Success in School* (Washington, D.C.: Public Affairs Press, 1963).

Phillips, Velma, *Home Economics Careers for You* (New York: Harper and Row, 1962).

Pierson, Irene, *Campus Cues* (Danville, Ill.: The Interstate Printers & Publishers, 1962).

Reid, Lillian N., *Personality and Etiquette* (Boston: D. C. Heath and Company, 1950).

Rogers, Carl R., *On Becoming a Person, A Therapist's View of Psychotherapy* (Boston: Houghton Mifflin Company, 1961).

————, *Understanding Ourselves* (Bloomington, Ill.: McKnight and McKnight Publishing Co., 1957).

Stearn, Esther W., and Allen E. Stearn, *College Hygiene* (Philadelphia: J. B. Lippincott Company, 1961).

Stoddard, George D., *On the Education of Women* (New York: Macmillan Publishing Co., Inc., 1950).

Sturm, Mary Mark, and Edwina H. Griesser, *Guide to Modern Clothing* (New York: McGraw-Hill Book Company, 1962).

Tate, Mildred Thurow, *Home Economics as a Profession* (New York: McGraw-Hill Book Company, 1961).

Turabian, Kate L., *A Manual for Writers of Term Papers, Theses and Dissertations* (Chicago: The University of Chicago Press, 1967).

Vail, Gladys E., Ruth M. Griswold, and Lucile Osborn Rust, *Foods* (Boston: Houghton Mifflin Company, 1967).

White, Philip L., *Let's Talk About Food* (American Medical Association, 1967).

Williams, Sue R., *Nutrition and Diet Therapy* (St. Louis, Mo.: C. V. Mosby Company, 1969).

PERIODICALS, PAMPHLETS, BULLETINS

Bear, Robert M., "How to Get the Most Out of Your Textbooks" (Robert M. Bear, Dartmouth College, Hanover, N.H., 1959).

Citron, B. P., "Necrotizing Angiitis in Drug Addicts." *New England Journal of Medicine*, 283, No. 19, 1970.

Czajkowski, Janina M., "Better Breakfasts." *Instructor,* LXXV (September 1965).

"A Girl's Guide to Good Make-up" (New York: Avon Products, Inc.).

Hirschhorn, K., "LSD and Chromosomal Damage" *Hospital Practice,* February 1969.

Imperi, L. L., "Use of Hallucinogenic Drugs on Campus," *Journal of the American Medical Association,* 204, No. 12, 1968.

Lieberman, C., and Lieberman, B., "Marihuana—a Medical Review," *New England Journal of Medicine,* 284, No. 2, 1971.

Metropolitan Life Insurance Company, *Four Steps to Weight Control* (New York: Metropolitan Life Insurance Company, 1969).

Miller, J. W., "Drug Abuse in the Western World" *Journal of the American Medical Association,* 213, No. 12, 1970.

Phi Eta Sigma, "Hints on How to Study" (n.p., Phi Eta Sigma, 1961).

Ray, Elizabeth M., "Professional Involvement in Education—Home Economics and the Time-Binding Values," *Journal of Home Economics,* 62 (December 1970).

Read, Merrill S., M.D., "Teen-Age Nutrition: Foundation for the Future," *Practical Forecast*, X (February 1965).

Sessoms, Deeda, "Learning to Like a New Food," *Instructor*, LXXV (September 1965).

Student Counseling and Testing Center, Office of Student Affairs, Southern Illinois University, "Study Hints" (Carbondale, Ill., n.d.).

Top Secrets from Toni (Chicago: The Toni Company, Division of the Gillette Company, 1967).

U.S. Department of Agriculture, "Food for Fitness," Leaflet No. 424 (Washington, D.C., 1964).

White, Philip L., "Fitness of Youth for the Challenge of Today," *School Lunch Journal*, 20:1 (January 1966).

Yolles, S. F., "Recent Research on Narcotics, LSD, Marihauana, and other Dangerous Drugs." Public Health Service Publication No. 1961, U.S. Government Printing Service, 1969.

A Sample Letter of Inquiry

144 Coral Circle
Palm Harbor Estates
South Daytona, Florida

Dear

Do you have a position in your business for an enthusiastic, well-trained interior designer? I can fill that position because of my training and background.

In August, I received a Bachelor of Science degree from Southern Illinois University. I was enrolled in the School of Home Economics, with a specialization in interior design in the Clothing and Textiles Department. Until March, I took additional courses in architectural technology, which provided training in various aspects of the architectural profession. Although I do not intend to obtain a degree in this field, these courses furthered my knowledge in a related area.

My undergraduate and postgraduate work at Southern has provided me with an excellent background. Fifty-six hours were directly related to the interiors curriculum. I took an additional twenty-six hours in the following areas: art appreciation, art history (oriental and nineteenth and twentieth century), pottery, industrial technology (mechanical drawing, upholstering, and design), product shelter, and principles of design. Specifically, I have been trained to do furniture arrangements, color scheming, and renderings in one- and two-point perspective and isometric drawings—all in watercolor or tempera.

If you have any questions that are not answered by the enclosed data sheet, I will be most happy to furnish additional information. I would appreciate your reply, as well as appropriate times that are convenient for you for an interview.

Sincerely,
Jill Denise Siwicki

PERSONAL DATA SHEET OF JILL DENISE SIWICKI

Personal Information
Age   22   Health   Excellent
Address   144 Coral Circle   Height   5' 2½"
            South Daytona, Florida
Telephone   252-4835   Weight   130 lb.

Education
  High School   Crete-Monee High School, Crete, Illinois
  Degree Received   High School Diploma
  Grade Average   C
  College   Southern Illinois University, Carbondale, Illinois
  School   Home Economics, Department of Clothing and Textiles
  Grade Average   Overall—3.5 (of 5.0); Department—4.7
  Degree   Bachelor of Science with Specialization in Interior Design
  Postgraduate   Southern Illinois University, Department of Archi-
  Work   tecture and Design (Vocational Technical Institute)

Practical Work Experience
  Waitress   Duties
    Lincolnshire Country Club,   Serving food to members and
    Crete, Illinois   guests

  Student secretary for
    Dr. Walter Welsh (retired)   Doing general office work—typing,
    Chairman of Botany Department   filing, dictation, receptionist
    Carbondale, Illinois

  Resident Fellow   Counselor and adviser in girl's
    Wilson Manor   dormitory in lieu of room, board,
    708 West Freeman   and tuition
    Carbondale, Illinois
    Mr. Robert Wilson, Manager

    600 West Freeman
    Carbondale, Illinois
    Mrs. Al Shafter, Manager
    Thompson Street, Carbondale, Illinois

References (by permission):
  Dean Eileen Quigley, School of Home Economics
    Southern Illinois University, Carbondale, Illinois
  Mr. Paul Lougeay, Chairman of Department of Architectural Design
    Vocational Technical Institute, Carterville, Illinois
  Mrs. Anita Kuo, Head of Off-Campus Housing
    Southern Illinois University Housing Office, Carbondale, Illinois

Mr. Thomas Cassidy, Professor of English
English Department, Southern Illinois University, Carbondale,
Illinois
Mrs. Lucy Stewart, Clothing and Textile Department,
School of Home Economics
Southern Illinois University, Carbondale, Illinois

College Extracurricular Activities
OBELISK Staff Member (Yearbook), Home Economics Counselor
University Choir—Secretary, Southern Belle
Oratorio Choir   Dormitory Judicial Board
New Student Week Leader, Steering Committee—Publicity Chairman
Newman Club Representative of Dormitory
Student Member of National Society of Interior Designers, Officer
Student Member of American Institute of Interior Designers
Homecoming Steering Committee—Secretary, Publicity Committee
Parent's Day Steering Committee, Coffee-hour Chairman
Christmas Week Steering Committee, Ed-Cult Committee Chairman
University Center Programming Board—Cochairman Ed-Cult Committee
Resident Fellow—Chairman and Secretary of Off-Campus Council

Specific Courses Related to Interior Design
APPLIED DESIGN—Theory of design
TEXTILES—Characteristics of commonly used fibers and fabrics
ADVANCED TEXTILES—Study of textile testing analysis
DISPLAY—Laboratory problems to provide experiments in planning execution, and evaluation of display
FURNITURE—AND INTERIORS—Study of furniture related to interior from antiquity through the eighteenth century
MODERN MOVEMENT IN INTERIOR DESIGN—Study of furniture related to interiors from the eighteenth century to the present
DECORATIVE ARTS—Study of ceramics, textiles, paper, plastics, lighting and lighting fixtures, metals and hardware, selecting and hanging pictures, window and wall treatment, floor coverings, and backgrounds
INTERIOR DESIGN FUNDAMENTALS—Analysis and practices of interior design with emphasis on present-day problems
ADVANCED INTERIOR DESIGN—Major problems and trends in interior design in residential and commercial interiors
PROFESSIONAL PRACTICE—Organization and methods of conducting an interior design business; production, management, customer relationships, and professional ethics

Index

ACTION: introduction as federal program, 113; programs included in, 114; source of additional information, 113. *See also* Community action programs

Adjustment: 86, 234–40

Agricultural Experiment Stations: 23

Albanese, Naomi: 28; Man Designs for Man, 72–74

American Association for Childhood Development: 111

American Dietetic Association: Headquarters staff, 74; membership requirements, 81. *See also* Dietetics

American Home Economics Association: first officers, 27–28; founding of, 27; headquarters, 35–36; membership, 27, 35; official symbol, 33, 34; original purpose, 27; subject matter and professional sections, 35. *See also* Objectives

American Institute of Interior Designers: 69, 71

American Vocational Association: 30–31, 115

Apparel design: advantages, 63; national organizations, 63; nature of the work, 62–63; possible disadvantages, 63–64; qualifications, 62–63

Archibald, Rosemary: The Home Economist in Business—Equipment, 128–30

Aristotle: 342–44

Atwater, Wilbur O.: 23–24

Bankhead-Jones, Bill: 33

Basic Four: 250–51

Beecher, Catherine: 16–18; A Treatise on Domestic Economy, 11; Domestic Receipt Book, 18; teaching of domestic economy, 17–18

Bell-shaped curve: 227–28

Berry, Charles A.: 89

Betty Lamp: 33–34. *See also* AHEA

Boston Cooking School: 21

Breakfast: 256

Brigham Young University: 7*f.*, 8*f.*, 174–75*f.*

Bryant, Shari G.: The Home Economist in Business—Finance, 144–46

Burkett, Lowell: 31

Burns, Kathryn Van Aken: 29–30

Byrd, Flossie M.: The NASULGC Home Economics Task Force, 45–46; predictions of significance to the home economist, 50

California, University of: 115

Calories: defined, 257; measured, 257; need for, 257

Carbohydrates, functions and sources: 248

Card catalog: 213–15

Careers in Home Economics: 53–180; apparel design, 62–64; child development and family relations, 104–16; clothing and textiles merchandising, 64–69; dietetics, 74–83; ethical dimensions of, 330–54; extension work, 99–104; home economists in business, 116–50; homemaking, 54–62; institution management, 83–88; interior design, 69–74; international programs, 154–62; nutritionist, 88–91; rehabilitation, 152–54; research, 162; social welfare and public health, 150–52; teaching, 92–99

Castellarin, Sheila A.: The Home Economist in Home Service with a Utility Company, 131–34

Cellulose: desirable forms of, 249; purpose in diet, 249; sources of high content, 249